A LEADER'S GUIDE

to Reading and Writing

in a PLC at Work®

ELEMENTARY

Kathy Tuchman Glass
Karen Power

EDITED BY
Mark Onuscheck
Jeanne Spiller

Solution Tree | Press

a division of
Solution Tree

555 North Morton Street
Bloomington, IN 47404
800.733.6786 (toll free) / 812.336.7700
FAX: 812.336.7790

email: info@SolutionTree.com
SolutionTree.com

Visit **go.SolutionTree.com/literacy** to download the free reproducibles in this book.

Printed in the United States of America

Library of Congress Cataloging-in-Publication Data

Names: Glass, Kathy Tuchman, author. | Power, Karen, 1967- author. |
  Onuscheck, Mark, editor. | Spiller, Jeanne, editor.
Title: A leader's guide to reading and writing in a PLC at work, elementary
  / Kathy Tuchman Glass, Karen Power, Mark Onuscheck, Jeanne Spiller.
Description: Bloomington, IN : Solution Tree Press, 2021. | Includes
  bibliographical references.
Identifiers: LCCN 2021017951 (print) | LCCN 2021017952 (ebook) | ISBN
  9781947604957 (paperback) | ISBN 9781947604964 (ebook)
Subjects: LCSH: Language arts (Elementary) | Professional learning
  communities. | Teacher-administrator relationships.
Classification: LCC LB1576 .G47477 2021 (print) | LCC LB1576 (ebook) |
  DDC 372.6--dc23
LC record available at https://lccn.loc.gov/2021017951
LC ebook record available at https://lccn.loc.gov/2021017952

Solution Tree
Jeffrey C. Jones, CEO
Edmund M. Ackerman, President

Solution Tree Press
President and Publisher: Douglas M. Rife
Associate Publisher: Sarah Payne-Mills
Art Director: Rian Anderson
Managing Production Editor: Kendra Slayton
Copy Chief: Jessi Finn
Senior Production Editor: Todd Brakke
Content Development Specialist: Amy Rubenstein
Copy Editor: Evie Madsen
Proofreader: Elisabeth Abrams
Text and Cover Designer: Abigail Bowen
Editorial Assistants: Sarah Ludwig and Elijah Oates

ACKNOWLEDGMENTS

As authors, we recognize that you are only able to read and comprehend our text because parents, teachers, and life experiences created the reader in you. We authored this book because of our overwhelming passion for educators to develop strong literacy skills in students and our understanding of how to lead this work. We realize you have tremendous choices for where to seek advice and support as a school or district leader. Therefore, we acknowledge and appreciate that you have selected our book to guide you on this altogether worthwhile and imperative enterprise.

To the reviewers who used their valuable time to provide suggestions for improvement, we thank you for your expertise. Your comments proved invaluable, and this book is stronger because of your insightful input. As always, the Solution Tree family deserves our abundant gratitude for providing the opportunity to publish our work.

And with full hearts, we each express gratitude to our husbands Mike and Wayne for their patience and understanding. Writing takes on a life of its own, and as we concentrated relentlessly on yet another draft, their endless support fueled our efforts.

—Kathy Tuchman Glass and Karen Power

Solution Tree Press would like to thank the following reviewers:

Casey R. Ahner
Solution Tree Associate
Los Lunas, New Mexico

Charles Ames Fischer
Educational Consultant
Decatur, Tennessee

Scott Hagerman
Superintendent
Tanque Verde USD
Tucson, Arizona

Lisa May
Literacy Coach
Kildeer Countryside School
   District 96
Buffalo Grove, Illinois

Erica Martin
Literacy Specialist
Kildeer Countryside School
   District 96
Buffalo Grove, Illinois

Kimberly Miles
Principal, East Gresham
   Elementary School
Gresham-Barlow School District
Gresham, Oregon

Visit **go.SolutionTree.com/literacy** to
download the free reproducibles in this book.

TABLE OF CONTENTS

Reproducible pages are in italics.

ABOUT THE AUTHORS

 **Kathy Tuchman Glass** strives to empower teachers to maximize student potential. She is a consultant, trainer, and former classroom teacher with more than twenty-five years of experience in education. Additionally, she is an accomplished author of more than a dozen books, including *The New Art and Science of Teaching Writing*, coauthored with Robert J. Marzano, the *(Re)designing Writing Units* series, and *Reading and Writing Instruction for Fourth- and Fifth-Grade Classrooms in a PLC at Work*.

Kathy provides dynamic and interactive professional learning to K–12 educators and is recognized for her expertise in myriad areas, such as differentiation, instructional strategies, assessments, standards work around English language arts, and unit and lesson design. She has consulted with over 150 collaborative teams in reading and writing, contributing to some receiving model PLC status. Taking the PLC culture to heart, she coaches teams with intensity and commitment to assist educators in improving their practice for the betterment of all students in their charge. She is a member of the International Literacy Association, National Council of Teachers of English, Association for Supervision and Curriculum Development, and Learning Forward.

Kathy has a bachelor's degree from Indiana University Bloomington and a master's degree in education from San Francisco State University.

To learn more about Kathy's work, visit Glass Educational Consulting (https://kathyglassconsulting.com).

Karen Power is a consultant and former teacher, principal, superintendent, and senior advisor for professional learning and leadership. Karen is coauthor of *Leading With Intention: Eight Areas for Reflection and Planning in Your PLC at Work* and contributed to the Canadian version of *Learning by Doing*. Karen also contributed to the anthology *Charting the Course for Leaders: Lessons From Priority Schools in a PLC at Work*.

Karen's work focuses on leadership coaching in schools and districts. She is passionate about growing leaders and improving schools. Karen's international experiences include building collaborative practices through professional learning community (PLC) implementation, district strategic planning, and developing effective instruction, assessment, and evidence-based decisions for long-term sustainability. Karen coaches and supports the implementation of the PLC process in many schools and districts and is both a district and school coach in priority schools development.

In 2010, 2011, and 2012, Karen was selected as one of Canada's Top 100 Most Powerful Women in the Public Sector by the Women's Executive Network. She also received the national *Reader's Digest* Leadership in Education Award, and Atlantic Canada's *Progress* magazine named her one of its Outstanding People in the Atlantic Region.

To learn more about Karen's work, visit her blog for school improvement at https://karenpower.blog and follow @power58karen on Twitter.

To book Kathy Tuchman Glass or Karen Power for professional development, contact pd@SolutionTree.com.

ABOUT THE SERIES EDITORS

 **Mark Onuscheck** is director of curriculum, instruction, and assessment at Adlai E. Stevenson High School in Lincolnshire, Illinois. He is a former English teacher and director of communication arts. As director of curriculum, instruction, and assessment, Mark works with academic divisions around professional learning, articulation, curricular and instructional revision, evaluation, assessment, social-emotional learning, technologies, and Common Core implementation. He is also an adjunct professor at DePaul University.

Mark was awarded the Quality Matters Star Rating for his work in online teaching. He helps to build curriculum and instructional practices for TimeLine Theatre's arts integration program for Chicago Public Schools. Additionally, he is a National Endowment for the Humanities' grant recipient and a member of the Association for Supervision and Curriculum Development, National Council of Teachers of English, International Literacy Association, and Learning Forward.

Mark earned a bachelor's degree in English and classical studies from Allegheny College and a master's degree in teaching English from the University of Pittsburgh.

 **Jeanne Spiller** is assistant superintendent for teaching and learning for Kildeer Countryside Community Consolidated School District 96 in Buffalo Grove, Illinois. School District 96 is recognized on AllThingsPLC (www.AllThingsPLC.info) as one of only a small number of school districts where all schools in the district earn the distinction of model professional learning community (PLC). Jeanne's work focuses on standards-aligned instruction and assessment practices. She supports schools and districts across the United States to gain clarity about

and implement the four critical questions of PLCs. She is passionate about collaborating with schools to develop systems for teaching and learning that keep the focus on student results and helping teachers determine how to approach instruction so all students learn at high levels.

Jeanne received a 2014 Illinois Those Who Excel Award for significant contributions to the state's public and nonpublic elementary schools in administration. She is a graduate of the 2008 Learning Forward Academy, where she learned how to plan and implement professional learning that improves educator practice and increases student achievement. She has served as a classroom teacher, team leader, middle school administrator, and director of professional learning.

Jeanne earned a master's degree in educational teaching and leadership from Saint Xavier University, a master's degree in educational administration from Loyola University Chicago, and an educational administrative superintendent endorsement from Northern Illinois University.

To learn more about Jeanne's work, follow @jeeneemarie on Twitter.

To book Mark Onuscheck or Jeanne Spiller for professional development, contact pd@SolutionTree.com.

INTRODUCTION

Leaders of Literacy

Wherever we work as leadership and literacy coaches, we consistently notice that districts and schools name literacy as a top priority. We see the phrases "increase reading comprehension" or "improving writing skills" as part of their strategic plans. Teams and leaders craft goals to encourage teachers to explicitly understand what progress should look like and what leadership will monitor. On paper, the goal of improving literacy appears obvious, but looming questions beg attention: What can leaders and teachers do to ensure that collaborative-team action and commitment align to these goals?

Furthermore, what is the goal of literacy? What does this subject entail? How do teachers plan and deliver effective literacy instruction? What do collaborative teams focus on to further students' achievement in literacy? Who is responsible for teaching literacy skills? What is the impact of district and school leadership in this critical work? These questions should permeate school and district leaders' thoughts as they reflect on schoolwide and districtwide reading and writing instruction.

Clearly, there is pressure to improve literacy rates. For example, the National Assessment of Educational Progress (NAEP, 2019) states 36 percent of fourth graders in U.S. public and nonpublic schools scored at or above the *proficient* level in reading. The NAEP does not have similar numbers for fourth-grade writing, but in 2002, it was just 28 percent (NAEP, 2002); a 2011 report on eighth-grade students reported just 27 percent, indicating the situation has not improved (NAEP, 2011). In another report, Donald J. Hernandez (2011), a sociology professor and senior advisor for the Foundation for Child Development, states, "one in six children who are not reading proficiently in third grade do not graduate from high school on time, a rate four times greater than that for proficient readers" (p. 3). The rates are highest for the low, below-basic readers: 23 percent of these children drop out or fail to finish high school on time, compared to 9 percent of children with basic reading skills and 4 percent of proficient readers, and below-basic readers account for a third of the sample but three-fifths of the students who do not graduate (Hernandez, 2011). Undeniably, there must be a clarion call to guarantee all students achieve a literacy level that positions them to fully function and engage in society.

Every Teacher Is a Literacy Teacher is a series of books designed to support teachers and other educators who interface directly with students to inform and enhance literacy instruction across all grade levels and content areas. The elementary-level books in this series focus specifically on classroom reading and writing instruction in a professional learning community (PLC) and comprise the following three titles from series editors Mark Onuscheck and Jeanne Spiller.

▸ *Reading and Writing Instruction for PreK Through First-Grade Classrooms in a PLC at Work* by authors Erica Martin and Lisa May (Onuscheck, Spiller, Martin, & May, 2020)

▸ *Reading and Writing Instruction for Second- and Third-Grade Classrooms in a PLC at Work* by authors Sarah Gord and Kathryn E. Sheridan (Onuscheck, Spiller, Gord, & Sheridan, 2020)

▸ *Reading and Writing Instruction for Fourth- and Fifth-Grade Classrooms in a PLC at Work* by author Kathy Tuchman Glass (Onuscheck, Spiller, & Glass, 2020)

This text—*A Leader's Guide to Reading and Writing in a PLC at Work, Elementary*—provides collective guidance applicable across the full set of elementary-level texts to myriad individuals who serve in a leadership capacity with respect to literacy goals. Throughout this book, we refer to this elementary-level collection as the *signature series*.

As a leader at a district, school, or collaborative-team level, you must vigilantly commit to ensuring teacher teams provide optimal literacy instruction so students can capably and adeptly read, write, and communicate. In truth, principals alone cannot lead a school to excellence. Rather, students make gains when invested individuals share their expertise and assume collective responsibility for contributing to students' success. Therefore, school and district leadership requires shared ownership to meet the ultimate goal of student achievement. School leadership refers to leaders who participate in various roles throughout the building. For example, a classroom teacher can serve as a team leader in a PLC, and an instructional coach or facilitator provides leadership support in one or more content areas. At the district level, assistant superintendents, supervisors, and district coaches can lead curriculum and instruction efforts more broadly. Steering the change process is a *guiding coalition*, a team usually comprised of select district and school leaders as well as representative coaches, specialists, and teacher leaders.

Many readily recognize the urgency to improve literacy rates; however, the real work lies in taking action to address deficiencies and obstacles that avert progress. This requires answers to numerous questions. As a leader, where do you focus your time and attention to ensure your students can read and comprehend grade-level content? Is the fundamental goal of a school or district's literacy initiative to know students can leave each grade reading, writing, and discussing grade-level content? How do you lead this work? What does it take to stay the course with intention? And lastly, where do you begin? In this text, we aim to position leaders to address these and other questions so they can succeed in supporting teachers on behalf of any school's most precious commodity: students.

In the following sections, we detail the content you will find in this book as well as establish several areas of focus that leaders must be aware of in facilitating the work of their school's collaborative teams.

About This Book

The nine chapters in this book align with the chapters in the three grade-level signature series books we identified in this introduction (preK–grade 1, grades 2–3, and grades 4–5). The chapters represent a natural progression of a team's work as members move from establishing a plan for a curriculum all the way through to determining the methods and strategies for classroom instruction. Each of the following chapters examines its topic through a literacy-focused lens with the spotlight on how leaders can drive and support the work of collaborative teacher teams. (Refer to the signature series books for a more in-depth discussion on each chapter's topic.)

▸ Chapter 1 addresses the importance of identifying *student learning expectations*; that is, what collaborative teams want students to learn based on content standards or learning outcomes. It introduces a specific protocol to assist teams in gaining clarity about what students should know and be able to do before beginning a unit of instruction.

▸ Chapter 2 defines types and formats of assessments and the purpose for administering them. It features a unit assessment continuum example and ways teachers can use each type of assessment within a unit of instruction.

▶ Chapter 3 shows how teams can create learning progressions for each learning standard in a curriculum. The learning progression assists teams in the development of learning target–aligned assessments and high-quality instruction. It also provides guidance about choosing appropriate complex texts.

▶ Chapter 4 details the importance of having collective understanding of learning expectations in the areas of student proficiency levels, use of various rubric types and their development, the benefits of student checklists, and the need for collaborative scoring.

▶ Chapter 5 addresses how teams use data and determine next steps to support students who have yet to achieve mastery or extend learning for those who have. The chapter focuses on establishing collective efficacy and the data-inquiry guidelines and process.

▶ Chapter 6 focuses on teams' methods of instruction, specifically the use of the gradual release of responsibility instructional framework and how leaders can ensure teacher teams implement it effectively. Through this model, teachers support student learning with adequate guidance and modeling as they gradually move students toward independent learning.

▶ Chapter 7 explains the importance of teams dedicating specific time to high-quality literacy instruction. It explains the structural and contextual components of literacy, which intertwine the domains of reading, writing, speaking, and listening.

▶ Chapter 8 details several strategies to facilitate high-quality literacy instruction, including vocabulary, and how leaders ensure teams understand how and when to use these strategies.

▶ Chapter 9 concludes the book by focusing on the importance of diversity and equity in literacy instruction and how leaders can help teams assess their invisible biases, ensure accessible instruction for all students, promote high expectations, and offer culturally appropriate resources.

We also include a pair of useful resources in this book's appendices. Appendix A consists of a variety of reproducible versions of tools in the book. Appendix B provides a list of the figures and tables featured throughout the book.

Leadership Areas of Focus

In their book, *Leading With Intention*, coauthors Jeanne Spiller and Karen Power (2019) identify eight leadership areas for reflection and planning that represent a wise direction for those who assume leadership roles within a PLC. The associated questions in the following list serve to elucidate these main guideposts, and figure A.1 (page 234 in appendix A) provides an in-depth overview of this model (Spiller & Power, 2019).

1. **Achieve focus and stay intentional:** How can you effectively spend time to guide, monitor, and support what you expect from teams and individuals?

2. **Establish and maintain organization:** How can you establish and maintain school organizational structures that connect to effective classroom practices?

3. **Build shared leadership:** How can you build collaborative teams and shared leadership to strengthen your ability and improve the school?

4. **Use evidence for decision making and action:** How can you use evidence of student achievement and the current state of the school to make decisions and take necessary actions?

5. **Prioritize students:** How can you maintain a primary focus on students vis-à-vis making student-centered decisions and establishing an equitable learning environment?

6. **Lead instruction:** How can you take an active role to lead effective instruction?

7. **Foster communication:** How can you foster strong communication skills between and among students and teachers?

8. **Develop community and relationships:** How can you build and promote relationships beyond the school community?

Within every chapter of this leadership guide, we highlight different leadership areas of reflection and planning that Spiller and Power (2019) articulate; these suggestions expressly support your districtwide and schoolwide efforts. In essence, we integrate their tenets of sound leadership into the action steps literacy-focused educators should undertake. Table I.1 (page 6) reflects the intersection between each chapter in this book and the aligned leadership-focus areas we highlight.

Table I.1: Intersection Between Building Literacy and Leadership Areas

Leadership Areas	Building Literacy in a PLC								
	Chapter 1: Establish Clarity About Student Learning Expectations	Chapter 2: Examine Assessment Options for Literacy	Chapter 3: Create a Learning Progression to Guide Instruction and Assessment	Chapter 4: Develop Collective Understanding of Learning Expectations	Chapter 5: Respond to Student Data to Ensure All Students Learn	Chapter 6: Design Lessons Using the Gradual Release of Responsibility Instructional Framework	Chapter 7: Plan for High-Quality Instruction in Literacy	Chapter 8: Select Appropriate Instructional Strategies	Chapter 9: Consider Equity in Literacy
Achieve Focus and Stay Intentional	✓	✓			✓				
Establish and Maintain Organization						✓	✓		
Build Shared Leadership	✓			✓					
Use Evidence for Decision Making and Action					✓			✓	
Prioritize Students		✓							✓
Lead Instruction			✓			✓	✓		
Foster Communication	✓								
Develop Community and Relationships									✓

Although several leadership areas can connect with each chapter's topics, we identified those that most aptly apply.

Throughout this book, leaders will have an opportunity to reflect on current practices and consider thoughtful actions and next steps to increase a focus on literacy within their school or district. We offer suggestions to those in various leadership roles—particularly leaders at the district and school levels, including coaches or instructional facilitators and teacher leaders—all of whom work with collaborative teams and individual teachers to maximize performance and facilitate student achievement. Each chapter begins with a summary of the content shared in the signature series books. Then we provide information and myriad resources, tools and templates, and reflective questions to support collaborative work on that topic. In addition, the leadership areas in each chapter conclude with a list of recommendations four types of leaders might consider for effectively implementing literacy within their systems: (1) district, (2) school, (3) coach, and (4) teacher. Leaders will determine which items on each are worthy of further action based on their current and future needs and where they are with regard to expertise—or lack thereof—in a particular area. We recommend that you read all columns to assist with alignment and next steps for all leaders in your building and district.

The PLC process has a fundamental focus on learning (DuFour, DuFour, Eaker, Many, & Mattos, 2016). Therefore, the comprehensive support in this text fuels action plans for leaders to ensure deep implementation of literacy through the PLC process. When a school or district functions as a PLC, educators collaborate and embrace high levels of learning for all students. This process is also results driven—educators set *SMART goals* (goals that are strategic and specific, measurable, attainable, results oriented, and time bound; Conzemius & O'Neill, 2014) and mutually agree on expectations of proficiency and how they will continuously monitor students' learning.

In a PLC culture, collaborative teams build shared knowledge through collective inquiry to develop new skills and capabilities (DuFour et al., 2016). As PLC architects and experts Richard DuFour, Rebecca DuFour, Robert Eaker, and Thomas W. Many (2010) note: "Gradually this heightened awareness transforms into fundamental shifts in attitudes, beliefs, and habits that, over time, transform the culture of the school" (p. 12). PLCs are also committed to continuous improvement, districtwide and schoolwide (DuFour et al., 2016). These schools and districts are constantly searching for ways to fulfill their vision of student success, and this book is dedicated to increasing student achievement through the successful attainment of literacy skills. Let's begin.

CHAPTER 1

Establish Clarity About Student Learning Expectations

Hands down, the students who read the most are the best at every part of school—reading, writing, researching, content-specific knowledge, all of it.

—STEPHEN D. KRASHEN

Getting started on curriculum design requires clarity on the *what*—what leaders want students to know and be able to do. In the signature elementary-level books in the *Every Teacher Is a Literacy Teacher* series, we introduce the pre-unit protocol (PREP) process, a valuable tool that collaborative teams use to take action as they prepare to write their units of instruction. This process requires teachers to identify what they believe to be the essential learnings based on each grade level's content standards. Using this process to plan in advance contributes to sound and effective curriculum design, and we provide a summary of each step of the PREP process in this chapter.

Editors and researchers Robert Eaker and Robert J. Marzano (2020) assert that each student is entitled to a guaranteed and viable curriculum. *Guaranteed* stipulates that all students are granted the opportunity to learn a core curriculum to position them for success. To deliver this guaranteed curriculum, it must be *viable*, meaning that schools ensure necessary time is available, as well as protected, for learning.

Further, there are four critical questions that drive the work of a PLC (DuFour et al., 2016).

1. What is it we want our students to learn?

2. How will we know if each student has learned it?

3. How will we respond when some students don't learn it?

4. How will we extend and enrich the learning for students who have demonstrated proficiency?

It's this first critical question that most directly aligns with the promise of delivering a guaranteed and viable curriculum. The signature, elementary-level books in the *Every Teacher Is a Literacy Teacher* series (see page 2) further state that before introducing complex texts, launching into an activity, or conducting assessments, collaborative team members must interpret standards in the same way and use them to guide a robust and rigorous instructional and assessment plan. If teachers do not sit down together to analyze literacy standards and reach a consensus on what they mean, students are not afforded access to the same content, knowledge, and skills. Simply put, any lack of clarity interferes with students' access to a guaranteed and viable curriculum.

School and district leaders have a responsibility to support, model, coach, and provide structures and common understanding to ensure teacher teams can deliver on a guaranteed and viable curriculum. Consider that part of a PLC culture is knowing what aspects of that culture are *loose* (anything individual teams or teachers can modify) or *tight* (anything that is non-negotiable; DuFour et al., 2016). As part of school and district non-negotiable tight expectations, it is necessary for leaders to facilitate processes that guide the development of this safeguarded curriculum and then communicate expectations regarding implementation. For example, district or school tight expectations might be that leaders expect to see grade-level work in classrooms, including the use of appropriately challenging complex texts and tasks aligned to the grade-level essential standards. Does this mean that you, as a leader, must provide the list of essential standards to teachers? This question is often one that causes the most discussion when we think about ensuring a guaranteed and viable curriculum for all students. Leaders should understand that *teachers* must prioritize and unpack standards to develop clear learning targets, as the PREP process supports. This often prompts leaders to wonder how they can get this work done quickly and efficiently.

Some believe the most efficient way to accomplish the work is for the district or school administrative team to prioritize and unpack standards. It's true, districts and schools will likely produce a product faster this way. However, we contend that teachers must directly engage in the process of determining need-to-know essential (or priority) standards, so they have the opportunity to deeply discuss the meaning, rigor, and value of each learning standard. For collaborative teams, this consensus around essential standards also establishes a sense of commitment to the process and its outcome. As author, educator, and motivational speaker Stephen Covey (2019) asserts, "Without involvement, there is no commitment. Mark it down, asterisk it, circle it, underline it. No involvement, no commitment."

In this chapter, we outline how you can use the PREP process with your collaborative teams to provide a reliable and effective six-step process for digging deeply into each essential learning standard. We also highlight three specific leadership areas school and district leaders should develop when attempting to ensure literacy is a vital component of school and district curricula.

Getting Clear About Student Learning Expectations: Pre-Unit Protocol (PREP) Process

Having a clear vision of what students must know and be able to do requires careful consideration of components that work in concordance to guide an effective instruction and assessment plan: standards, knowledge, skills, depth of knowledge, and learning targets. To address them, a week or more prior to conducting a unit, teams utilize the six-step PREP process. Adhering to this process safeguards student learning by establishing distinct expectations for learners across all classrooms and sets the groundwork for team collaboration in developing a unit of instruction.

REFLECTION

How can you reinforce the purpose and value of the PREP process? What artifacts can you collect and observe as evidence of teacher teams implementing this process?

Figure 1.1 (page 12) provides the six steps, along with guiding questions you can ask to assist teachers as they implement the PREP process with their teams. While working on each step, teachers complete a blank PREP template (see the reproducible "PREP Template" in appendix A, page 239). Chapter 1 in each elementary signature series book includes completed examples of templates for specific units by grade band: preK–1 (on Friendship and Acceptance), grades 2–3 (on Exploring Elements of Fiction), and grades 4–5 (on The Power of Dialogue Within a Narrative). As collaborative teams participate in various exercises to lead them through completing each step for a targeted unit of study, leaders support, provide guidance, and monitor the work. By posing the questions in figure 1.1, leaders help teachers ensure their team discussions are focused and intentional.

PREP Step	Questions for Collaborative Teams to Guide Exercise
1. **Enter unit standards onto the template.** Input the entire set of standards onto the PREP template.	• How can we work as a collaborative team to initiate and proceed with the steps this chapter outlines? • What if I am in a situation where I do not have a collaborative team and am a singleton in my building or district?
2. **Indicate (or determine) priority standards.** Distinguish priority from supporting standards by bolding, underlining, or color-coding them. If the team has not yet prioritized standards, see Step 2: Indicate (or Determine) Priority Standards (page 16) for guidance. Then, return to the unit template and mark essential standards.	• Which standards does our team deem priority or essential? • Which priority standards are appropriate for our targeted unit of study? • Are all team members clear that we are held accountable for students learning the priority standards? Do they understand that these priority standards become the focus for teaching and assessing and for interventions? • Which standards serve as supporting and, as such, are subsumed under which particular priority standards? • Are we all clear that we still address and teach supporting standards; however, they do not receive the same time and attention as priority standards?
3. **Unwrap unit priority standards.** Refer to the PREP template, and annotate priority standards to uncover smaller, incremental learning goals.	• What priority standards are we targeting for this unit? • What verbs can we capitalize or circle to indicate skills students will need to be proficient? • What nouns or phrases can we underline to show the content and concepts to teach in a particular context? • Are there conjunctions, such as *and* or *or*, that need deciphering to help unwrap these standards?
4. **Identify knowledge items.** Add knowledge items that align to the unwrapped standards, paying attention to what they imply. The team might generate a list, reference a page number from a source (for example, a diagram or a vocabulary list), or create a graphic organizer.	• What should students know relative to a priority standard targeted for this lesson? • What explicitly stated knowledge items do we expect students to know? • What might be implicit in the standard and require us to make inferences? For example, a standard about complex sentences requires an inference that students need to know dependent and independent clauses and subordinating conjunctions.
5. **Determine skills.** Use the unwrapped, annotated standards and	• What cognitive process can students employ to show they can apply what they've learned?

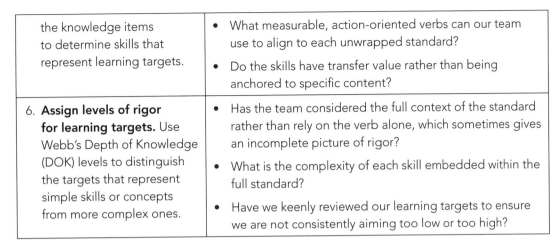

the knowledge items to determine skills that represent learning targets.	• What measurable, action-oriented verbs can our team use to align to each unwrapped standard? • Do the skills have transfer value rather than being anchored to specific content?
6. **Assign levels of rigor for learning targets.** Use Webb's Depth of Knowledge (DOK) levels to distinguish the targets that represent simple skills or concepts from more complex ones.	• Has the team considered the full context of the standard rather than rely on the verb alone, which sometimes gives an incomplete picture of rigor? • What is the complexity of each skill embedded within the full standard? • Have we keenly reviewed our learning targets to ensure we are not consistently aiming too low or too high?

Figure 1.1: PREP steps and guiding questions for teams to consider.

*Visit **go.SolutionTree.com/literacy** for a free reproducible version of this figure.*

How do you, as a leader, ensure teachers understand and deeply implement the PREP process, addressing pertinent guiding questions as a team? What does this look like at each step along the way? Figure 1.2 (page 14) shows a completed example PREP template from the grades 4–5 text in our signature series.

The following sections take you, step by step, through the six-step PREP template so you can see how teams arrive at the final product. You will find leadership suggestions throughout you can ask to assist teams in this endeavor and understand certain roadblocks that teams often face doing this work.

Step 1: Enter Unit Standards Onto the Template

As teams begin step 1 of the protocol, leaders must ensure they have access to all relevant state or provincial standards and can identify *all* standards collaborative teams will address throughout a specific unit of study. A *unit*, which can vary in length from a mini-unit of two weeks to a comprehensive one of possibly eight weeks, represents a subdivision of instruction within a content area and might be interdisciplinary. Teams might use published resources, district or school curriculum maps, teacher-developed materials, or a combination of these to determine all standards for the unit they are preparing. As teachers work through step 1, leaders pay attention to the discussion regarding the standards teams indicate for a given unit to be sure they are selecting them intentionally. For example, leaders help teams avoid the common mistake of teachers simply copying and pasting from a published resource. Rather, they encourage them to take time to ensure they have consensus and clarity on all standards within a unit.

Unit 2: The Power of Dialogue Within a Narrative | **Time Frame:** Approximately two weeks in October | **Grade:** 4

Unit Standards (Priority standards are in bold and italic typeface.)

Strand: Reading for Literature

- ***Refer to details and examples in a text when explaining what the text says explicitly and when drawing inferences from the text. (RL.4.1)***

- Describe in depth a character, setting, or event in a story or drama, drawing on specific details in the text (e.g., a character's thoughts, words, or actions). (RL.4.3)

- Compare and contrast the point of view from which different stories are narrated, including the difference between first- and third-person narrations. (RL.4.6)

Strand: Writing

- Write narratives to develop real or imagined experiences or events using effective technique, descriptive details, and clear event sequences. (W.4.3)

  - Orient the reader by establishing a situation and introducing a narrator and/or characters; organize an event sequence that unfolds naturally. (W.4.3a)

  - ***Use dialogue and description to develop experiences and events or show the responses of characters to situations. (W.4.3b)***

  - Use a variety of transitional words and phrases to manage the sequence of events. (W.4.3c)

  - Use concrete words and phrases and sensory details to convey experiences and events precisely. (W.4.3d)

  - Provide a conclusion that follows from the narrated experiences or events. (W.4.3e)

- Produce clear and coherent writing in which the development and organization are appropriate to task, purpose, and audience. (W.4.4)

- With guidance and support from peers and adults, develop and strengthen writing as needed by planning, revising, and editing. (W.4.5)

- With some guidance and support from adults, use technology, including the Internet, to produce and publish writing as well as to interact and collaborate with others; demonstrate sufficient command of keyboarding skills to type a minimum of one page in a single sitting. (W.4.6)

Strand: Language

- ***Use correct capitalization. (L.4.2a)***

- ***Use commas and quotation marks to mark direct speech and quotations from a text. (L.4.2b)***

- ***Choose words and phrases to convey ideas precisely. (L.4.3a)***

- Use context (e.g., definitions, examples, or restatements in text) as a clue to the meaning of a word or phrase. (L.4.4a)
- Explain the meaning of simple similes and metaphors (e.g., as pretty as a picture) in context. (L.4.5a)

Unwrapped Unit Priority Standards	Knowledge Items	Skills (Learning Targets and DOK Levels)
RL.4.1 (A): Refer to details and examples in a text when explaining what the text says explicitly.	Literal and explicit details from a text are directly stated. Terms: *Literal, explicit*	Identify details and examples in a text to explain what it says explicitly. (DOK 1)
RL.4.1 (B): Refer to details and examples in a text when drawing inferences from the text.	Inferences—implied information that is not directly or explicitly stated. Terms: *Imply, infer, inference*	Make inferences using details and examples in a text. (DOK 2)
W.4.3b (A): Use dialogue to develop experiences and events or show the responses of characters to situations.	Purpose and function of dialogue Dialogue is meaningful and serves a function—to develop the plot or to show characters' responses to situations.	Write dialogue to develop a plot or to show characters' responses to situations. (DOK 2)
W.4.3b (B): Use description to develop experiences and events or show the responses of characters to situations.	Descriptive details—precise nouns, vivid verbs, and colorful adjectives	Write descriptive detail to develop a plot or show characters' responses to situations. (DOK 2)
L.4.2a: Use correct capitalization. **L.4.2b:** Use commas and quotation marks to mark direct speech and quotations from a text.	Punctuation and capitalization rules for the different types of dialogue or speaker tags	Use proper conventions when writing dialogue. (DOK 1)
L.4.3a: Choose words and phrases to convey ideas precisely.	Types of dialogue (or speaker) tags—beginning, middle, end, or no tag Dialogue tag verbs provide description to indicate how characters speak to one another. Term: *Dialogue tag (speaker tag)*	Use words and phrases to convey ideas in a dialogue tag. (DOK 1)

Source for standards: National Governors Association Center for Best Practices (NGA) & Council of Chief State School Officers (CCSSO), 2010.
Source: Onuscheck, Spiller, & Glass, 2020, pp. 12–13.

Figure 1.2: PREP process example for grade 4—Dialogue.

Step 2: Indicate (or Determine) Priority Standards

In step 2, collaborative teams determine which standards from those listed in step 1 qualify as essential or priority standards. These vital standards students must learn become the basis for instruction, assessment, and intervention. If a team has already identified grade-level priority standards, they designate them in the PREP template by either bolding, underlining, or color-coding them. This indication distinguishes priority from supporting standards. If teams have yet to establish priority standards, members participate in a process that takes into consideration these key factors or criteria: *endurance, leverage, readiness,* and *high-stakes exams.* Figure 1.3 provides a snapshot of these criteria. For a more detailed discussion about them, along with a process teams can use to identify priority standards, refer to appendix B in the elementary-level books in this series.

Criteria for Prioritizing Standards

- **Does the standard have endurance?** Are the skills and knowledge embedded in the standard critical for students to remember beyond the course or unit? For example, the ability to coherently summarize complex text is a skill that extends beyond a particular unit of instruction. Teachers expect students to be able to summarize key details from their reading throughout high school and even into their professional careers. Therefore, summarizing is an enduring skill worth teaching.

- **Does this standard have leverage?** Are the skills and knowledge in the standard applicable across several disciplines? For example, summarizing complex text might be taught in ELA when students experience a literary work, but it is equally valuable when reading content in social studies and science. If the skills embedded in a standard have value in other content areas, the standard has leverage and should become a priority.

- **Is the standard needed for student readiness?** Does the standard include prerequisite skills and knowledge necessary to prepare students for the next grade? For example, when students learn the structure and elements of an opinion paper, it equips them with skills they need to tackle the more rigorous works of argumentation writing. Therefore, when prioritizing standards, consider the progression of skills from one grade level to the next, and choose those that build the foundation for future learning.

- **Will the standard be needed for high-stakes exams?** Will students need to know and apply the skills and knowledge of the standard on external exams? For example, in district, state or provincial, college, or vocational exams, students might need to respond to questions or writing prompts geared to the standard. Teachers should consider this when discussing which standards are necessary for student preparedness.

Source: Adapted from Ainsworth & Viegut, 2015; Bailey, Jakicic, & Spiller, 2014; Reeves, 2002.

Figure 1.3: A snapshot of the criteria for prioritizing standards.

*Visit **go.SolutionTree.com/literacy** for a free reproducible version of this figure.*

As the leader of this work, what are your look-fors to ensure teachers understand and take the time to determine the absolute, most important essential learnings for students? What can go astray with this step?

The main priority of the leader here is to focus on ensuring collaborative teams stay true to the criteria of endurance, leverage, readiness, and high-stakes exams as the criteria for determining what is essential. Note, however, that a particular standard does not need to meet all four criteria to qualify as priority. For example, if a standard aligns to a high-stakes exam requirement, it is deemed essential. Leaders should be on the lookout for too-shallow and too-loud conversations.

▸ **Too shallow:** These conversations occur when teachers either do not take the time to look at each standard through the lens of the established criteria of endurance, leverage, readiness, and high-stakes exams or the conversation deteriorates into discussions around standards less complicated to teach, those easier for students to learn, or the number of resources a team has already collected or developed around a standard.

▸ **Too loud:** These conversations usually involve one or more teachers on the team feeling their past experiences overshadow using the criteria to determine what students must know and be able to do. This often ensues innocently, perhaps when someone has taught the same grade and content level, and he or she honestly believes it's unnecessary to examine, through established criteria, what is important.

In both cases, you may need to bring the conversation back to the criteria to ensure the team does not fall into the trap of repeating past behaviors that derail the goal. Strict adherence to the criteria can help prevent teachers from espousing merely opinions regarding what teams want students to know and be able to do in each unit of study. Rather, they must support their positions using the criteria as evidence for designating certain standards as priority.

Step 3: Unpack Unit Priority Standards

After determining priority standards for the target unit, collaborative teams *unwrap* (or *unpack*) these standards to examine the explicit and implicit knowledge and skills embedded within each standard. Doing so helps teams develop assessments and design instruction. To unwrap, teams annotate standards using three steps.

1. **What priority standards are we targeting?** Focus on a priority standard.

2. **What will students need to do to be proficient?** Find and capitalize (or circle) pertinent verbs in the standard. The verbs—together with the

content and context (the next step in this list)—pinpoint the exact skills students need to achieve proficiency in a standard.

3. **With what content and concepts?** Find and underline the nouns and phrases that represent the content and concepts to teach within each standard.

Figure 1.4 shows a snapshot example of an annotated unwrapped priority standard for fourth grade.

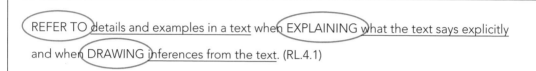

Source for standard: NGA & CCSSO, 2010.

Figure 1.4: A snapshot of unpacked (unwrapped) standards.

It's important for leaders supporting the unwrapping process to guide and practice this step with collaborative teams. Teacher teams are often tempted to skip this step, explaining (or rationalizing) they have taught this standard before and students understand it. Again, in our experience, as with step 2 in the PREP process, leaders must ensure teachers take the time to complete this step thoroughly and carefully so they identify both the skills and concepts teachers will expect of students. If individual teachers argue against this step, remind them that without unwrapping, it's common for them to tackle only the easiest skills and concepts. As a result, they run out of time to address the more rigorous parts of the standard. Or they neglect to divide a comprehensive standard to address a more complex part of it with more focused teaching.

Teachers should not ignore or dilute any verb in the standard, which could result in overlooking or discounting critical learning opportunities. As a case in point, in figure 1.4, teachers may look quickly at the standard and expect that students merely refer to details and examples in a text, missing the notation to do this by explaining what a text states explicitly *and* by making inferences. The latter is more sophisticated in that students must first draw an inference and then cite text to justify it. To teach all of the standard in one lesson is a tall order; unwrapping it to discover the skills embedded within it allows teachers to target their teaching precisely. Teachers also might consider how students demonstrate understanding, as in the phrase *explaining what the text says*. Students could ostensibly explain orally; however, requiring students to write about their reading experience raises the rigor of expectations.

Steps 4 and 5: Identify Knowledge Items and Determine Skills

In step 4 (identify knowledge items) and step 5 (determine skills), collaborative teams use their unpacked standards to expand and identify what they will actually teach and assess. The knowledge items include facts, dates, people, places, examples, vocabulary, and terms—including concept words. However, not all lessons or units necessarily include each of these categories. Knowledge items derive from explicitly and implicitly stated information from a standard that students will need to *know*. When formulating knowledge items, teachers record nouns and noun phrases rather than line items beginning with verbs, which would reflect what students *do*. The following examples for *imagery*, a type of figurative language, qualify as knowledge items and complete the frame *I want students to know . . .*

- A sentence that includes a statement of fact:

  - Types of figurative language include simile, metaphor, personification, hyperbole, and imagery.

  - Imagery, also called *sensory details*, is writing that appeals to the five senses.

  - Writers use imagery so readers visualize a setting, character, or event in their mind's eye.

- A bulleted list of items:

  - *Sight (visual)*—Descriptions of colors, shapes, sizes, movement, or appearances

  - *Sound (auditory)*—Loud or soft sounds; someone's speech (for example, *chatter, scream,* or *whimper*)

  - *Taste (gustatory)*—What food or something other than food tastes like (for example, *bitter, bland, crisp,* or *tangy*)

  - *Touch (tactile)*—Texture or what someone feels (for example, *bumpy, cool, greasy, rough,* or *slippery*)

  - *Smell (olfactory)*—Nature, foods, or scents (for example, *rotten, perfumed, fresh,* or *musty*)

- A graphic, such as a diagram or map, which teachers can reference from an existing resource

In step 5, teams review the unwrapped standards and knowledge items to determine skills—what students actually *do*. Skills begin with concrete verbs, such as *define*, *analyze*, or *compare*, rather than unobservable words like *understand* or *know*. Educators often refer to these as *learning targets*—the incremental and specific skills students must be able to do to achieve mastery of the entirety of the standard.

Throughout this book, we reference both *learning targets* (the skills embedded within the standards) and *standards* (overall learning goals). With a collective understanding of *what students need to know* (knowledge) and *be able to do* (skills), teachers can design instruction that addresses these skills explicitly. Therefore, teams pay careful attention to the verb so the rigor of instruction matches the expectation for students.

REFLECTION

As a leader, how do you ensure collaborative teams take the time to correctly unpack priority standards to inform what they will teach and assess through this process? How can you support and lead this work?

In step 4 and step 5, leaders can support the work of collaborative teams by participating and paying close attention to the knowledge and skills they identify. It may be necessary to ask probing questions to ensure teachers acutely understand their unpacked standards. For example, they can pose the following questions.

▶ "Are there vocabulary words or terms students should learn?"

▶ "What assumptions might you be making that students know? For instance, you have *compound sentences* listed, so should you also include *independent clauses*, *simple sentences*, and *coordinating conjunctions*?"

▶ "Since you include that you want students to know the writing process, do you want to clarify and include the stages: prewrite, draft, revise, edit, publish, and reflect?"

Review the team's identified lists of knowledge items to create more awareness of anything that might be inadvertently or overtly missing.

Step 6: Assign Levels of Rigor for Learning Targets

The final step of the PREP process supports the collaborative team's need to ensure students can access appropriate grade-level expectations. It is not enough for teams to identify the standards, knowledge, and skills; they must also ensure they teach those standards, knowledge, and skills at the appropriate level. In our experience, teachers still struggle with upholding high expectations for students even when they follow all the steps to this point in the PREP process. We often see low-level instruction and assessment design despite teachers' best efforts. Leaders must ensure teams adhere to this critical step, so rigor makes its way to the classroom. Once teachers finish this step, they are positioned to design or access curricula that contribute to a successful and effective program in literacy or any content area.

When concentrating on this step, teams conscientiously assign Norman L. Webb's (2002) *Depth of Knowledge (DOK)*, a thinking taxonomy, to the skills to ensure each learning target contains the appropriate and intended challenge level. *DOK* is a scale of cognitive demand that includes the following four levels (Francis, 2017; Hess, 2013).

1. **Recall:** Level 1 requires rote recall of information of facts, definitions, terms, or simple procedures. The student either knows the answer or does not.

2. **Skills and concepts:** Level 2 requires the engagement of mental processing or decision making beyond recall or reproduction. Items falling into this category often have more than one step, such as organizing and comparing data.

3. **Strategic thinking:** Level 3 requires higher-level thinking than levels 1 and 2 and could include activities or contexts with more than one possible solution, thereby requiring justification or support for the argument or process.

4. **Extended thinking:** Level 4 requires high-cognitive demand tasks in which students are synthesizing ideas across content areas or situations and generalizing that information to solve new problems. Many responses in this category require extensive time as they imply students complete multiple steps, as in a multivariant investigation and analysis.

Teams often wonder which DOK level correctly aligns to a particular skill. This is a common concern since the high-inference nature of a standard can result in various interpretations. As a leader, you must emphasize or facilitate teams (if needed) to arrive at a consensus so everyone on the team interprets a standard's rigor level uniformly and correctly. Clearly make the point that consensus is necessary since DOK levels guide how teachers instruct and, ultimately, the assessments they design. Communicate that teachers must match the challenge level to the expectations on state or provincial assessments; therefore, teachers must incorporate rigor into both instruction and assessment.

As leaders support teams in completing this six-step process, they must reflect and act on the impact they can potentially have on the work of collaborative teams. Use figure 1.5 to consider guiding questions as you visit with collaborative teams using the PREP process and template.

For more guidance, let's go deeper into the leadership work involved with guaranteeing curriculum for students. In the introduction to this book (page 1), we familiarized you with eight areas for reflection in *Leading With Intention* (Spiller & Power, 2019). In the remainder of this chapter, we use pertinent areas as the lens for supporting your role as a literacy leader.

Leadership Area: Achieve Focus and Stay Intentional

Leading by example with intentionality requires an ongoing commitment to understanding what you value and prioritize and dedicating time and actions around these commitments. "As a school leader, what you spend your time doing, what you focus on, speaks volumes to others about what is important" (Spiller & Power, 2019, p. 10). When you apply this thinking to support teams in formulating the PREP process, maintain intentionality in your message of what actions you expect from them and monitor to ensure these actions align to goals. In other words, leaders must determine their tights, create the conditions and resources to support this work, and then monitor to celebrate and adjust as needed. For example, if you expect collaborative teams to use the PREP process to begin their standards-based planning, then leaders must take steps to ensure teams understand the *why* and *how*, arrange training and leadership support to do this work, and provide time and necessary resources. As a leader, keep the focus on the work, remove the distractors, and celebrate with teams when they are successful. It also means taking action to adjust and attend to misconceptions or noncompliance. You lead with intention so others can follow.

Leadership: Guiding Questions for the PREP Process and Template	Collaborative Team Notes and Next Steps
What steps have you collaboratively taken to agree that necessary standards are recorded on the template? What can I do to support your work as you build a guaranteed and viable curriculum?	
How are you using the criteria of endurance, leverage, readiness, and high-stakes exams as the criteria for determining what is essential? What can I do as a leader to help you interpret these criteria items consistently and apply them uniformly? How can I provide more time or support with this step in the protocol?	
How is your understanding of what students must *know* clearer by unpacking the standards? How is unpacking helping you see the factual and foundational information embedded in the standard, including key terms and vocabulary? What can I do to help with this step?	
How is your understanding of what students must *be able to do* clearer by unpacking the standards? How is it helping you see the more rigorous requirements embedded in the standard? What can I do to help with this step?	
What assumptions can you make about what will be required for students to master this standard? What might you have inadvertently missed or overlooked?	
How are you working collaboratively to reach consensus on the DOK level of the unpacked standard? How can this help you match the challenge level to the expectations on state or provincial assessments? How will this impact your instruction?	

Figure 1.5: Leadership guiding questions for the PREP process.

Visit **go.SolutionTree.com/literacy** *for a free reproducible version of this figure.*

In *Good to Great*, author Jim Collins (2001) uses a hedgehog analogy from Aesop's fable "The Fox and the Hedgehog" (Long, n.d.) to help readers understand successful leadership. The hedgehog knows to repeat the same, simple practices that always guarantee safety. Rather than creating change just for the sake of change, this animal relies on repeating focused and effective routines and procedures. Author and former administrator and ELA teacher Mike Schmoker (2018) uses Collins's (2001) hedgehog analogy to articulate the critical need for leaders to simply and carefully accomplish the following:

- Carefully determine and [significantly] reduce your focus to the fewest and most manageable priorities,

- Emphatically and repeatedly clarify and repeat these priorities throughout your organization, and

- Ensure everyone stays focused on these priorities and fully commits to them through practice, reflection, and refinement. (pp. 13–14)

This leadership-focus area and intentionality center on the question: *How can you effectively spend time to guide, monitor, and support what you expect from teams and individuals as they gain clarity about student learning expectations*? Consider your job as a leader. Is there a specific role in the area of literacy if you are a lead teacher on a collaborative team? Is there a role in supporting the *what* if you are an instructional coach? Is it important for a school administrator to be part of the PREP work, and in what capacity? Lastly, does district leadership impact the implemented curriculum for the student sitting in the classroom?

The answer to all of these questions is an emphatic *yes*. There are opportunities at all levels of leadership that will impact what a student has access to in the curriculum. For direction and even validation, review figure 1.6 to determine how you might apply (or have applied) intentionality in your own role as you support literacy expectations and instruction. The items in this figure are suggestions that you might consider addressing based on your role as a leader and the needs of teams based on their level of expertise.

Leadership Area: Build Shared Leadership

Leading a school or district does not mean leading alone. Too often, capable and focused leaders attempt to do everything by themselves. In the work of authentic PLCs, shared leadership is developed to ensure shared ownership of successful school improvement (DuFour et al., 2016). "Shared leadership may have its greatest

Leadership Area: Achieve Focus and Stay Intentional			
District Leader	**School Administrator**	**Instructional Coach**	**Lead Teacher**
☐ Develop tight expectations for collaborative teams to identify essential student learning outcomes. ☐ Create professional learning opportunities to support the tight expectations so teachers will know the *why* and *how* of getting clear on student learning expectations. ☐ Provide ongoing support to principals and other leaders to ensure strong school leadership in curricula. ☐ Develop reciprocal accountability tools that enable school teams to monitor their work and receive feedback, coaching, and training as needed to ensure that clarity on student learning expectations is a focus of teams' work. ☐ Prevent distractors from taking the focus away from ensuring a guaranteed and viable curriculum for all students.	☐ Ensure a professional learning plan for the school builds deep understanding of the PREP process. ☐ Identify expectations of team leader, instructional coach, and other support staff in leading this work. ☐ Define tight expectations for collaborative teams by modeling the PREP process as the right work to answer the first critical question of a PLC. ☐ Work with leaders to ensure a consistent format (such as a template) is available for teams to use for the PREP process. ☐ Develop an accountability plan to create time and space for observations, feedback, and monitoring of teams' work with the PREP process.	☐ Support collaborative teams in using the PREP process and template. ☐ Lead and support discussions of the instructional components of standards-based planning. ☐ Provide resources for teachers to deepen their understanding of the *why* and *how* of clarifying what is guaranteed and viable in a curriculum.	☐ Develop norms with teams that include tight expectations of using the PREP process and template. ☐ Model the PREP process and provide support to complete it. ☐ Ensure the PREP process is implemented with fidelity to answer the first critical question of a PLC. ☐ Invite all team members to contribute fully and hold everyone accountable to the norms and work established through the PREP process. ☐ Work with other team leaders to participate in the guiding coalition and shared-leadership model for the school.

Figure 1.6: Leadership area guidelines for learning expectations—Achieve focus and stay intentional.

*Visit **go.SolutionTree.com/literacy** for a free reproducible version of this figure.*

impact by reducing teacher isolation and increasing commitment to the common good" (Louis, Dretzke, & Wahlstrom, 2010, p. 318). The following guiding question aligns to this area: *How can you build collaborative teams and share leadership to strengthen your ability and improve district and school outcomes for students?*

For the purpose of this chapter, consider how a shared-leadership model in a district or school can contribute to ensuring teachers implement a guaranteed literacy curriculum based on essential grade-level expectations in all classrooms. One of the most common concerns educators express to us as we coach this work is the worry that teachers will select the wrong standards to focus on or pace the work inappropriately. If so, this could result in inadequate time for essential learnings and a surplus of time spent in less-important areas. We understand these concerns, and we believe this creates even more urgency to have a strong shared-leadership model where all stakeholders maintain a common understanding of why the work around what students must know and be able to do and what that work entails is imperative.

Consider sending off every teacher in your district or school to decide what to teach on a given day. Each has his or her own notion about what is salient among the grade-level standards and an interpretation of them. Perhaps, for example, in one kindergarten classroom, students spend the entire year learning only the alphabet. In another, the teacher moves from the alphabet to blending sounds to reading and introducing writing during the year. As a first-grade teacher receiving these students, how difficult will it be to grow readers when your students have had access to a very different curriculum? In other words, because these two kindergarten teachers were not required to collaborate and consider essential grade-level expectations together, a classroom full of students will enter first grade below grade level and unprepared to tackle first-grade text, tasks, or questions. As a leader, how do you avoid this disservice to students in your school or district? How does a shared-leadership model—such as among a guiding coalition, collaborative-content teams, or grade-level teams—support this work?

We believe each student must have equal access to learn at high levels. This situation can only be accomplished when starting with the critical first step of achieving consistency among colleagues on grade-level expectations and all they entail as dictated by the components of the PREP process. It should not be "the luck of the draw" or which teacher a student gets each year that dictates his or her success. Therefore, leaders must ensure teachers collaborate to reach initial agreement on priority standards and acutely dissect and interpret them as a team since this exercise launches instruction and assessment. Shared leadership is critical, both at the district and school levels. It isn't as simple as putting teachers on teams and giving them time to work. Although surely imperative, the real value lies in providing ongoing training, support, coaching, and guidance to ensure teacher team members understand what they are to accomplish and how they go about it when they meet.

As DuFour and his colleagues (2016) proffer, PLCs' foundational focus rests on three big ideas (1) student learning, (2) collaborative culture, and (3) a results orientation. When districts and schools function as PLCs, leaders and educators (which include classroom teachers, special education teachers, and those who teach second-language learners) understand that they work interdependently to impact student learning. They share ownership of learning and student achievement through evidence-based and student-centered collaborative discussions. The shared-leadership model develops this ownership; guiding coalitions champion the effort of districts and schools, and collaborative teams own the work at the grassroots level. A guiding coalition, for example, often includes lead teachers and instructional coaches who have a dual responsibility of being members at the school or district level spearheading the PLC process *and* also leading the work of their collaborative teams. This includes, of course, determining essential grade-level expectations before creating assessments and instructional plans. Leaders must ensure that all guiding coalition members understand the necessity of this task and how a protocol (such as PREP) will support consistent grade-level expectations in all classrooms and schools.

To safeguard deep implementation of this work, leaders must arrange consistent support, training, communication, and dialogue within a shared-leadership model. For concrete suggestions on how leaders in various capacities in schools and districts can support this endeavor, review figure 1.7 (page 28).

Leadership Area: Foster Communication

As a leader invested in literacy, you must ensure you articulate your priorities for high expectations in communications, through words and actions. It must be a clear focus in the district or school. This includes attention to listening, reflecting, asking questions, and deepening your understanding of the root causes that create literacy issues. But fostering communication as a leadership area encompasses much more.

Can you recall a time when you had a miscommunication with someone in your district or school because you were not listening attentively or asking the right questions? Do you assume others understand your message? How do

Leadership Area: Build Shared Leadership			
District Leader	**School Administrator**	**Instructional Coach**	**Lead Teacher**
☐ Create a district guiding coalition to share leadership and to build a common understanding of the what and how of a guaranteed and viable curriculum.	☐ Create a school guiding coalition to build common understanding and to implement the PREP process as a tight expectation for all collaborative teams.	☐ Participate with the guiding coalition to build shared leadership of the PREP process in your school or district.	☐ Participate with the school's guiding coalition to support shared leadership of the PREP process.
☐ Ensure the district guiding coalition meets regularly and that agendas focus on building equal and equitable access of grade-level essential expectations for every student.	☐ Ensure the school's guiding coalition meets regularly and agendas focus on building equal and equitable access of grade-level essential expectations for every student.	☐ Learn to use the PREP process and prepare to lead collaborative teams, if necessary, in this work.	☐ Ensure collaborative team meeting agendas focus on answering the first critical question of a PLC.
☐ Adopt a protocol (such as PREP) for all school-based collaborative teams to use as they determine essential expectations.	☐ Develop progress-monitoring tools and practices with the guiding coalition to celebrate and adjust grade-level essential expectations as needed.	☐ Observe collaborative teams and classroom practices to provide feedback and coaching support in ensuring teams implement essential grade-level expectations with fidelity.	☐ Learn to use the PREP process and prepare to lead collaborative teams in this work.
☐ Provide ongoing training and support through the guiding coalition and school administrators to ensure consistent implementation of the protocol.	☐ Observe and provide feedback to collaborative teams that focus on the first critical question of a PLC. Provide support as needed to deepen implementation of the PREP process based on observations.	☐ Provide checks for vertical alignment of grade-level expectations.	☐ Support and lead collaborative teams' conversations as they determine essential grade-level literacy expectations and develop unit plans.
☐ Observe and give feedback to school administrators, instructional coaches, and lead teachers of collaborative teams' work focused on the first critical question of a PLC.	☐ Provide training and support to lead teachers and instructional coaches both in leadership skills and in how to use the PREP process with teams.		☐ Help other teachers deepen their understanding of the purpose of determining essential grade-level literacy expectations as a collaborative team.
☐ Create monitoring tools to celebrate and readjust actions that demonstrate shared leadership of a guaranteed and viable curriculum.			

Figure 1.7: Leadership area guidelines for learning expectations—Build shared leadership.

*Visit **go.SolutionTree.com/literacy** for a free reproducible version of this figure.*

communication skills affect your leadership impact? In this section, we explore the benefits of building productive listening skills and seeking ways to ensure your message is clear and understood. To do so, we address the following guiding question: *How can you foster strong communication skills with and among district and school administrators, teachers, and students?*

Build Productive Listening Skills

In almost every leadership conversation we engage in as coaches, we learn of communication mishaps. The smallest missed opportunity to communicate effectively often devolves into a much larger issue; emotions get in the way, feelings are hurt, and it sometimes becomes necessary to start over to fix the situation. Consider your own personal leadership style and take time to dissect what happens when you participate in a conversation. How do you ensure you are giving the conversation your undivided attention? How do you show you are actively listening? How do you honor the other person's contributions to a conversation?

When we unpack productive listening skills and intentionally consider the word *productive*, we should consider the desired outcome of the conversation before it takes place. If you are initiating the dialogue, then you want to envision the purpose of the exchange and how you wish the flow of discussion to progress prior to starting it. Productive listening skills necessitate that you willingly close your mind to other thoughts when someone asks you to engage in conversation. This often means showing attentiveness by putting down your phone, shutting your laptop (or turning away from an electronic screen), and making eye contact with the person speaking. Listening also requires deepening your understanding of what individuals say. When in doubt, you might reframe what someone says to you and also ask clarifying questions.

Teachers and others with whom you work will appreciate ways you demonstrate this leadership skill and look forward to learning with you. Support deeper communication skills with leaders by clarifying and continuing to message your top priorities and commit to keeping them there. To grow as a leader who earnestly listens and to make yourself understood, you must first realize people's perspectives and their situations influence what they say, do, and feel.

Seek First to Understand

Imagine this scenario: as a school leader, you observe a collaborative team meeting. A teacher shows a great deal of frustration and emotion when the team displays its latest literacy data from a common assessment. Her class failed to score as high as students in the other classes, but her frustration and especially her comments surprise you. Clearly defensive, she begins to blame the students and parents for their lack of literacy acumen. She voices her opinion by stating, "These kids are all from one neighborhood. My class is stacked with kids from the lowest socio-economic neighborhood, and now I am supposed to teach them to read. They just aren't able to master the required skills to read well!" Your first instinct is to meet with her to tell her exactly how you feel about her display of anger. Thinking twice, you decide to avoid an inevitable confrontation, so you return to your office and send her an email. In it, you state that you will be writing her a letter for her file as disciplinary action for her poor professional behavior.

Now picture the same situation, but this time, you ask her to meet after school in your office. You begin the conversation by telling her how her reaction stunned you. You then invite her to articulate why she was so upset, emphasizing that you want to better understand her feelings. You remind her that we often look at data this way, but you have never seen her respond so emphatically. She becomes very emotional again as she explains that she was surprised and caught off guard by how poorly her students performed and wanted to conceal it from others. The more she talks, the more obvious it is to you that she was embarrassed in front of you and her peers. As the conversation continues, you ask clarifying questions about what she thought she might have done differently with her instruction than her peers and what else might have caused the unsatisfactory scores. You continue to find ways for her to reflect on her actions without blaming the students or worrying about her peers' responses. At one point, she admits that she didn't really believe she knew how to implement the expected school-adopted close-reading strategy and test students on it. She was afraid to admit she felt inadequate to capably teach this strategy. She breathes a sigh of relief when you offer to invite an instructional coach to model a lesson in her classroom the next day, and her students can retake the assessment.

Consider how listening and asking clarifying questions can change the outcome of a situation, not only for the teacher but her students, as well. In this section's two examples, the personal meeting versus the email was obviously a better mode of communication that spawned a genuine conversation. It's through these sorts of conversations that leaders uncover the root of an issue, which simultaneously promotes learning for all. An effective way to increase your ability to communicate impactfully begins with removing barriers that lead to one-way discourse, such as directing from a position of telling (too often through email). Instead, ask or seek personal communication that builds relationships and deepens understanding.

Leaders confront these and similar situations on a constant basis, so be mindful to focus on solutions that benefit teachers and their students. Create the opportunity and environment for teachers to honestly emote and share concerns so you can problem solve together. Figure 1.8 lists myriad examples of how to infuse best practices for listening, understanding, and communicating, particularly for literacy support.

Leadership Area: Foster Communication			
District Leader	**School Administrator**	**Instructional Coach**	**Lead Teacher**
☐ Maintain focus and consistently message the purpose and intended actions of establishing essential grade-level learning expectations for students. ☐ Take every opportunity to communicate tight expectations for how collaborative teams will use the PREP process. ☐ Develop strategies to observe, listen, receive feedback, and understand the needs of school leaders, coaches, and teachers in implementing the PREP process with fidelity.	☐ Support district common messages that explain the purpose and intended actions of establishing essential grade-level learning expectations for students. ☐ Take every opportunity to communicate tight expectations for how collaborative teams will use the PREP process. ☐ Observe collaborative team meetings and classrooms with the intended purpose of seeking to understand the concerns, struggles, and successes of identifying and implementing essential grade-level student expectations. ☐ Create monitoring tools that assist in learning, communicating, and readjusting actions around the first critical question of a PLC. ☐ Practice productive listening skills by asking clarifying questions, reframing the conversation, and closing your mind to other thoughts. ☐ Celebrate and provide ongoing feedback to teachers and collaborative teams as they increase their ability to deepen clarity on essential expectations.	☐ Support collaborative teams in understanding how to use the PREP process through modeling, messaging, and coaching. ☐ Create every opportunity to communicate expectations on why answering the first critical question of a PLC is so important. ☐ Observe, model, and provide feedback in classrooms specifically supporting grade-level expectations.	☐ Communicate with the same voice as the district and school leaders and instructional coaches. ☐ Learn how to answer the *why* questions and the common questions of resistance involving the PREP process. ☐ Facilitate the PREP process during collaborative team meetings. ☐ Provide support and feedback to teams as they complete the PREP process.

Figure 1.8: Leadership area guidelines for learning expectations—Foster communication.

*Visit **go.SolutionTree.com/literacy** for a free reproducible version of this figure.*

The Final Word

In a PLC, tight and loose expectations coexist. A non-wavering expectation might be that teams develop a standards-based unit map comprised of the PREP template components, which all teachers must use to develop curricula. Each teacher on a team, however, may choose to conduct lessons using different instructional strategies.

As a leader, you adopt tight expectations about the rigor of grade-level work in classrooms. As a result, teachers collaborate to gain clarity on what students will be proficient in accomplishing. It is not a "'Tyranny of the OR'—the purely rational view that says you can have either A *OR* B" but the "'Genius of the AND'—the paradoxical view that allows [pursuit of] both A *AND* B at the same time" (Collins & Porras, 2002, p. 10). Education leadership expert and author Jane A. G. Kise (2019) describes the pursuit of two competing leadership priorities as the need to think in terms of *both-and* to maximize effectiveness. As a leader, your first responsibility is to define the tight expectation that teachers must provide all students a guaranteed opportunity to learn grade-level essential standards *and* that teachers will work together to define expectations related to them.

District leaders often ask us how they ensure that their teachers are providing a guaranteed and viable curriculum if they are not providing the essential standards. We believe this is the purest form of the genius of the *and*: support the work with tight expectations that the PREP protocol will be used to establish essential expectations while at the same time allow teachers the professional autonomy to consider what students must know and be able to do. In the next chapter, you will learn how you can support teacher teams on their assessment journey.

CHAPTER 2

Examine Assessment Options for Literacy

Using assessment well means capitalizing on the information collected and using those insights to facilitate learning and foster hope for students.

—NICOLE DIMICH

As you gain experience supporting team participation in the PREP process, and as teams develop a deeper understanding of planning a guaranteed and viable curriculum, consider how you will know what students are learning. By establishing clarity on the priority standards teams will assess *and* the specific knowledge and skills students must acquire to show proficiency, teachers set the groundwork to answer the second critical question of a PLC: *How will we know if each student has learned it?* (DuFour et al., 2016).

As a school or district leader, it's your role to secure sufficient time for teachers to engage in assessment planning, just as you did with the PREP process in chapter 1 (page 9). Consider: What is your vision for how you want students and teachers to gauge the learning that actually takes place? What will be your role in ensuring teachers understand and use effective assessment practices that provide them and their students with valuable information to advance learning? Do teachers and students know why assessment is critical and how it contributes to student achievement? In *Softening the Edges*, assessment expert Katie White (2017) reminds leaders:

> Traditionally, planning has often meant devoting a great deal of time to thinking about what students would be *doing* and not nearly enough time thinking about *why* they would be doing it and *what they would be thinking and learning.* (p. 32)

To provide educators with the tools and guidance to eventually design assessments, this chapter focuses on collecting evidence to measure to what degree students master essential standards. Your role as the leader of assessment practices in your school or district means you must champion and advance a deep understanding of what assessment tools teams can use effectively and when. Most important, you ensure teams understand *why* they assess. In this chapter, we examine the use of formative and summative assessments, along with various assessment types and formats that support this thinking and learning, and your role as a leader in this literacy work. We conclude with an examination of two leadership areas related to assessment: (1) achieve focus and stay intentional and (2) prioritize students.

Note that assessments are just a starting point for answering the second critical question of a PLC. Subsequent chapters address the learning progressions (chapter 3, page 59), rubrics and collaborative scoring (chapter 4, page 83), and data-analysis practices that support the making and use of high-quality assessments (chapter 5, page 101).

Formative and Summative Assessment Overview

To ensure students practice skills and strategies and for teachers to measure standards-based learning targets, teachers "assess to gather information about student learning and either use that information *formatively* to advance learning or use it *summatively* to verify that it has occurred" (Schimmer, 2019). Teachers historically consider formative assessments opportunities to check in on student learning (assessments *for* learning) and summative as a culmination at the close of a unit (assessments *of* learning). Education and assessment expert Dylan Wiliam (2018) offers a useful summation of formative assessment:

> An assessment functions formatively to the extent that evidence about student achievement is elicited, interpreted, and used by teachers, learners, or their peers to make decisions about the next steps in instruction that are likely to be better, or better founded, than the decisions they would have made in the absence of that evidence. (p. 48)

In terms of *summative*, a broader definition includes assessing students after a cluster of lessons and not only at the end of the unit. In this regard, *summative assessments* represent touchpoints to ascertain students' understanding at significant junctures throughout—as well as at the end of—a comprehensive unit of study.

Throughout an instructional cycle, teams design and issue both common formative and summative assessments against a common rubric that members also create together. During collaborative scoring, teams establish that each teacher interprets the rubric uniformly to maintain consistency in assessing students' work. Teachers also administer individual classroom assessments to collect additional data on student progress. The data teachers compile and review from all assessments provide information daily and weekly to advance students' learning.

Within the classroom, teachers conduct both informal and formal formative assessments consistently; the latter can represent common assessments if collaborative teams create them together. When doing so, they design, find, or revise existing assessments that give students multiple opportunities to demonstrate their learning in myriad ways. Whether creating assessments from scratch or planning to administer prepared assessments from a purchased literacy program, teachers ensure that each assessment clearly measures students' understanding of priority learning standards.

Although the convenience of prepackaged assessments entices teachers, they review and sometimes revamp those assessments to make sure they evaluate precisely the right skills. Richard DuFour (2015) states:

> When students struggle on tests created by others—the textbook, the district, the state—it is uncommon for educators to attribute their struggles to the poor quality of the test. That likelihood is diminished when the teachers themselves create an assessment that they agree is a valid way to gather evidence of student learning. (p. 176)

A critical role of leaders in building common, team-level understanding of assessments is making certain teachers know how to use prepackaged assessments (if they choose this option) or design their own to align with the essential learnings from the PREP process.

Complicating this work is the reality that *assessment*—a term used pervasively in education—causes much confusion with its varied terminology of types and formats, such as *formative, summative,* and *performance*; *formal* and *informal*; *obtrusive, unobtrusive,* and *student-generated*; *selected-* and *constructed-response*; and so on. Although we lay a foundation for leading assessment work in this chapter, as mentioned in this chapter's introduction, we address related assessment topics to ensure you, as a leader, see an extensive scope of this altogether pivotal component in ensuring all students learn. To begin, let's look at a snapshot of the assessment types and formats we describe in our signature series; refer to those books for additional in-depth explanations and examples.

REFLECTION

As the leader of assessment work in literacy, where do you begin building a common understanding of how to use assessment to inform your teachers' next steps? What dialogue will you initiate with teachers to help them understand the different uses of formative and summative assessments? What examples can you model for them?

Types of Formative Assessment Practices in the Classroom

Marzano (2017) identifies three types of formative assessments embedded in classroom practice: (1) unobtrusive, (2) obtrusive, and (3) student-generated. *Unobtrusive* are assessments that do not require teachers to interrupt their instruction. Rather, they observe and listen to students. For example, teachers pay attention to whether students actively listen as they model a strategy. They walk around the classroom to take a peek while students complete a graphic organizer or listen in on group conversations. When necessary, teachers approach students to redirect, pose questions, or provide clarification. They might even take informal notes on a recordkeeping sheet to track students' level of understanding. Figure 2.1 shows a sample unobtrusive data-recording tool instructional facilitators or coaches can replicate in blank form for teachers to use.

Obtrusive assessments mean that teachers stop instruction and ask students to work on an individual, pair, or group activity. For example, a teacher projects a passage from a complex text on an interactive screen to model and explain how readers use context clues to determine meanings of unknown words. After taking questions and clarifying any confusion, she instructs students to work with a partner to practice this task as she circulates around the room assessing needs.

Student-generated assessments allow students to choose the way they demonstrate their understanding of a learning target. As teachers involve students in self-assessment practices, the opportunities for students to understand learning targets and establish their own goals support their independence and responsibility. White (2019) reminds educators that students who self-assess can "reframe their own ideas of what it means to be successful in school by asking them to explore the

Concept or Skill: Determine whether a sentence is a statement or a question.

Student Name	Demonstrates mastery and can apply the concept or skill in an advanced way (4)	Demonstrates mastery of the concept or skill (3)	Has some understanding of the concept or skill (2)	Demonstrates limited understanding of the concept or skill (1)
John D.			Can explain the difference between statements and questions but can't correctly identify examples of them ✓	
Suzy S.		✓		
Darel J.	✓			
Aditi V.			Inconsistently identifies examples of questions and statements ✓+	

Source: Onuscheck, Spiller, Martin, & May, 2020, p. 45.

Figure 2.1: Unobtrusive student data-recording form—Example.

Visit go.SolutionTree.com/literacy for a free reproducible version of this figure.

relationships between their attempts at new approaches and what they are hoping to achieve" (p. 94).

As a leader, your classroom observations and look-fors should align to the formative assessment practices you expect. Consider creating a tight expectation that teachers use formative assessment in their literacy practices on a daily basis to collect information about student learning that is timely and appropriate to their instructional plan. However, you might want to be loose on the formative assessment type as long as teachers understand the critical need to be well informed of ongoing student learning during literacy instruction and that the instruction and assessment align to the rigor of each learning standard.

Assessment Formats or Methods

In our signature series, we explore four formats or methods of assessing students: (1) selected-responses, (2) constructed-responses, (3) student-generated assessments, and (4) performance assessments. Leaders should build their own knowledge and skills in this area so they can support teachers in understanding assessment formats and how to use them. Here is a short summary of each format with more detailed explanations and resources in chapter 2 of the signature series books.

- **Selected-responses:** This format measures knowledge of factual information, main ideas, and basic skills that involve one correct answer. Examples of this format include multiple-choice, matching, fill-in-the-blank, and true-or-false prompts. Students can take these assessments quickly; teachers score them easily to obtain a broad overview of students' knowledge of foundational information.

- **Constructed-responses:** Through open-ended tasks, this format measures deeper understanding and might span one to three class periods. Responses can be short or expanded, ranging from one or two sentences to a developed essay; or students might produce a graphic organizer, brief summary, or descriptive paragraph. Sometimes students examine, read, watch, or listen to a stimulus as the basis for their response, such as a graphic, photograph, text, short video, or audio recording.

- **Student-generated assessments:** An underutilized but potentially valuable form of assessment, this involves students self-selecting and choosing ways in which they can demonstrate what they learn. This type of formative assessment promotes self-agency and engagement as students determine the best way to provide evidence of their learning.

▸ **Performance assessments:** Perhaps spanning a few days, weeks, or even a semester, this format measures multiple learning outcomes. Teachers gather evidence from not just a product, presentation, or performance but also the process students use to complete it.

Teachers must write both valid *and* reliable assessments. To address *validity*, teams defer to the learning targets and DOK levels the PREP process template identifies so the assessment aligns to the cognitive demand in the learning target. This prework is invaluable for teachers in determining how to assess students. In terms of *reliability*, teachers trust that the results indicate which students have and which have not reached proficiency based on the learning target. Education authors and consultants Kim Bailey and Chris Jakicic (2017) explain two aspects that contribute to reliability:

> The first is to make sure to include enough questions for each of the assessed learning targets. While there is no one piece of research that supplies the answer to how many questions this would be, most researchers suggest that at least three to four selected-response questions per learning target will eliminate lucky guessing (Gareis & Grant, 2008). For constructed-response questions, one well-written question should instill confidence in a team that it can decide on next steps. (p. 70)

The other component pertaining to *reliability* is to write the question or task in accessible language students clearly understand. If the directions in an assessment hamper students because they trip over the language, their misinterpretation can skew the results.

As a leader, look for teachers to match the learning target and its DOK levels with their method of assessment. Selected-response items alone do not allow students to demonstrate high-level understanding of learning standards, which constructed-response items and performance assessments can achieve. However, teachers can couple selected-response items with another assessment format to determine a more robust awareness of students' mastery. If teachers are measuring a DOK 1 learning standard, selected-response items work well to ascertain students' grasp of foundational and factual information. Further, teachers can efficiently score them. However, teachers can also use a constructed-response to measure a DOK 1 learning standard.

To illustrate, primary teachers might ask students to describe through dictation what an individual looks like and draw a picture to address standard W.K.2: *Use a combination of drawing, dictating, and writing to compose informative texts in which they name what they are writing about and supply some information about the topic* (NGA & CCSSO, 2010). A teacher might say, "Aunt Kathy has blue eyes and black hair. Her hair is shorter than Mrs. Andolina's hair, and it sticks out. She wears black pants, high heels, and a black sweater with a white shirt under it. She has a ring on her finger, and she wears earrings and a watch." Figure 2.2 illustrates what a student might then produce (assume the colors are correct). This example is indicative of a constructed-response in that it represents a basic task that requires students to recall or reproduce knowledge they observe from a familiar individual to provide information through a description, which applies to DOK 1.

Figure 2.2: Constructed-response example to a teacher prompt.

As stated, posing at least four selected-response questions or prompts will likely render an assessment valid since teachers can safely conclude that students acquire understanding when they correctly answer three or four items (Bailey & Jakicic, 2017). For example, to design a selected-response assessment to address standard RL.1.4, *Identify words and phrases in stories or poems that suggest feelings or appeal to the senses* (NGA & CCSSO, 2010), teachers can share the following quotes from *Chrysanthemum* (Henkes, 1991).

1. "Chrysanthemum loved her name. She loved the way it sounded when her mother woke her up. She loved the way it sounded when her father called her for dinner. And she loved the way it sounded when she whispered it to herself in the bathroom mirror."

2. "Chrysanthemum wilted. She did not think her name was absolutely perfect. She thought it was absolutely dreadful."

3. "Chrysanthemum thought her name was absolutely perfect."

4. "But when Mrs. Chud took roll call, everyone giggled upon hearing Chrysanthemum's name."

5. "'If I had a name like yours, I'd change it,' Victoria said as the students lined up to go home. I wish I could, thought Chrysanthemum miserably."

Next to each quote, teachers place a sad and happy emoji along with words such as *sad*, *happy*, and even *I'm not sure*. Students circle the face and word that indicate the mood the text evokes. Alternatively, teachers can issue a constructed-response by asking students to write *happy* or *sad* next to each quote and circle or underline text that provides evidence for this mood.

Teachers can also conduct an active participation assessment to informally gather information about individual students' understanding, then augment with a more formal assessment to collect additional data to determine next steps in instruction. For example, figure 2.3 (page 42) shows an assessment prompt teachers can issue to address a learning target in which students identify a character's trait in a complex text and support it by citing specific details from the story.

The Illinois Assessment of Readiness Digital Item Library (https://il.digitalitemlibrary .com) houses a repository of assessment items that grades 3–11 teachers can choose from to help build their own assessments or add to their current inventory. It provides myriad selected- and constructed-response items by grade level and ELA or mathematics standards. These assessments complement many state and provincial

Selected-Response (Active Participation)		
Thumbs-up: Yes, the trait describes the character.		
Thumbs-down: No, the trait does not describe the character.		
Fist: I am not sure.		
a. Adventurous	c. Brave	e. Respectful
b. Shy	d. Dishonest	f. Independent

Constructed-Response	
Circle two traits from this column that you think best describe the main character of the story.	Use examples from the story to provide detailed support for each of these character traits.
Adventurous	
Shy	
Brave	
Dishonest	
Respectful	
Independent	

Figure 2.3: Assessments using textual evidence to describe a character.

standards if you are in a state or province that has not adopted these U.S. standards. Most K–12 education publishers include these types of assessments, as well.

To obtain substantive diagnostic data, be sure your teachers know how to choose questions wisely. Each assessment question teachers select must allow them to ascertain students' proficiency levels based on specific learning targets. A group of questions can address the same standard, whereby each one enables teachers to elicit specific data. Consider standard RL.3.3: *Describe characters in a story (e.g., their traits, motivations, or feelings) and explain how their actions contribute to the sequence of events* (NGA & CCSSO, 2010). One question might state something a character does (the cause) and ask students to indicate which effects result from his or her action from a provided list. Other prompts can focus on students' ability to describe a character's appearance and his or her feelings about a situation. Students then cite text evidence to support their thinking. Remember, teachers must collect enough data to ascertain students' understanding of skills. Therefore, if teachers use provided selected-response items, they will need to find a sufficient number of questions that assess the same learning target or augment the items with their own.

Additionally, teachers can pose constructed-response prompts, such as this example for assessing the same third-grade standard (RL.3.3):

As you read _____, pay attention to details from the story that help you identify a personality trait to describe _____ (include character's name). Then write to explain this character's trait by using details and examples from the story.

When teachers confidently understand the different types of assessments and have opportunities to discuss and ascertain the most appropriate formats that align to their grade-level expectations, they afford students a variety of ways to demonstrate their learning. As a leader, continue to build common understanding of assessments and ensure teachers can differentiate between the usages and purposes of formative versus summative measures. In figure 2.4 (page 44), you may use the guiding questions to lead dialogue and build assessment literacy with teachers. You can frame these questions differently so that they address in-class formative assessments that teachers conduct as well as teams' common assessments.

As we have explained, your job as a leader is to make certain that teachers understand why they assess students' work. When you support teachers in realizing the purpose, they achieve clarity for selecting or designing the type, format, and quality of assessments they administer. To lead well, it is necessary to focus on the leadership areas we discuss next.

Leadership: Guiding Questions for Examining Assessment Options for Literacy	Collaborative Team Notes and Next Steps
In building an assessment plan, how are you integrating both assessing *for* learning (formative) and assessment *of* learning (summative)? How are you considering both informal and formal formative assessments in this plan?	
Will you be using prepackaged assessments or creating your own? How are you ensuring both validity and reliability of the assessment? If you are creating your own, how have you applied the PREP process as prework?	
How are you planning to balance unobtrusive, obtrusive, and student-generated assessments in your everyday classroom practice? How will the information gathered through these formative practices assist you in understanding student learning?	
How will you determine if you will use selected-response, constructed-response, student-generated, or performance assessments? What steps will you take to ensure the questions and prompts are providing the information that you need about student learning (reliability)?	

Figure 2.4: Leadership guiding questions for examining assessment options for literacy.

*Visit **go.SolutionTree.com/literacy** for a free reproducible version of this figure.*

Leadership Area: Achieve Focus and Stay Intentional

After completing the PREP process, teams planning a unit must consider the kinds of assessments they can use with students, which requires focus and intentionality. Depending on your leadership role, you are responsible for supporting teachers and collaborative teams in some capacity by educating, guiding, or monitoring as they come to understand why assessment is critical; the types and functions of different assessment options; and which ones to use within instruction. Let's consider some of the missteps that might occur so you can help teams stay squarely focused on the right work. Once aware of these potential obstacles, we present specific suggestions for achieving focus and intentionality.

Although teams should receive strong guidance while completing the PREP template, leaders sometimes mistakenly assume teachers understand why they assess and also know how to select the appropriate assessment types and formats. Unfortunately, teams are often left to figure out assessment plans on their own. Without sufficient professional learning to build their capacity around assessment practices, they quickly go to the internet and pull questions from a website. They may not have engaged in discussion or participated in training about what information an assessment should yield, why they are conducting it, or what method of assessing is most suitable based on the unwrapped standard (or standards) from their PREP template. In fact, they might forget to refer to that template and their previous hard work. When that happens, the bridge between answering the first critical question of a PLC (*What is it we want our students to learn?*) and the second critical question (*How will we know if each student has learned it?*) collapses.

Unless leaders intentionally focus efforts on building common awareness of the *why* and *what* before teachers create assessments, teams will likely struggle to confidently know what students can and cannot do with regard to essential learnings. As a leader, ask yourself: "Am I confident that teachers know the difference between formative and summative assessment practices? Do they know why they are assessing and which type and format are optimal? How will they use the data from each?"

To uncover answers, preassess teachers' knowledge and experience around this topic, and directly address any deficits, visit a team meeting, and pose pertinent questions, like the following. You might also revisit figure 2.4 and pose any of those questions to preassess.

▸ "Why are you giving this assessment?"

▸ "Are you planning to use it formatively or summatively?"

▸ "Why are you checking in at this particular point in instruction?"

▸ "What kind of assessment will you administer?"

▸ "How will you conduct it?"

▸ "How will the assessment indicate to what degree students have mastered essential knowledge and skills?"

▸ "How do you intend to use the data?"

Based on teacher responses, suggest particular resources and plan professional development opportunities so they understand and use assessments effectively.

In our work with school and district leaders, we often witness teachers (and sometimes leaders) misidentify the purpose of formative and summative assessment. For example, members of a collaborative team sometimes begin to discuss moving the date of a common formative assessment back because students are unprepared. This communicates teachers' lack of understanding regarding the purpose of formative assessment, which should serve as a check-in point for them to gauge students' capabilities at a particular point in instruction. The data analysis the team conducts from the formative assessment reveals concrete information that guides their next instructional moves (see chapter 5, page 101). Therefore, communicate to your teachers they should not wait until they feel students have acquired more knowledge and skills. Rather, they administer the assessment to ascertain what students need in order to advance their learning. You must instill (or reinforce) in teams the necessity to create district- and schoolwide formative practices that provide ongoing and timely information to both teachers and students about what they are or are not mastering.

Another observation we notice involves some teachers' preoccupation with grading and reporting rather than the major premise of assessing. As a leader, strive for teachers to answer the following types of questions so they grasp *why* assessment is critical.

▸ "What are your intent and purpose of assessing?"

▸ "How do they support student learning?"

▸ "How do strategies connect with assessments?"

Dedicate concentrated time to develop assessment awareness with your teachers by guiding teams to realize the purpose of common assessments and reinforcing why developing, collecting, and using data from them are critical. How teachers and teams use the information assessments generate matters most because all assessments should clearly indicate to teams what they need to do to ensure success for all. Let teachers know that although they are identifying assessments they might conduct at this juncture in students' learning, they will eventually administer an assessment and then critically analyze the data.

With the *why* clearly established, teams begin to consider the most applicable assessment types and formats. As a leader, we caution you to avoid assuming teachers can write quality assessments or know which format to use. Time and professional learning around this work are necessary so teachers design or find valid and reliable assessments that will aptly solicit what students have learned. In addition to conveying the information from this chapter, a leader can share exemplars, model how to design effective assessments, and explain the thinking behind assessment types. This strategy is akin to teachers showing mentor texts to illustrate examples of sound aspects of writing students can emulate.

Teams also benefit from reviewing assessments others design. Team members should read and discuss levels of rigor and expectations of these assessments to examine what other teams create in response to a grade-level standard they will also address. Instructional coaches or facilitators can collect assessments and share artifacts between teams and even from other schools within the district or in different states or provinces. Any leader who has expertise in building assessments can walk teachers through the exemplars to articulate how they best assess students' knowledge and skills. For suggestions about how you might achieve focus and intentionality in your role as an assessment leader, review figure 2.5 (page 48).

As always, when district, team, and classroom expectations align, the likelihood of success around this work increases. For example, as a principal, it would be valuable for you to create a professional learning plan for the school that builds a deep understanding of assessment planning. Lead teachers, in turn, understand common assessment development and how to align assessments to the rigor of the standards. A district leader develops tight expectations and intentionally creates assessment systems, guidelines, or protocols and communicates them to school leaders and teachers. This might mean working with others to devise a flowchart detailing these expectations in the district or school. For example, figure 2.6 (page 49) exemplifies how staff at Kildeer Countryside Community Consolidated School District 96 in Buffalo Grove, Illinois, created tight expectations for assessment planning in all schools. This continuum, centered around the four critical questions of a PLC, demonstrates assessment as part of a learning journey rather than a separate entity.

Leadership Area: Achieve Focus and Stay Intentional			
District Leader	**School Administrator**	**Instructional Coach**	**Lead Teacher**
☐ Develop tight expectations within the district that all teachers will build a common understanding of the types and formats of assessments. ☐ Provide ongoing support to principals and others in leadership positions to ensure strong school leadership in the area of assessment, including professional learning. ☐ Develop reciprocal accountability tools that enable school teams to monitor their work and receive feedback, coaching, and training as teachers select assessment methods and formats. ☐ Prevent distractors from taking the focus away from building assessment literacy in the schools.	☐ Ensure a professional learning plan for the school builds a deep understanding of assessment planning. ☐ Identify expectations of team leader, instructional coach, and other support staff in leading assessment work. ☐ Define tight expectations for collaborative teams to answer the second critical question of a PLC effectively, with appropriate types and formats of assessment. ☐ Work with leaders to ensure resources are available and teams use them. ☐ Develop an accountability plan to create time and space, as needed, for observations, feedback, and monitoring assessments.	☐ Lead and support discussions at team meetings. ☐ Help teachers to ascertain which assessment types and formats are needed in common planning and classroom practice. ☐ Offer input and suggestions on types and formats of classroom and common assessments for a featured unit. ☐ Intentionally observe classroom assessment practices to provide feedback, coaching, and modeling of effective practices. ☐ Ensure there is a plan to match assessments with learning targets and levels of rigor. ☐ Suggest evidence that individual teachers can collect based on assessments. ☐ Find and share resources with teachers.	☐ Develop norms with teams that include tight expectations of common assessment planning. ☐ Ensure your team uses assessment types and formats that appropriately provide teachers with timely information about student learning. ☐ Model and facilitate discussions about building a common understanding of assessments (for example, facilitate discussion for an exercise to generate a list of assessments teachers might potentially use). ☐ Ensure collaborative teams answer the second critical question of a PLC with fidelity. ☐ Invite all team members to contribute fully and hold one another accountable to team norms and assessment work. ☐ Use the signature series and other resources to support and broaden team learning concerning assessments. ☐ Record and distribute (via hard copy or electronically) team-generated lists of classroom and common assessments to use for next steps in developing a learning progression.

Figure 2.5: Leadership area guidelines for assessment—Achieve focus and stay intentional.

*Visit **go.SolutionTree.com/literacy** for a free reproducible version of this figure.*

PLC critical question 1:
What is it we want our students to learn?*

*Team should engage in the pre-unit protocol (PREP) before beginning the unit of instruction.

PLC critical question 2:
How will we know if each student has learned it?

Assessment Continuum and Data Analysis:
Repeating Cycle for Units of Instruction

Optional preassessment with data conversation

Data-driven instruction

Formative classroom assessments

Data-driven instruction

During-unit common formative assessments with data conversation

Data-driven instruction

End-of-unit common formative assessment with data conversation

Preassessment
- Administered at least one to two weeks in advance
- Used to determine what students already know to tailor the instructional unit plan and differentiate to meet specific student needs
- May or may not be common

Formative Classroom Assessments
- Administered daily
- Used to make decisions in the moment or day to day (checklists, observations, conferences, and so on)
- May or may not be common

During-Unit Common Formative Assessments
- Administered during the unit of instruction within a defined window
- Used to check in on student progress toward mastery of essential learning outcomes
- Are common at the team or district level

End-of-Unit Common Formative Assessment
- Administered at the end of a unit of instruction within a defined window
- Used to assess students' current level of mastery after a significant amount of instruction
- Is common at the district level

PLC critical question 3:
How will we respond when some students don't learn it?

PLC critical question 4:
How can we extend the learning for students who have demonstrated proficiency?

Source: Onuscheck, Spiller, & Glass, p. 52; adapted from © 2016 Kildeer Countryside Community Consolidated School District 96, Buffalo Grove, Illinois.

Figure 2.6: Assessment continuum example.

As you can see, the district elects to use the term *common formative* instead of *common summative* for its end-of-unit assessments, thus indicating an unwavering belief in the ongoing and recurring cycle of instruction and assessment. In other words, assessment is part of a balanced literacy instructional plan rather than a separate task for collaborative teams or individual teachers to work on in isolation. As a leader in any capacity, the important message is that you clarify your beliefs and use common language to communicate your expectations.

REFLECTION

Consider the sample expectations in figure 2.5 (page 48) and the continuum in figure 2.6 (page 49). As a leader, what would be your next steps in creating a focus of assessment practices in your district or school? How can you support this work more intentionally in your role? How do you keep this focus as an ongoing expectation and commitment in your district, school, or teams?

Leadership Area: Prioritize Students

Think about this: a teacher adamantly asserts that she knows her students best and does not require concrete evidence to understand what they need. She plans her lessons and, when you observe her class, it becomes obvious that she moves on with her teaching despite whether her students master skills. She has a plan and is sticking to it. It reminds us of the cartoon *Mr. Magoo*, an oblivious character who ignores the disasters happening around him. He appears to be nearsighted and unable to see the problems that abound in his midst. Unfortunately, this might serve as an apt comparison to what you see in some teachers' classrooms— a well-orchestrated lesson devoid of an assessment plan that provides ongoing feedback to teachers *and* students about learning or perhaps stagnation. Without that information, teachers are merely covering material, not securing what students absorb and can apply. Undoubtedly, you do not want to observe this scenario in your school.

With an intentional focus on students, teachers and leaders create authentic opportunities for their literacy assessment planning to inform learning. When students can explain information and skills they've acquired or have yet to master based on feedback from formative assessments, they take ownership of their own learning. The assessment reveals a story that helps learners understand their personal journey. When students describe the expectations, compare them to how they performed, and most important, plan what to do next (given an analysis of errors and thoughtful reflection), it truly epitomizes the meaning of formative assessment. Teachers must create a situation in which students help to guide their own learning trajectory. Authors Connie Moss and Susan Brookhart (2019) emphasize the influential and synergistic relationship between student and teacher in feedback and formative assessment:

> We believe that the central idea behind formative assessment is improved student learning that comes from informed actions taken by the students themselves. Engaged in the formative assessment process, students develop the capacity to monitor the quality of their own work, so that they can move from teacher-supplied feedback to expert self-monitoring. (p. 192)

As a leader, always be mindful that teachers conduct assessments so they and their students gain clarity about points along their learning path. In other words, teachers and students understand the milestones students make as they incrementally progress and what needs to happen next as they strive to achieve a learning target.

Spiller and Power (2019) say that *putting students first* means ensuring equity of access to learning for all students:

> This means quality instruction with rigorous learning opportunities and fair assessment practices that give all students differentiated and various chances to demonstrate what they know and do. We understand that this is a tall order for both teachers and school leaders. (p. 110)

This passage poses several questions: Why is this a tall order? What makes it so challenging to create equitable opportunities for students to learn and the teacher to assess that learning? How can you, as a leader, work with teachers to ensure your students, whether district- or schoolwide, receive equitable assessment opportunities with appropriate types and formats?

In *Building Equity: Policies and Practices to Empower All Learners*, coauthors Dominique Smith, Nancy Frey, Ian Pumpian, and Douglas Fisher (2017) challenge readers to imagine a school in which the opportunity roadblocks that result in the *haves* receiving higher-quality education than the *have-nots* are identified and removed, so that all students benefit from high-quality learning experiences.

To achieve this reality, teachers must consider and understand their students' background knowledge and avoid biased assumptions when selecting assessment questions. For example, consider this: you are a principal in Los Angeles, California, and your students receive a common assessment question that a collaborative team selected from a mathematics test bank. The word problem asks students to work through a situation involving a corn maze in a farmer's field. As you enter the classroom, you immediately recognize that the mathematics required to solve the problem is not causing an issue for the students. Rather, what interferes with them demonstrating understanding of the targeted mathematics skills is their lack of background knowledge about a corn maze (such as various designs or the word *maze*) and even the configuration or mental picture of a farmer's field. Similarly, teachers might administer a writing assessment in which students have little or no prior knowledge about the topic that forms the basis for the essay. For instance, the teacher tasks students in Miami, Florida with writing a descriptive piece about skiing down a mountain in the midst of a blizzard.

These kinds of assessments jeopardize students' ability to accurately reflect their true capabilities; hence, they skew the results, making it difficult to measure strengths and weaknesses that align to learning targets. As a leader, what might you do to help teachers understand how to put students first as they consider which assessment format and types they will use?

In 2020 and 2021, the world dealt with challenges surrounding COVID-19, forcing educators to confront and adjust to new expectations, such as learning how to support parents and students remotely. In responding to unforeseen circumstances such as these, leaders must work with their teams to create equitable learning experiences even in the most unsettling times. For example, teachers and administrators must seek solutions to ensure all students engaged in remote learning receive support even if they are without internet access, do not own an electronic device, or have one that lacks internet capabilities.

In figure 2.7, review the suggestions for how you, as a leader, can prioritize students and place them at the forefront when designing or finding assessments. Perhaps as a district leader, you can support assessment awareness by creating opportunities for all school leaders and teachers to understand the purposes, types, and formats of assessments. As a school leader, you might follow up on professional learning and create tight expectations for collaborative teams to create common formative and summative assessments that align to grade-level standards' levels of rigor. As an instructional coach, you make certain you grasp assessment practices in order to support teams' common understanding of assessment literacy and perhaps

Leadership Area: Prioritize Students			
District Leader	**School Administrator**	**Instructional Coach**	**Lead Teacher**
☐ Develop and reinforce tight expectations within the district that the student is the focus of all assessment plans. ☐ Provide ongoing support to principals and other leaders to ensure strong school leadership regarding equitable assessment practices. ☐ Communicate regularly that students should be involved in their learning journey through self-assessment strategies.	☐ Define tight expectations for collaborative teams to answer the second critical question of a PLC effectively, with appropriate types and assessment formats that are equitable for all students. ☐ Consistently reinforce and communicate the district expectation that the student is the focus of all assessment plans. ☐ Ensure a professional learning plan for the school builds a deep understanding of assessment planning. ☐ Identify expectations and monitor assessment practices of the team leader, instructional coach, and other support staff to ensure equitable practices for all students. ☐ Expect student understanding of their learning journey by sharing information with them through assessment practices.	☐ Ensure your personal understanding of assessment strategies that focus on a commitment to all students. ☐ Lead and support discussions at team meetings that focus on the student as the reason for assessment. ☐ Help teachers to ascertain which assessment types and formats provide equitable assessment practices for all students. ☐ Offer input and suggestions on types and formats of classroom and common assessments with an equitable student lens. ☐ Observe classroom assessment practices to provide feedback, coaching, and modeling to ensure a student-centered culture. ☐ Support teacher and student understanding of how students can use assessments to own their learning journey.	☐ Model and facilitate discussions for building a common understanding of equitable assessment practices for all students. ☐ Be responsible for helping create fair and equitable common assessments for all students. ☐ Support collaborative teams in deepening their understanding of why assessments must focus on the student. ☐ Ensure teachers have timely information about student learning through their assessment plan. ☐ Ensure collaborative teams address the second critical question of a PLC with fidelity by keeping a focus on putting students' needs first.

Figure 2.7: Leadership area guidelines for assessment—Prioritize students.

*Visit **go.SolutionTree.com/literacy** for a free reproducible version of this figure.*

provide pertinent resources. Or, as a team leader, you can assume responsibility for assisting teams in creating valid and reliable common assessments that align to learning targets.

As a leader, you aim to achieve a level of confidence so your teachers understand why they assess and can select the most appropriate assessment types and formats. Additionally, as you listen to collaborative team discussions and observe members' assessment planning, convey points that support a balanced literacy focus. Remind teachers to pay attention to text complexity, the importance of reading and writing across content areas, plus students as the priority. In particular, emphasize the following as teams generate a list of potential in-class and common formative assessments. Later, they will select from this list those to use in a learning progression—the focus of the next chapter.

- ▸ Reading standards pertain to complex texts of various lengths; therefore, assessments allow students to demonstrate an understanding of both shorter and longer works they experience.

- ▸ Teachers must take into account their students' schema when selecting text as the basis for an assessment to avoid unintentional bias assumptions. When considering their students' background knowledge, the assessment can more acutely and accurately reflect how well they can demonstrate understanding of reading skills.

- ▸ Since students write to demonstrate an understanding of the content they read, teachers must consider an appropriate task that provides students ways to show what they glean from a complex text. For example, an assessment might instruct students to create an objective summary or a literary critique, paraphrase a text excerpt, or draw a picture and a caption of something noteworthy (such as a significant event or the main character).

- ▸ Assessments that align the complex processes of reading and writing, as in the previous bullet, take longer to complete. Since students must employ a number of skills and strategies across literary strands, teachers must allow enough time for students to address this kind of task.

- ▸ Students also write to show how well they can incorporate the characteristic elements of a particular text type and adhere to its structure. For instance, when they write a mystery, students include elements pertaining to this genre, such as establishing a crime has been committed and including witnesses, victims, an alibi, and so on. Since mysteries are categorized under a narrative-text type, students' writing must also reflect their knowledge of a plot structure.

▸ Support teachers in reviewing and determining which types and formats are in any prepackaged literacy program. Ask them to consider the following questions: "Are the assessments rigorous enough? Do they align to the learning targets? Do we need to revise or augment them to be more robust or complete? Are they fair and equitable?"

▸ Teachers should understand and articulate the differences of the types and formats of assessments. How does obtrusive differ from unobtrusive? What are ways teachers can collect these assessments informally and formally? What is the rationale for using selected- and constructed-response items?

▸ Teachers can ask students to create their own assessments to demonstrate understanding of a learning target. As a leader, you can discuss how teachers can conduct a brainstorming session with students to collect ideas for student-generated assessments. As a resource for teachers to help prompt students to create a list of options, share selected items in figure 2.8 with students as the basis for them to choose their own assessments.

Assessment Options A to Z				
A	**B**	**C**	**D**	**E**
• Academic notebook entries	• Bibliography	• Cartoons	• Descriptive writing (of setting, character, individual, event, and so on)	• Editorial
• Advertisement (newspaper, TV, magazine, radio script)	• Billboard	• Case study		• Essay
	• Biography	• Catalog		• Eulogy
• Advice column	• Blog	• Chapter	• Dictionary with pictures	• Exit card
• All-about book	• Book	• Character sketch		• Explanatory essay or paper (how-to)
• Allegory	• Book cover	• Comedy (play script)	• Documentary script	
• Alphabet book	• Brochure	• Comic book		• Eyewitness account
• Anecdote	• Bulletin board	• Convention program	• Drama	
• Annotation	• Business plan	• Creation myth		
• Announcement		• Critique		
• Argumentation essay or speech				
• Autobiography				

Figure 2.8: Writing assessment options A to Z.

continued ⟶

F	G	H	I	J–K
• Fable • Fairy tale • Fantasy story • Feature story	• Glossary • Graph with analysis • Graphic organizer • Greek myth • Greeting card	• Handbook • Headlines • Historical fiction • How-to paper	• Informational essay or report • Interview (questions or complete script) • Invitation (personal or business)	• Job descriptions • Journal entries (such as personal and historical accounts)

L	M	N	O	P
• Lab report • Labeled diagram • Laws for organization • Legal document • Legend • Lesson plan • Letter (personal or business; résumé and cover letter) • Letter of recommendation • Letter to the editor • List • Literary critique or analysis • Lyrics	• Magazine article or layout • Manual • Memoir • Menu • Multimedia project • Mural • Mystery story • Myth (creation, Native American, Greek, and so on)	• Narrative • Nature log • Newsletter • Newspaper • News story • Notes (Cornell, observational, and so on) • Novel • Novella	• Obituary • Opinion piece • Organization bylaws, vision or mission statement • Outline	• Pamphlet • Parody • Pattern book • Personal narrative • Petition • Poem • Political cartoon • Portfolio • Poster • Pourquoi tale • Presentation using PowerPoint, Keynote, or Prezi • Press release • Program

Q–R	S	T–U	V	W–Z
• Questions and answers • Reader's theater • Recipe • Research report or project • Résumé • Review of a book, movie, experiment, or presentation	• Satire • Science fiction • Scrapbook (annotated) • Short story • Song lyrics • Speech • Storyboard • Summary	• Technology project • TED Talk or television show script • Timeline • Travelogue • Trickster tale	• Venn diagram • Video	• Written response

Source: Adapted from Glass & Marzano, 2018.

*Visit **go.SolutionTree.com/literacy** for a free reproducible version of this figure.*

The Final Word

As leaders whose mission is to support teachers, look, listen, and participate, as needed, to move educators along in their commitment to students. No matter what challenges students face, teachers should effectively and appropriately assess their learning and provide useful feedback to move students forward in their learning. Leading this work means you, as a leader, must truly maintain focus on ensuring your students receive the education they rightly deserve in every classroom in your school. Inspiring teachers to understand the *why* and *how* of student-centered assessments is an important step in creating the equitable opportunities you want for your district or school. Now, let's turn the focus to developing learning progressions that guide both instruction and assessment as your next step as a literacy leader.

CHAPTER 3

Create a Learning Progression to Guide Instruction and Assessment

Life is a journey, not a destination.

—RALPH WALDO EMERSON

Visualize this: you embark on an enjoyable country walk and come upon a river, but to continue strolling, you recognize the need to cross it. Knowing this is your end goal, you consider ways to reach the other side. Rocks that visibly protrude from the water might be of help. To *progress* across the river, you must identify and carefully leverage the rocks you need to follow, making sure to intentionally take each step in an appropriate order. As you begin, you stop a few times to evaluate your progress. Is this direction getting you where you want to go? Do you have enough rocks in the plan to support your journey? Are they spaced too far apart? Do you land on a larger boulder after much effort and skip more easily to a smaller rock? Does the progression make sense to you? If you rush and skip a rock, you may stumble and risk not completing your goal, or worse, it could set you back significantly. Or the rocks you select might not actually direct you to the opposite shore. To successfully reach your destination, you must navigate the journey strategically in terms of direction as well as what steps you take next.

As a leader, you guide teams to establish the learning progression of both instruction and assessment that help members cross the metaphorical river to successfully plan. So teachers do not skip any steps along their journey, you must help them understand the need to proactively and effectively plan an *organized learning progression*, which teacher and author W. James Popham (2011) defines as:

> A sequenced set of subskills and bodies of knowledge (*building blocks*) a
> teacher believes students must master en route to mastering a demanding

cognitive skill of significant curricular importance (a *target curricular aim*). . . .
[A] formal, thought-through outline of the *key content of instruction*—what's
pivotal to be taught and mastered, and in what sequence. As such, it's a foundation for sound instruction and effective planning. It's also the backbone of
a sensible, *planned* approach to formative assessment. (p. 10)

In our work as coaches, we often hear teachers grumble about the instructional
planning school leaders require of them. Often, teachers assume they can move
from the *what*—knowing what standard to teach—to the *do*, leaving out the *how*
in between. As a leader, it is incumbent on you to adhere to tight expectations
around the need for teachers to intentionally plan useful instructional learning
experiences. So instead of leaving this to chance, provide a protocol and help
teacher teams organize their work; teach them to begin with the end in mind.

In this chapter, you will address these kinds of questions with teacher teams: In
what order and when do we teach each learning target and knowledge item? What
will be the timing of the assessment plan? Why is the progression of both instruction and assessment so crucial? To do so, you'll learn about guiding teams to use
specific planning steps that create natural progressions for learning. These *learning
progressions* delineate the order teams should teach, assess, and intervene for each
learning target team members unwrapped from a standard. Teams then focus on
assessments and devise a calendar that presents the timeline for assessments and
interventions. The clarity of a learning progression and accompanying timeline also
provides teams with a framework for formative assessment that allows teachers to
systematically collect data, adjust their instruction, and respond to students' needs
as they strive toward mastering each standard. We conclude by examining how a
focus on leading instruction will help leaders better support their teams as teachers
collaborate to design learning progressions. Are you ready to lead this work?

REFLECTION

As you read this chapter, consistently ask yourself: "What can I do
to ensure teachers understand how to plan a learning progression,
and why is it critical to student achievement? What conversations
do I need to have with teachers to assist them in understanding the
importance of planning well?"

Learning Progression Design

After completing the PREP template, the team begins to construct learning progressions for the unit. Some progressions will focus on one priority standard; others might integrate two or more priority standards. The team creates several learning progressions within a particular unit of study depending on the number of essential standards within the unit.

Begin With the End in Mind

Using priority standards, teachers engage in *backward planning* or *backward analysis*, a process that means beginning with the end goal in mind and then determining the steps necessary to reach it. In *Leading Modern Learning, Second Edition*, authors Jay McTighe and Greg Curtis (2019) describe the importance of backward planning for curriculum development: "We find that the intentional use of backward design for curriculum planning results in more clearly defined goals, more appropriate assessments, and more purposeful teaching" (p. 37).

To help teachers understand the importance of planning and focusing on mastery of target standards, we recommend the following steps for designing a learning progression. Teams can use the "Learning Progression and Assessments Template" (page 242 in appendix A) as they proceed through each step.

1. **Select unwrapped priority standards:** Place one unwrapped priority standard or integrated, aligned standards on the top rung of the learning progression template to represent the overarching goal. (You will see an example of this template in the next section.)

2. **Sequence the learning targets (skills):** Use backward analysis to determine the order of teaching each skill and input the skills onto the template in this sequence.

3. **Sequence the knowledge items:** On the in-progress template, input knowledge items—facts, dates, people, places, examples, concepts, vocabulary—which indicate what students should know in order to perform skills.

4. **Determine all assessments:** Teams review the brainstormed list referenced in the Leadership Area: Prioritize Students section of chapter 2 (page 50) and assign assessments to each step on the ladder, including the top rung with priority standards, for students to show evidence of learning. They consider the level of rigor (DOK) for the intended learning target

or knowledge item to choose an assessment method that matches the cognitive demand.

5. **Identify and design common assessments:** Teams determine which assessments are common formative assessments to measure student progress on critical and more complex learning targets (rather than on knowledge items teachers typically assess within their classrooms). Teams also agree on the common summative assessment and indicate both common assessments on the template. Then, members design the assessments or find them from an existing source, making specific adjustments as needed.

6. **Discuss options for complex texts:** This step provides teachers an opportunity to investigate and suggest possible complex texts to use for classroom instruction. To select appropriate texts, teachers consider three criteria that gauge a text's complexity level: (1) quantitative features, (2) qualitative features, and (3) reader and task considerations. (See more in the Text Complexity section, page 72.) Teachers must also attend to cultural diversity. (For expanded discussions about these topics, refer to chapters 3 and 9 in the signature series, respectively.)

Teams can choose to reverse steps 2 and 3 if that approach appears more prudent as they are devising this document. Be sure to refer to the appropriate grade-level texts within the signature series with your teachers to build a deep understanding of the details in each step.

You will note that this method for designing a learning progression constitutes one among many possible options, and teams might devise an alternative route for these steps. With so many options and approaches to instruction, teachers might ask, "How will we know we got it right? Is our sequence for instruction correct?" According to Popham (2007), with few exceptions, "there is no single, universally accepted and absolutely correct learning progression underlying any given high-level curricular aim" (p. 83). Popham (2007) asserts that separate teams of committed educators can unwrap identical standards and generate diverse learning progressions, and that is perfectly acceptable. The fact that collaborative teams take the time to think seriously about learning, discuss the nuances of the targets, and carefully sequence a learning progression will benefit student learning far better than students whose teachers do not make this collaborative attempt. As you lead this work, it is of utmost importance that you help teams understand the critical value of working together to make key decisions about students' learning based on priority standards and proactively choreograph a plan for their success.

As the literacy leader, impress on teams that a learning progression meets the needs of students by setting the stage for well-planned instruction, assessment, and interventions. Through this process, teams work together to sequence knowledge items and skills into a clearly articulated continuum of learning that essentially maps out the step-by-step journey students will take toward mastering each standard. Figure 3.1 provides examples of guiding questions for you to use with your collaborative teams as they apply the steps of building a learning progression. For each step, consider the questions that you could ask to deepen the teams' understanding of the *what*, *how*, and *why* of the work. Use the third column to record notes or additional questions that will prepare you to lead teams through this planning tool.

Steps for Building a Learning Progression	Leadership: Guiding Questions to Support Designing Learning Progressions	Other Questions, Notes, or Comments
1. **Select unwrapped priority standards:** Place one unwrapped priority standard or integrated, aligned standards on the top rung of the learning progression template to represent the overarching goal.	• Which unwrapped priority standards from the PREP template are the focus for the targeted unit? • What priority standards might the team use singularly or integrated together in each learning progression? • How many learning progressions does the team envision this unit requires?	
2. **Sequence the learning targets (skills):** Use backward analysis to determine the order of teaching each skill and input the skills onto the template in this sequence.	• Has the team articulated the right skills from the unwrapped priority standard or standards? How can the team review this to ensure that they have not omitted skills? • Do skills reflect the appropriate rigor?	

Figure 3.1: Leadership guiding questions to support designing learning progressions.

continued →

Steps for Building a Learning Progression	Leadership: Guiding Questions to Support Designing Learning Progressions	Other Questions, Notes, or Comments
	• Some teams might devise a learning progression to begin with DOK 1. Other progressions might begin with DOK 2 and focus on higher-level thinking initially, then return to DOK 1. How should the team sequence the skills to reflect the order in which they teach the unit? What is the rationale?	
3. **Sequence the knowledge items:** On the in-progress template, input knowledge items—facts, dates, people, places, examples, concepts, vocabulary—which indicate what students should know in order to perform skills.	• Has the team identified all knowledge items (facts, dates, people, places, examples, concepts, vocabulary) that are explicit as well as implicit? • What can the team do to double-check that all items are important for students to know from the standard and that none are inadvertently omitted?	
4. **Determine all assessments:** Teams review the brainstormed list compiled in the Leadership Area: Prioritize Students section of chapter 2 (page 50) and determine an assessment plan, assigning assessments to each step on the ladder for students to show evidence of learning. They consider the level of rigor (DOK) for the intended learning target or knowledge item to choose an assessment method that matches the cognitive demand.	• How does the team use its assessment plan to assign assessments based on what students should know and be able to do for each step on the ladder? • How does the team determine the level of rigor (DOK) based on the intended learning targets?	

5. **Identify and design common assessments:** Teams determine which assessments are common formative assessments to measure student progress on critical and more complex learning targets (rather than on knowledge items teachers typically assess within their classrooms). They also agree on the common summative assessment and indicate both common assessments on the "Learning Progression and Assessments Template" (page 242). Then, members design these assessments or find them from an existing source, making specific adjustments as needed.	• What support does the team or individual teachers need to develop quality common assessments? • How do team members determine which assessments from their plan will be common formative assessments? • How will team members work together to create common summative assessments? What should be their first step?	
6. **Discuss options for complex texts:** This step provides teachers an opportunity to investigate and suggest possible complex text to use for classroom instruction.	• What is teachers' understanding of the three-part complexity model they use to select appropriate complex text? (See Text Complexity, page 72.) • How can you help with complex-text decisions? What resources do team members need to find or acquire appropriate texts, including those that reflect cultural diversity?	

*Visit **go.SolutionTree.com/literacy** for a free reproducible version of this figure.*

Build the Learning Progression

As previously mentioned, once teams use the PREP to select the unwrapped priority standard or standards—along with pertinent associated supporting standards—they begin to develop a learning progression. To design this document, which drives instruction and assessment choices, teams follow the steps in the previous section while using the "Learning Progression and Assessments Template" (page 242) or a similar template teams devise to catalog their work. Figure 3.2 and figure 3.3 (page 68) feature examples from the signature series for grades 2–3 and 4–5, respectively. (See an example of a preK–1 progression in Onuscheck, Spiller, Martin, & May, 2020, p. 64.)

Priority Standard: Describe characters in a story (e.g., their traits, motivations, or feelings) and explain how their actions contribute to the sequence of events. (RL.3.3)

Learning Progression Steps	Learning Progression Components	Assessments	Texts for Assessment
Step 8	**Priority Standard** Describe characters in a story (e.g., their traits, motivations, or feelings) and explain how their actions contribute to the sequence of events. (RL.3.3)	***Common Summative Assessment: Short Constructed-Response Assessment** In a well-developed paragraph response, describe a character in a story and explain how one of the character's actions impact the sequence of events in the story. (Summative and formal)	*Brave Girl* (Markel, 2013)
Step 7	**Learning Target (Skill)** Explain how characters' actions contribute to the sequence of events.	***Short Constructed-Response Assessment** In a two- to three-sentence response, explain what happens as a result of a character's action. (Formative and informal)	*The Sign* (Wrang, 2015)
Step 6	**Knowledge** Plot development is affected by the characters and their actions.	**Constructed-Response Graphic Organizer** Complete a graphic organizer to show the cause-and-effect relationship between a character's action and what happens next in a story. (Formative and informal)	*The Sign* (Wrang, 2015)

		Knowledge	Teacher Observation	*The Sign* (Wrang, 2015)
	Step 5	Plot is the sequence of events in a story.	Arrange details from a story into the correct sequence of events using a flowchart. (Formative, informal, and unobtrusive)	
	Step 4	**Learning Target (Skill)** Describe characters by their traits, feelings, and motivations.	***Common Formative Assessment: Short Constructed-Response Assessment** In a two- to three-sentence response, describe a character from a story and use evidence from the text to support your thinking. (Formative and formal)	*The Sign* (Wrang, 2015)
	Step 3	**Knowledge** Motivation is the reason why a character acts a certain way.	**Teacher Conference** Meet with the teacher to describe characters and their motivations in a story. (Formative and informal)	Excerpt from *Sarah, Plain and Tall* (MacLachlan, 1985)
	Step 2	**Knowledge** Characters' feelings and emotions are expressed through details in a text.	**Teacher Observation** Identify traits that describe characters in a story, and determine a character's feelings based on story details. (Formative, informal, and unobtrusive)	Excerpt from *Sarah, Plain and Tall* (MacLachlan, 1985)
	Step 1	**Knowledge** Traits are words used to describe a character.		

Optional texts to consider for instruction or assessment:

- Excerpts from *Charlotte's Web* (White, 1980)
- *The 13 Clocks* (Thurber, 1978)
- *Poppleton in Winter* (Rylant, 2008)

*Grade-level teams will analyze and discuss data collected from common formative and summative assessments.

Source for standard: NGA & CCSSO, 2010.
Source: Onuscheck, Spiller, Gord, & Sheridan, 2020, pp. 64–65.

Figure 3.2: Unit learning progression and assessments for grades 2–3—Exploring Elements of Fiction unit.

Priority Standards:

- Use dialogue to develop experiences and events or show the responses of characters to situations. (W.4.3b [A])
- Use correct capitalization. (L.4.2a)
- Use commas and quotation marks to mark direct speech and quotations from a text. (L.4.2b)
- Choose words and phrases to convey ideas precisely. (L.4.3a)

Learning Progression Steps	Learning Progression Components	Assessments
Step 9	**Priority Standards** • Use dialogue to develop experiences and events or show the responses of characters to situations. • Use correct capitalization. • Use commas and quotation marks to mark direct speech and quotations from a text. • Choose words and phrases to convey ideas precisely.	***Common Summative Assessment: Constructed-Response Assessment (Dialogue Writing)** Write a final version of purposeful dialogue passages that develop a plot or show characters' reactions; include verbs that depict how characters speak, feel, or act; use proper mechanics. (Summative and formal)
Step 8	**Learning Target (Skill)** Use words and phrases to convey ideas in a dialogue tag.	**Short Constructed-Response Assessment (List)** Add to list of verbs and categorize them; use the list as a resource for writing dialogue tags. (Formative and formal)
Step 7	**Knowledge** Dialogue tag verbs provide description to indicate how characters speak to one another. (Connects to supporting standard L.4.6)	**Constructed-Response Assessment (Dramatic Enactment)** Find and circle dialogue passages from complex text where the author uses strong dialogue tag verbs. With a partner, act out a few of these passages using the dialogue tag verbs as a guide to show how characters speak to one another. Record verbs in academic notebooks or journals. (Formative and formal) **Selected-Response Assessment (Mini-Whiteboards)** Using mini-whiteboards, write dialogue tag verbs and chorally identify each verb. Record verbs in academic notebooks or journals. (Formative and formal)

		Learning Target (Skill)	Constructed-Response Assessment (Dialogue Writing)
	Step 6	Use proper conventions when writing dialogue.	Revise dialogue passages within your story to ensure proper use of conventions. (Formative and formal)
	Step 5	**Knowledge** • Types of dialogue (or speaker) tags—beginning, middle, end, or no tag • Punctuation and capitalization rules for the different types of dialogue or speaker tags	**Short Constructed-Response Assessment (Exit Slip)** Using proper conventions, write three sentences of dialogue: one with a beginning dialogue tag, one with a middle dialogue tag, and one with an end dialogue tag. Label each sentence appropriately as *beginning tag*, *middle tag*, and *end tag*. (Formative and formal)
	Step 4	**Learning Target (Skill)** Write dialogue to develop a plot or to show characters' responses to situations.	***Common Formative Assessment: Constructed-Response Assessment (Dialogue Writing)** Write dialogue passages throughout a story draft that develop the plot or show characters' responses to situations. (Formative and formal)
	Step 3	**Knowledge** • Purpose and function of dialogue • Brainstorming is a form of planning—an initial step in the writing process. (Connects to supporting standard W.4.5)	**Teacher Conference** Meet with the teacher to show your plans for inserting meaningful dialogue into your story draft, and provide a rationale. (Formative and informal) **Constructed-Response Assessment (Brainstorming)** Prepare for writing dialogue passages by brainstorming a plan for where to insert dialogue and for what purpose. (Formative and formal)
	Step 2	**Knowledge** Dialogue is meaningful and serves a purpose—to develop the plot or to show characters' responses to situations.	**Constructed-Response Assessment (Annotation)** Read dialogue and the surrounding text, and underline what you think is meaningful. Explain the purpose of what you underlined, and provide your opinion about why it is important. (Formative and formal)

Figure 3.3: Unit learning progression and assessments for grades 4–5—Dialogue in a Narrative unit.

continued →

			Selected-Response Assessment (Hand Signals)
			Determine the purpose of each dialogue passage your teacher reads. If it moves the plot forward, signal with one finger. If it reveals characters' responses to situations, signal with two fingers. If you're unsure, make a fist. (Formative and informal)
	Step 1	Knowledge Purpose and function of dialogue	Selected-Response Assessment (Voting Techniques) Determine to what degree a dialogue passage is important in developing the plot. For each passage your teacher reads, raise one hand if the dialogue is not very important, raise two hands if it is important, or stand up if it is extremely important. (Formative and informal)
*Grade-level teams will analyze and discuss data collected from common formative and summative assessments.			

Source for standards: NGA & CCSSO, 2010.
Source: Onuscheck, Spiller, & Glass, 2020, pp. 61–63.

Notice how these progressions establish priority standards—a single one for the learning progression in the grades 2–3 book and an integrated-standards learning progression in the grades 4–5 example—and then provide the option of identifying a learning target (skill), knowledge, or both for each step in the progression. Some teams might suggest complex texts within their learning progression, as the grades 2–3 example shows (see figure 3.2, page 66); some grades might opt to discuss them within the team and omit them from the document. In terms of the number of steps, each progression varies depending on the way a team approaches how to teach the priority standards. These variances indicate that each learning progression is distinctive because teams customize it for specific purposes.

If teams use a purchased literacy program with prepared lesson progressions, instruct them to review the progressions together to ensure they address the unwrapped priority standards and align to the intentions of the units they plan to teach. With prepared, purchased lessons or through their own design, the planning of the instruction, assessments, and interventions must align to agreed-on progressions for students' learning.

With rigor in mind, teachers list learning targets in the order they will teach them, working up the proverbial ladder to mastery of the standard. The upward arrow in this section's templates reflects an upward trajectory since it mimics the graduated order that teachers present instruction; however, teachers may not always begin with rudimentary skills and knowledge and move to more complex ones in an orchestrated, methodical fashion. The progression can be flexible based on instructional needs and teachers' preferences about how they choose to choreograph the unit. For example, to address a learning target related to using imagery, teachers might begin the lesson more conceptually by providing students with a passage from a mentor text that includes imagery. They then devise a task, saying to students, "Read the passage I gave you, and underline words and phrases you find most interesting and engaging. Be ready to share what you marked and why." Afterward, students contribute words and phrases they underlined as the teachers record a class-generated list. Teachers then ask, "Why do authors use these kinds of words and phrases in their writing? What is the effect on the reader?" In another approach, teachers might give a definition for imagery and ask students to read and annotate a writing sample to identify instances of sensory detail.

With well-defined learning progressions that one priority standard or integrated standards guide, teachers plan high-quality instruction necessary to move students forward in their learning. They also develop target-aligned assessments that pinpoint students' performance and calibrate their instruction at each step along the way. Doing so sets the stage for differentiated instruction. For those students missing essential building blocks, teachers may need to backtrack along the progression and reteach a concept or offer remediation on a particular skill. In other instances, students might already possess the knowledge and skills they need to advance further on the continuum, prompting teachers to increase the pace of instruction and provide extended learning opportunities for a target. In both situations, the learning progression that guides assessments provides data that allow teachers to appropriately match their instruction to the specific learners' needs.

A Focus on Assessments

To design valid assessments for each step of a learning progression, teams should consider the level of rigor (DOK) for the intended learning target and choose an assessment method that matches the cognitive demand of the learning. They must also consider the knowledge items and design pertinent assessments to measure students' takeaway of factual information. As discussed in chapter 2 (page 33), your role as a leader includes ensuring that you continue to build common understanding within teams of the types and ways teachers can assess. At each step of the learning progression, you can engage in conversations with teachers that guide their thinking in the right direction. For example, you might focus team conversation on how their assessment questions align to the rigor of the standard and learning target. You can provide professional development and coaching opportunities to create a broader understanding of how teachers collect information about what their students learn and, through your teacher observations, give feedback on formative classroom assessment practices. You can do all this through the lens of the learning progressions the collaborative team identifies as you support their work. The following sections focus on two critical areas related to assessment: (1) text complexity and (2) the assessment calendar. Once again, refer to our signature series for more detailed descriptions about what assessment literacy means for each grade band and how it applies to your school or district. Considering the field of assessment presents a vast amount of information, this book only scratches the surface, so add to your existing knowledge base where you feel deficient in this area.

Text Complexity

Teachers and teams alike must consider text complexity when planning instruction and creating or choosing assessments since students should experience rich, grade-level text. When teams secure learning progressions that incorporate reading for students, they should select appropriately complex text that aligns to reading standards and best addresses the demand of the knowledge and skills they will assess. Teachers sometimes assess a student's reading capabilities using a text below grade level; however, this will incorrectly measure how well students can master a grade-level reading standard. Literacy expert Timothy Shanahan (2020b) advisedly responds to a query in a blog post asking whether students can meet a standard while accessing below-grade-level texts:

> If a student is able to identify a main idea in a second-grade text, then he is meeting the second-grade standard. Students need to be able to demonstrate that they can make sense of texts in the ways described in the standards, but they have to be able to do this with texts commensurate with their grade levels.
>
> At the end of the year, they'll be tested on fourth grade, not second grade, texts. And, of course, if they continually are working with texts that are a year

or two behind their grade level, when they leave high school they'll be at a horrible disadvantage.

As a leader, help teams realize this astute and noteworthy message.

To determine the appropriate text-complexity level, which might appear as suggestions on a learning progression for classroom instruction as well as on assessments that address reading standards, make sure teachers use the following three-part complexity model.

1. **Quantitative:** These are countable items, such as word length and frequency, sentence length, syllables, and other calculable properties. Computer software can generate quantitative measures, such as Lexile (https://lexile.com) and Flesch-Kincaid (Achieve the Core, n.d.b; Kelly, 2020).

2. **Qualitative:** This part measures language sophistication, complexity of ideas, and text attributes—for example, structure, style, and levels of meaning. See the rubrics in appendix A of the signature series books to identify the qualitative nature of literary and informational texts.

3. **Reader and text considerations:** These are the characteristics of the students in a classroom (such as readers' cognitive abilities, motivation, knowledge, and experiences); the tasks teachers assign and questions they pose; and the selection of complex texts that take into account demographics, cultural relevancy, and diversity (see Offer Culturally Appropriate Resources, page 219 in chapter 9).

Teachers must consider all three aspects for selecting the right text. For example, author and Nobel Prize in Literature winner John Steinbeck's (1939/1993) *The Grapes of Wrath* measures at a second- to third-grade level band quantitatively, yet the qualitative and reader considerations dictate this text to a much higher grade level.

Your leadership role necessitates communicating to teachers the imperative of why text choice is critical in teaching grade-level standards. Despite an unwrapped standard's rigor and the diligent work of many collaborative teams in planning learning progressions, we often see many teams completely ignore the need to select appropriate text for both instruction and assessments. Time and time again, we conduct classroom visitations in schools, as well as accompany principals on classroom observations, only to find teachers execute an excellent, well-planned lesson using text far below grade level. As a consequence, students are not engaged, challenged, or prepared to read and respond to the more rigorous grade-level text they later encounter on state or provincial assessments. With little practice with appropriately challenging grade-level texts, students will lack the stamina or comprehension skills to manage them. As part of your tight expectations as an instructional leader, you should create a tight (non-negotiable) practice: teachers must use grade-level complex text well-suited for specific students during instruction and for reading assessments. By planning learning progressions that include text identification on the template or on an external document, you begin to communicate this critical expectation.

Assessment Calendar

Teams generate an assessment calendar that pinpoints dates for instruction, intervention, and assessments as detailed in the following bullets. They consider time issues, like the frequency and length of these meetings. Since the calendar must reflect realistic situations, if teams have limited opportunities to convene, they take this into account when entering information on the calendar. As well, teams record time for engaging in the PREP process.

- **Instruction:** Enter the priority and supporting standards; units should typically have no more than five priority standards.

- **Intervention:** Offer corrective instruction for students who have yet to master standards and provide extensions for those who have achieved mastery; this addresses the third and fourth critical questions of a PLC (DuFour et al., 2016).

- **Assessments:** Designate meetings for creating or finding assessment tasks, designing rubrics, discussing the administration of the assessment, scoring collaboratively, and analyzing the data. Every unit should have mid-unit check-ins; longer units will have briefer ones. For example, the team might issue a common formative assessment every three weeks in a twelve-week unit; however, in a three-week unit, issuing a common formative assessment each week may be unrealistic.

Each grade-level book in the signature series includes an example calendar that illustrates plans for both daily instruction and assessments for a unit; figure 3.4 shows an example from the grades 2–3 text. As the literacy leader of this work, again, ensure you have a tight expectation for the collaborative team to create a calendar of the workflow for their instruction, assessment, and intervention plans.

Unit: Exploring Elements of Fiction

Time Frame: Four weeks in October **Grade:** 3

Today's Date: September 16 (two weeks prior to unit)

Monday, 9/16	Tuesday, 9/17	Wednesday, 9/18	Thursday, 9/19	Friday, 9/20
Instruction for the current unit takes place while the team engages in the PREP process for the upcoming Exploring Elements of Fiction unit beginning on 9/30.				
Monday, 9/23	**Tuesday, 9/24**	**Wednesday, 9/25**	**Thursday, 9/26**	**Friday, 9/27**
Instruction for the current unit takes place while the team engages in the PREP process for the upcoming 9/30 Exploring Elements of Fiction unit.		Preassessment		
Monday, 9/30 **Day 1**	**Tuesday, 10/1** **Day 2**	**Wednesday, 10/2** **Day 3**	**Thursday, 10/3** **Day 4**	**Friday, 10/4** **Day 5**
Instruction on Priority Standards: RF.3.4 (LP steps 1 and 2) W.3.2a (LP step 1) **Instruction on Supporting Standards:** RL.3.1 **Assessment:** RF.3.4 (informal and unobtrusive for five students based on a common rubric)	**Instruction on Priority Standards:** RL.3.3 (LP steps 1 and 2) RF.3.4 (LP steps 3 and 4) W.3.2a (LP step 2) **Instruction on Supporting Standards:** RL.3.1 L.3.4a **Assessment:** RL.3.3 (LP steps 1 and 2; informal and unobtrusive) RF.3.4 (informal and unobtrusive for five students based on a common rubric) **Team Literacy Meeting**	**Instruction on Priority Standards:** RL.3.3 (LP step 3) RF.3.4 (LP step 5) W.3.2a (LP step 2) **Instruction on Supporting Standards:** RL.3.1 **Assessment:** RL.3.3 (LP step 3; informal) RF.3.4 (informal and unobtrusive for five students based on a common rubric)	**Instruction on Priority Standards:** RL.3.3 (LP step 3) RF.3.4 (LP step 6) W.3.2a (LP step 3) **Instruction on Supporting Standards:** L.3.4a **Assessment:** RF.3.4 (informal and unobtrusive for five students based on a common rubric)	**Instruction on Priority Standards:** RL.3.3 (LP step 4) RF.3.4 (LP step 7) W.3.2a (LP step 3) **Instruction on Supporting Standards:** RL.3.1 **Assessment (Team CFA):** RL.3.3 (LP step 4; formal CFA) W.3.2a (LP step 3; formal CFA) RF.3.4 (informal and unobtrusive for five students based on a common rubric)

continued →

Figure 3.4: Team calendar for the Exploring Elements of Fiction unit.

Monday, 10/7 Day 6	Tuesday, 10/8 Day 7	Wednesday, 10/9 Day 8	Thursday, 10/10 Day 9	Friday, 10/11 Day 10
Instruction on Priority Standards: RL.3.3 (LP step 5) W.3.2a (LP step 4) RF.3.4 (LP step 7)	**Instruction on Priority Standards:** RL.3.3 (LP step 5) RL.3.2 (LP step 1)	**Instruction on Priority Standards:** RL.3.3 (LP step 6) RL.3.2 (LP step 1) W.3.2a (LP step 5)	**Instruction on Priority Standards:** RL.3.3 (LP step 6) RL.3.2 (LP step 2) W.3.2a (LP step 5)	**Instruction on Priority Standards:** RL.3.3 (LP step 6) RL.3.2 (LP step 3) W.3.2a (LP step 6)
Instruction on Supporting Standards: W.3.2b RF.3.3a	**Instruction on Supporting Standards:** W.3.2b	**Instruction on Supporting Standards:** W.3.2b RF.3.3a	**Instruction on Supporting Standards:** L.3.4a	**Instruction on Supporting Standards:** None
Assessment: W.3.2a (LP step 4; informal and unobtrusive)	**Assessment:** RL.3.3 (LP step 5; informal and unobtrusive)	**Assessment:** RL.3.2 (LP step 1; informal and unobtrusive)	**Assessment:** RL.3.2 (LP step 2; informal and unobtrusive) W.3.2a (LP step 5; informal and unobtrusive)	**Assessment:** RL.3.3 (LP step 6; informal)
	Team Literacy Meeting	**Corrective Instruction or Extension for RL.3.3 and W.3.2a (based on data inquiry)**	**Corrective Instruction or Extension for RL.3.3 and W.3.2a (based on data inquiry)**	
	Team Data-Inquiry Meeting: Discuss RL.3.3 and W.3.2a CFA data from 10/4 and running-record data collected for RF.3.4.			

Monday, 10/14 Day 11	Tuesday, 10/15 Day 12	Wednesday, 10/16 Day 13	Thursday, 10/17 Day 14	Friday, 10/18 Day 15
Instruction on Priority Standards: RL.3.3 (LP step 7) RL.3.2 (LP step 3) W.3.2a (LP step 6)	**Instruction on Priority Standards:** RL.3.3 (LP step 7) RL.3.2 (LP step 4)	**Instruction on Priority Standards:** RL.3.2 (LP step 5)	**Instruction on Priority Standards:** RL.3.3 (LP step 8) RL.3.2 (LP step 5)	**Instruction on Priority Standards:** RL.3.2 (LP step 6) RL.3.3 (LP step 8) W.3.2a (LP step 9)
Instruction on Supporting Standards: RL.3.1	**Instruction on Supporting Standards:** None	**Instruction on Supporting Standards:** RF.3.3a	**Instruction on Supporting Standards:** None	**Instruction on Supporting Standards:** L.3.4a

	Monday, 10/21 Day 16	Tuesday, 10/22 Day 17	Wednesday, 10/23 Day 18	Thursday, 10/24 Day 19	Friday, 10/25 Day 20
(top row)	**Assessment:** RL.3.2 (LP step 3; informal and obtrusive) RF.3.4 (informal fluency check based on common rubric for students that have not yet mastered)	**Assessment:** RL.3.3 (LP step 7; informal and unobtrusive) RF.3.4 (informal fluency check based on common rubric for students that have not yet mastered) **Team Literacy Meeting:** Begin to look ahead at the next unit.	**Assessment:** W.3.2a (LP step 6; informal and obtrusive) RF.3.4 (informal fluency check based on common rubric for students that have not yet mastered)	**Assessment:** RL.3.3 (LP step 8; formal and obtrusive CSA) RL.3.2 (LP step 4; formal and obtrusive CFA)	**Assessment:** RL.3.2 (LP step 5; informal and unobtrusive)
(bottom row)	**Instruction on Priority Standards:** RL.3.2 (LP step 7) W.3.2a (LP step 6) **Instruction on Supporting Standards:** L.3.4a **Assessment:** RL.3.2 (LP step 6; informal and unobtrusive)	**Instruction on Priority Standards:** RL.3.2 (LP step 7) **Instruction on Supporting Standards:** W.3.2b **Assessment:** Determine assessment based on corrective instruction or extension provided to students. **Team Meeting** **Team Data-Inquiry Meeting:** Discuss RL.3.2 and RL.3.3 data from 10/17.	**Instruction on Priority Standards:** Provide corrective instruction or extension based on all previous assessments. **Assessment:** Determine assessment based on corrective instruction or extension provided to students.	**Instruction on Priority Standards:** Provide corrective instruction or extension based on all previous assessments. **Assessment:** W.3.2a and RL.3.2 formal and obtrusive CSA	**Instruction on Priority Standards:** Provide corrective instruction or extension based on all previous assessments. **Assessment:** Determine assessment based on corrective instruction or extension provided to students.

LP = Learning progression

Source: Onuscheck, Spiller, Gord, & Sheridan, 2020, pp. 89–91.

Leadership Focus: Lead Instruction

Imagine that you are a first-year teacher attending your first faculty meeting at School A, one of several elementary schools in your district. An administrator hands you a folder of the state standards for the content area you will teach and reminds the faculty to submit the first three weeks of lesson plans to the office by the following Monday. Today is Thursday. You have not been assigned to a collaborative team and are the only one teaching at this grade level (a *singleton*). You open the folder and struggle to know where to begin. Although you had coursework for lesson planning during your credentialing program and created, found, or were provided lessons for student teaching, you lack the confidence to plan a lesson or series of lessons on your own. You ask yourself: "What lesson should I teach first? How should the lessons progress? What exactly should I teach? Which of these standards should I omit?" You feel compelled to throw in the towel before you even begin!

Now imagine you are a beginning teacher at School B. Before school starts, your principal connects you with a collaborative team. Even though you are a singleton, reading and writing teachers in other grades assure you that you will plan together with the team. Team members explain that they have already planned the first unit—narrative—which you can easily adapt to your grade level. Team members will review the unit with you and explain the templates they use to create a step-by-step plan for instruction, assessment, and intervention to orient you to their process and resources. The principal arranges for an instructional coach to provide modeling and feedback on your instruction to improve your practice and impact on students. The principal ends the conversation by telling you that instructional planning is the first priority, so your support will begin with this aspect of teaching.

Obviously, School B's principal understands the critical role she plays in leading instruction. She institutes clear, PLC-aligned processes and team tools for planning, and she expects a focus on instruction and learning as the outcome of the collaborative work. She understands that learning to teach well requires a direct-instruction model, like gradual release of responsibility (Fisher & Frey, 2014) and dedicated support.

In *Get Better Faster*, author Paul Bambrick-Santoyo (2016) offers a map for coaching and supporting new teachers, which has implications for more seasoned educators as well. He explains that support must be from the "quarter-inch view" (Bambrick-Santoyo, 2016, p. 28), with bite-sized action steps for teachers to understand. Building learning progressions as part of instructional planning provides that granular-inch view for teachers, and each step thoughtfully delineates assessments and appropriate complex-text suggestions. How much easier and more effective is it to teach a unit when this preplanning is done together with a team? How different would a teacher from School A feel if he or she had this kind of instructional focus and support from the school leader? To actualize leadership from a similar high-achieving school, review the action steps in figure 3.5. As you peruse this figure, consider your potential next steps to support and guide teams in step-by-step instructional planning with a focus on understanding and setting a path for the progression of learning.

Leadership Area: Lead Instruction			
District Leader	**School Administrator**	**Instructional Coach**	**Lead Teacher**
☐ Develop tight expectations within the district that teachers collaborate to plan step-by-step learning progressions with assessments. ☐ Create professional learning opportunities to support the tight expectation that teachers understand how to create learning progressions as part of their instructional planning.	☐ Develop and communicate tight expectations to team leaders, instructional coaches, and other support staff for instructional planning that include developing a learning progression and aligned assessments. ☐ Support collaborative teams with templates (or feedback on templates they design) for instructional planning and assessment expectations. ☐ Monitor and provide feedback on instructional planning, ensuring a focus on learning progressions with assessments and complex text recommendations to meet students' needs.	☐ Ensure your personal understanding of the what, how, and why of learning progressions with aligned assessments as part of instructional planning. ☐ Lead and support discussions at team meetings that help teachers understand the benefit of planning learning progressions for both teachers and students. ☐ Help teachers to ascertain the step-by-step planning from the priority standard that will lead to instruction, assessment, and interventions. ☐ Observe, model, or demonstrate classroom instruction, specifically providing feedback on learning progressions. ☐ Recommend appropriate complex text for steps of the learning progression and assessments, as needed.	☐ Model and facilitate a deeper understanding of instructional, step-by-step planning. ☐ Identify teachers, perhaps new or less experienced, who need more support in understanding the value of step-by-step planning. ☐ Support collaborative teams working together to use the PREP template and then the learning progression and assessments template in their planning. ☐ Lead discussion about the suitability of complex texts choices for learning progression steps and assessments, as needed.

Figure 3.5: Leadership area guidelines for learning progressions—Lead instruction.

*Visit **go.SolutionTree.com/literacy** for a free reproducible version of this figure.*

As Spiller and Power (2019) explain:

> Gone are the days of teachers pulling out the previous year's laminated lesson plans without a thought of their students' individual learning needs. The complexity of instruction can be dizzying; differentiating lessons, grouping and regrouping students based on learning needs, providing additional time for learning, reteaching when necessary, and knowing exactly what a student will need to move to the next level of learning are non-negotiable expectations in schools today. (p. 117)

Spiller and Power (2019) further explain that, in their work in schools as leadership and instructional coaches, teachers often tell them that they are either unsure of how to improve instruction or they don't know where to go for support. Without the assistance and guidance of school leaders, teachers can feel the challenges of instruction are insurmountable. To avoid this sentiment, stay steadfast in helping seasoned and beginning teachers to proactively plan by working from the prioritized standards through the learning progression. This support will bolster their confidence and expertise to produce more effective and focused lessons with thoughtful assessments.

As we have previously discussed, the four critical questions of a PLC require teachers to collaborate around the following (DuFour et al., 2016).

1. What is it we want our students to learn?
2. How will we know if each student has learned it?
3. How will we respond when some students don't learn it?
4. How will we extend and enrich the learning for students who have demonstrated proficiency?

Learning progressions provide a tool for teachers to methodically sequence and orchestrate a series of instructional moves and generate accompanying assessments. To help them with this altogether worthwhile endeavor—and in consideration of the four critical questions of a PLC—review the following reflection box to prepare for how to proceed.

REFLECTION

How do collaborative teams benefit when they discuss answers to the four critical questions of a PLC as they devise learning progressions? How can you help teams to realize their impact on student learning when they integrate the process of step-by-step planning of the learning journey into their work together? What should be your first steps to move your teams to this type of instructional planning?

The Final Word

District and school leaders frequently ask how they can possibly focus on instruction amid the frequent barrage of managerial issues they must address within district and school systems. In fact, collaborative team meetings and classrooms are often the last places leaders spend their time. If, however, leaders fail to pay attention to teachers' instructional planning and assessments, it will be difficult to ascertain whether or not students participate in the most opportune learning experiences. It is through the planning of learning progressions—the intentional and coordinated development of what and how teachers will teach and assess students—that teams identify the most critical learning essentials that better equip members to assume a more effective role in student advancement. In doing so, teachers gain confidence in determining students' levels of mastery and what areas still require more instruction, assessment, and intervention. In the next chapter, you will learn more about how teachers collaborate and develop common understanding of proficiency expectations.

CHAPTER 4

Develop Collective Understanding of Learning Expectations

The biggest mistake is to deprive yourself of proficiency.
—LUC DE CLAPIERS, MARQUIS DE VAUVENARGUES

Through the processes in chapter 3 (page 59), teams design one or more learning progressions and determine which assessments to use for each step and perhaps complex text recommendations, as well. The focus of this chapter shifts to a collective understanding of proficiency since part of the PLC process necessitates that teams collaborate to determine what exactly *proficiency* means (DuFour et al., 2016).

Unfortunately, some teachers work in isolation to decide what constitutes success. They might evaluate student performance and assign grades or marks based on, for example, their impressions of students or by arbitrarily comparing student work products and rating the strongest of the class high and the rest against them. Such narrow approaches are anathema to the goals of a guaranteed and viable curriculum. Further, they result in undesirable situations, such as parents requesting a specific teacher for their child because of a teacher's supposedly more lenient grading practices.

When teachers work in teams to design rubrics and reach consensus on student performance, they eradicate any such perception. Marks or grades are criterion-based and define specific levels of student achievement. Teachers develop collective understanding of what defines *proficiency* (also called *mastery*), ensuring students all access the same guaranteed and viable curriculum.

To accomplish this step, teams address the following questions: What does proficiency look like? How will teachers know when a student has mastered a learning standard? How will teachers uniformly measure student proficiency? These questions remain firmly within the scope of the second critical question of a PLC because they reflect a need to know what qualifies as learning (DuFour et al., 2016). By reaching an agreement on grade-level expectations and proficiency, collaborative teams also hold students to a common understanding of success. This work represents important next steps in effective instruction because it enables teams to address the third and fourth critical questions of a PLC.

Specific and distinct descriptions form the basis of establishing student expectations. As a leader, how will you support teachers as they begin to clarify exactly what students will know and be able to do to exhibit proficiency? What conversations will be important in building a common understanding of mastery? To answer these and related questions, this chapter revolves around rubrics (understanding rubric types, rubric development, and using rubrics as instructional tools), student checklists (creating a list of items an assignment requires), and collaborative scoring (calibrating and consistently scoring and collecting anchor papers). It also explores their application in the context of shared leadership.

Rubrics and Student Checklists

You receive a parcel in the mail. Opening it, you discover a random bag of jigsaw puzzle pieces. Intrigued, you begin putting the pieces together. As time progresses, you realize the difficulty of the task but not the benefit of looking at the end product. Absent this big-picture view, you know that you can continue to assemble the puzzle; however, not seeing the final outcome impedes staying on task. Therefore, you lack an understanding of how you are progressing and what mastery will resemble.

Unfortunately, teachers often work this way as they create assessment and instructional plans—without clearly defining the outcome or expectation for themselves and for students, success is nebulous. Like the puzzle analogy, without the ability to visualize the end product, the task is rendered all the more difficult. Therefore, students (the puzzle builders) benefit from—or actually are entitled to—a common understanding of the requirements and clear expectations of what they will need to accomplish to achieve success. Otherwise, it proves challenging for students when the target moves or appears unknown. Psychologists and educators Thomas R. Guskey and Eric M. Anderman (2013) proffer that understanding mastery can be the "learners' purpose for engaging in a task or activity" (p. 20). They share further motivational research that indicates "students who focus on mastery are more likely to persist at academic tasks, particularly challenging ones" (Guskey & Anderman, 2013, p. 21). Consider the puzzle analogy: What would motivate you to finish it? Would it be helpful if you could visualize what a successful finish looks like?

Leading this work requires a continuous commitment to ensuring teachers address critical questions 1 and 2 of a PLC: *What is it we want our students to learn?* and *How will we know if each student has learned it?* (DuFour et al., 2016). Collaborative teams must continuously return to these questions as they work through the learning progression, identify assessments, and understand what constitutes proficiency based on essential standards. For example, what will a fourth-grade student be able to do if he or she can *Determine the main idea of a text and explain how it is supported by key details* and *summarize the text* (NGA & CCSSO, 2010)? What conversation do teachers need to engage in to truly articulate how students in fourth grade will show proficiency on this standard? What will the teachers accept as mastery of this standard? How will they share the requirements and expectations of a standards-based task with students? What measurement tools will they use?

As a leader, ensure collaborative teams build in the time it takes to define *proficiency* through rubrics and develop collaborative-scoring practices as part of their PLC process. As we often state in this book, a critical role for leaders is to create every opportunity for teachers to understand the *why*; in this case, why they must dedicate time to determine proficiency expectations and how teams are going to know, collectively, what their students can and cannot do. Rubrics, used to describe performance levels, and student checklists for listing requirements are two essential tools for this purpose.

Holistic and Analytic Rubrics

Susan Brookhart (2013) describes a *rubric* as a clear set of criteria for student work that ascribes levels of performance quality to each criterion. She adds:

> Rubrics are important because they clarify for students the qualities their work should have. This point is often expressed in terms of students understanding the learning target and criteria for success. For this reason, rubrics help teachers teach, they help coordinate instruction and assessment, and they help students learn. (Brookhart, 2013, p. 11)

In our signature series, we discuss two specific types of rubrics: (1) holistic and (2) analytic. We detail each in the following sections.

Holistic Rubrics

Teachers typically use *holistic-scoring rubrics* for school, district, or state or provincial on-demand assessments. This type of scoring guide groups together multiple skills to reveal a general picture of student performance within overarching categories. For instance, the New Meridian Resource Center (n.d.), which aligns its assessments to the Common Core, includes these grade 3–11 expectations for a 3 of 3 score under Knowledge of Language and Conventions:

> The student response to the prompt demonstrates *full command* of the conventions of standard English at an appropriate level of complexity. There *may* be a *few minor errors* in mechanics, grammar, and usage, but *meaning is clear*.

For another example, review this grades 3–8 narrative writing rubric excerpt from the Smarter Balanced Assessment Consortium (2014):

> The organization of the narrative, real or imagined, is fully sustained and the focus is clear and maintained throughout:
>
> - an effective plot helps to create a sense of unity and completeness
> - effectively establishes a setting, narrator/characters, and/or maintains point of view*
> - consistent use of a variety of transitional strategies to clarify the relationships between and among ideas; strong connection between and among ideas
> - natural, logical sequence of events from beginning to end
> - effective opening and closure for audience and purpose
>
> *point of view begins at grade 7 (p. 8)

District and school leaders, as well as teachers, can use holistic-scoring rubrics to help generally determine the proficiency levels of students in a district or school. In the New Meridian Resource Center (n.d.), leaders and teachers gain a good snapshot of student performance for grammar and convention skills. The Smarter Balanced Assessment Consortium (2014) combines objectives, which makes it more challenging for leaders and teachers to ascertain students' strengths and weaknesses for specific narrative skills, such as developing a plot, establishing a setting, or using transitional techniques. However, they can glean an overall picture of students' abilities to write using a combination of story elements. This information can help determine which areas might need more emphasis in curriculum design, instructional focus, and even professional development support. Since the categories are rather broad, educators are wise to use the scores from one writing assessment in conjunction with multiple assignments throughout the year—

or even several years—to look for trends. To accomplish this, leaders need to shore up a team's capacity to notice patterns.

Once teams identify patterns, they begin asking questions to dive into assessing problems to address. For example, Do students still struggle with the same areas? What are teachers successfully able to teach, or are they unsure how to teach a skill or related skills? What assistance might they need from an instructional coach to improve their classroom practice? If observing longitudinal trends, was there a year when students did particularly well, and teachers taught a skill in a unique way that begs investigation and strategy sharing? If a particular category is too broad and teachers lack clarity about specific weaknesses after holistically scoring, they can issue a classroom assessment and use an analytic rubric to more directly diagnose discrete skills that present difficulties. In short, holistic-scoring rubrics provide leaders information about teaching *and* learning in a broader context.

Analytic Rubrics

Unlike holistic rubrics, *analytic rubrics* are educative in that each criterion is devoted to a specific skill that students must master. Consequently, these rubrics provide teachers, as well as students, with feedback for improvement. In this regard, analytic rubrics are a highly effective tool for classroom instructional purposes and for scoring in-class and common formative assessments since they uncover more specifically to what degree students have mastered each skill. Teams can also use them for summative assessments. For example, teachers can create an analytic rubric for a lengthy summative assessment that indicates what students are to produce for a writing task. Throughout the unit, though, teachers select line items to assess formatively to ensure students are mastering key skills for each facet of the comprehensive writing product. If teachers have formatively assessed along the way, they can create a holistic rubric and use it for scoring the final summative piece.

REFLECTION

How can you make sure teachers know the difference between an analytic and holistic rubric and the circumstances when each are prudent to use? How can you support teachers in understanding the benefits of developing a rubric as they create assessments and instructional plans?

An analytic rubric entails the following three components. See figure 4.1 for a fourth-grade example from our signature series, paying attention to how the figure treats each skill separately in its own row.

1. **Scoring criteria:** The learning targets (or skills) to measure indicate a rubric's scoring criteria (for example, draw inferences using key details, use sensory details to describe a setting, differentiate between fact and opinion). Each criterion is dedicated to a separate skill and positioned in its own row.

2. **Levels of performance:** Most rubrics have between three and six levels of performance. If possible, teams should use the same number system as the school or district report card. This is especially important in a standards-based grading system where report cards list the same learning standards to report on outcomes (Townsley & Wear, 2020). Use numbers, terms, or both, such as *extends* for level 4; *mastery* for level 3; *developing mastery* for level 2; and *novice* for level 1. Avoid judgmental language (for example, *excellent, fair*, and *poor*).

3. **Criteria descriptors:** Write descriptors that match each level of performance. Either begin with the Mastery column, which represents the grade-level expectations and aligns with the standard, then build up or down from there, or begin with the Extends column, describing what student work looks like when they move beyond the grade-level mastery expectation, which is more sophisticated. From this point, describe performance levels moving down.

A first step to lead this work is to ensure teams create (or revise existing) rubrics to account for the three components. When finished, teams test the rubric by analyzing and scoring actual student work or teacher-created exemplars. This way, teams might discover the rubric needs revising before they use it to score actual student work, which is a sound proactive measure.

Teams must also take time to create the analytic rubric prior to developing the assessment. Leading this work in a school provides several opportunities for you, as a leader, to support conversations pertaining to why teams assess, what they expect students to be able to do, and how they (and you) will know if students are proficient with specific skills. In fact, instructional coaches and principals who develop a clear understanding of rubrics' purpose and an expectation for creating rubrics prior to assessing and instructing model a non-negotiable expectation for collaborative teams to effectively impact student achievement. Consider the questions in figure 4.2 (page 90) to assist your work with teachers as they create or revise an analytic rubric for a common assessment.

Levels of Performance

Scoring Criteria	4.0 Extends	3.5	3.0 Mastery	2.5	2.0 Developing Mastery	1.5	1.0 Novice
Dialogue to develop plot: Write dialogue to develop a plot or to show characters' responses to situations.	Completely meaningful and sophisticated dialogue moves the plot forward and enhances story development.		Dialogue moves the plot forward and meaningfully adds to the story development.		Weak dialogue somewhat moves the plot forward; some dialogue is unnecessary.		Little, if any, dialogue is used; dialogue might confuse readers.
Word choice for dialogue tags: Use words and phrases to convey ideas in a dialogue tag.	Descriptive and sophisticated word choice for dialogue and dialogue tags deeply enhances what characters say and how they say it.		Strong and varied verb use for dialogue tags conveys characters' feelings or reactions.		Somewhat repetitive verb use for dialogue tags sometimes conveys characters' feelings or reactions.		Repetitive and weak verb use for dialogue tags makes how characters feel or react unclear.
Dialogue mechanics: Use proper conventions when writing dialogue.	Minimal or no errors in dialogue mechanics		Minor errors in dialogue mechanics		Some errors in dialogue mechanics		Serious errors in dialogue mechanics, which might make reading or what speakers say difficult to understand

Criteria Descriptors

Source: Onuscheck, Spiller, & Glass, 2020, p. 98.

Figure 4.1: Dialogue common analytic rubric.

Leadership: Guiding Questions for Rubric Design	Collaborative Team Notes and Next Steps
For what common assessment will your team use this rubric? What point scale will you use on the rubric? Why? How did you determine this?	
How can you include numbers as well as phrases, such as *novice, developing mastery, mastery,* and *extends* on the rubric's performance levels?	
What are the scoring criteria and associated descriptors for this common assessment?	
Is there a rubric you currently use that you can adjust to ensure it includes the essential components? What areas require adjusting?	
Is each row in the rubric dedicated to a discrete skill so it is clear what team members are discussing?	

Figure 4.2: Leadership guiding questions for rubric design.

*Visit **go.SolutionTree.com/literacy** for a free reproducible version of this figure.*

Student Checklists

While a rubric defines the quality of each scoring criterion along with levels of performance, and teachers use it for scoring or reporting purposes, a *student checklist* itemizes an assignment's requirements and serves as a guide and self-checking tool for students as they work to complete a task such as a project, piece of writing, or performance. Leading this work requires you to build a common understanding among teachers that the items on the checklist align to a standards-based task and with expectations on a rubric. Checklists are a tool to support students as they complete the task, but neither students nor teachers use them for evaluative purposes. To help students become keenly aware of and make a connection between learning requirements and expectations, teachers refer to items on both the checklist and rubric as they conduct lessons since they are companion pieces.

Teams can complete a common rubric first and use it to design an accompanying student-writing checklist for a common assessment or vice versa. They write the checklist in first-person, with present-tense verbs and accessible language, so students can use it as a guide while they complete their learning task. Figure 4.3 provides an example of a student checklist for an informational paper in grades 2 or 3.

Writing prompt: After reading the article _____ by _____, write a paper in which you describe two important people in our community. Use evidence from the article to explain why they are important.

☐ I include a topic sentence with the title and author of the text.

☐ I name two important people in the community.

☐ I describe two people by telling who they are and what they do.

☐ I include evidence from the text to explain why both people are important.

☐ I use complete sentences in my response.

Figure 4.3: Student checklist for a writing assignment.

Both rubrics and student checklists can serve as instructional tools in various ways. In *The School Leader's Guide to Grading*, independent consultant and grading and reporting expert Ken O'Connor (2013) writes:

> There can be no disagreement that learners control their own learning, and so they must be actively involved in the learning and assessment process. The ability to self-assess, reflect, and set goals is critical to successful learning whether you are five, twelve, or sixteen. (p. 61)

These tools can help students set goals, track their progress, and self-assess; communicate the expectations for success; critique student and published samples; and guide peer and teacher feedback. As stated, to use them instructionally, the language in rubrics and checklists must be accessible to students.

Always with an eye on the learning targets, teachers develop a checklist or rubric and share it with students, or sometimes students cocreate these tools with teacher guidance to be sure students include line items relative to priority standards. To do this successfully, educators and consultants Kathleen Gregory, Caren Cameron, and Anne Davies (2011) write:

> Teachers can set criteria for their students. Teachers can set criteria with their students. Students can set or negotiate their own criteria. . . . when students take part in developing criteria, they are much more likely to understand what is expected of them, 'buy in,' and then accomplish the task successfully. (p. 13)

As a leader at any level, you can observe and pose questions or prompts to both students and teachers as they create checklists. For example, a principal attending a collaborative team meeting might ask probing questions to ensure teachers write the checklist in first-person and in language accessible to students. Instructional coaches and lead teachers will also want to guide the conversation to ensure the level of rigor is not lost in translation from the standard to the rubric to the checklist. As you lead a deeper understanding of the *what* and *how* of student checklists, consider the questions in figure 4.4 to support your collaborative teams.

Through sharing or cocreating rubrics and checklists, teachers provide opportunities for ownership of learning and afford students the advantage of full awareness of what an assignment entails and its expectations, which positions them for success.

Students can explain their own learning journey through an understanding of analytic rubrics, holistic rubrics, and student checklists. If teachers make a student-friendly version of the rubric for students to use, they should ensure the rigor and intention of the criteria mirror the teacher version. To make both the checklist and rubric powerful instruments for growth, teachers conduct lessons that introduce the academic vocabulary and format and familiarize students with how to use each tool, isolating or chunking line items in digestible pieces.

As a leader, you can establish classroom observation protocols that include conversations with students about their work. Intentional questions that clarify what students understand about what teachers expect and how they show proficiency

Leadership: Guiding Questions for Student Checklists	Collaborative Team Notes and Next Steps
What items on the checklist did you align to standards and the rubric (unless you develop the checklist first, in which case the reverse applies)?	
Is each item written in first-person point of view with present-tense verbs and student-friendly language, so students use it as a guide while they write? If not, what changes do you need to make to the checklist?	
How can you make the assessment task clear to students? Did you write it at the top of the checklist? Can I share resources to help you write more clearly defined tasks?	
How will you introduce the checklist so it captures students' attention, and they use it as a useful tool to guide their writing? Would you like me to explain the lesson in chapter 4 of the signature series books that you can conduct for this purpose?	

Figure 4.4: Leadership guiding questions for designing student checklists.

*Visit **go.SolutionTree.com/literacy** for a free reproducible version of this figure.*

will assist your understanding of how teachers are using requirements of an assignment and success criteria to inform students of their learning. Prior to conducting classroom visits, set your intention. Purposefully consider what you want to learn from students and establish questions or prompts to guide your observation and conversations with them. For example, as students work, pose the following prompts or questions that compel them to engage in discussion with you to uncover their degree of learning and how teachers relay expectations.

▶ "Tell me about what you are working on today."

▶ "How do you know what you have to do? What are the requirements of this assignment?"

▶ "Can you show me a student checklist or rubric? How are you using it? Tell me how it helps you understand what to do. Did you create it, or did your teacher hand out a checklist?"

▶ "How will you know when you are successful with this task? What are the expectations for this assignment?"

▶ "How do you know what to do with your checklist or rubric? What is its purpose? How does it help you work on this task?"

When students understand teacher expectations and requirements for their performance of a learning task, it increases the effectiveness of classroom practice. In other words, by using tools such as rubrics and checklists, teachers create assessment opportunities that provide timely feedback to students about their learning progress. Next, we will look at how they use these tools to calibrate and score student work.

Collaborative Scoring

Teachers oftentimes interpret items on a rubric for assessing reading and writing skills slightly differently since the criteria can lean toward subjectivity. To help ameliorate this potential problem, collaborative teams work together to ensure consistency of scoring so that together they clarify and agree on expectations for student mastery. This requires teams to calibrate *how* they will score students' work. We refer to this process as a *calibration session*.

When participating in this process, teams make certain the rubric serves as an instrument that guides them to fairly and accurately measure students' performance and achievement. When teams convene for a calibration session, they collectively score student work for the same assessment task using an agreed-on common analytic rubric they've designed together. The task that teachers assign must be administered in the same way; otherwise, it will have unfair, skewed results. For example, if one teacher assists students with the introduction of an informational writing task by leading a class brainstorming session to generate options for strategies and other teachers do not, this support—or lack of support—will impact student performance, causing a loss of equity.

Teachers reach consensus about student examples of proficiency for each performance level of criteria items, so they have consistent impressions of what each level on the rubric means. These samples—called *anchor papers*—give expression to a rubric since they serve as a reference and the best representation of what writing at different performance levels looks like for each scoring criterion. Anchor papers that reflect high-quality characteristics that meet or exceed the criteria on the rubric are called *exemplars*. Further, teachers use anchor papers during parent conferences to make family members and guardians aware of how to interpret rubric scores. They also use them during instruction so students are aware of what to avoid or aspire to based on writing skills. To this point, teachers can conduct activities in which students critique and score (unidentified) anchors against the rubric; next, they compare their impressions with the pre-calibrated anchors.

Consequently, participating in the collaborative-scoring process ensures that teachers establish and maintain a shared understanding of the rubric, uniformity in their evaluation of student work, and common expectations of mastery for all students in every grade-level classroom. The byproduct of participating in this exercise increases the assessment data's reliability. Afterward, teachers can independently continue to score their students' papers, confident that all team members share a consistent interpretation of rubric criteria.

REFLECTION

As a school or district leader, what can you do to ensure educators work collaboratively to score student work? How can you verify that their protocol is effective? Might you suggest that teachers read and participate in a calibration session using the detailed protocol in chapter 4 of the signature series?

Reeves (2016) describes collaborative scoring as "a superb professional learning experience, allowing teachers to improve the quality, consistency, and timeliness of their feedback to students" (p. 69). He continues with this explanation:

> The most effective collaborative scoring processes I have observed follow a consistent protocol in which the identities of the students and teachers are unknown to the teachers who are doing the scoring. The only question is, "Given this particular piece of student work and the scoring rubric I have available, what is my assessment of the work?" Accuracy not only improves because practice with a rubric leads to consistency but also because teachers have constructive discussions about their disagreements. This leads to an improvement in the clarity and specificity of the scoring rubric. (Reeves, 2016, p. 69)

As a leader, you will have several opportunities to support collaborative scoring of student work by creating tight expectations for it. Professional development opportunities include modeling of rubrics, scoring criteria, student checklists, anchor papers, and the actual process of collaboratively scoring student work. Instructional coaches support the development of anchor papers and exemplars and ensure teachers understand how to use these with both the students and other educators. Lead teachers create space and time for the professional discussions needed to agree on proficiency, develop scoring criteria, and collaborate about the scoring of student work. As you lead a deeper understanding around collaborative scoring, consider the questions in figure 4.5 to support your collaborative teams.

Leadership Area: Build Shared Leadership

A shared-leadership model is critical to the success of the collaborative work necessary for all teachers to build collective understanding of learning expectations. About this, Spiller and Power (2019) write:

> Often in schools where deep implementation of shared ownership is a priority, school leaders take the time to build leadership in teachers who are facilitating collaborative teams. This important focus helps teachers build leadership skills so they are prepared to effectively facilitate collaborative discussions, support members, and develop other leadership abilities to guide team success. (p. 73)

For teachers (and students) to develop a common understanding of what *proficiency* means and exemplifies explicitly, leaders at all levels must participate to support, guide, and monitor teams. Of course, this begins with district and school leaders recognizing the need to empower and ensure that teacher leaders agree on

Leadership: Guiding Questions for Calibration	Collaborative Team Notes and Next Steps
How are you engaging in discussions with colleagues to achieve a common understanding of expectations for student work? How can I assist with this discussion?	
During the collaborative-scoring (calibration) sessions, what can I do as a leader to help you interpret each level of the rubric consistently and apply the rubric uniformly?	
How are you interpreting high-inference rubric items using evidence from students' work?	
How does the collaborative-scoring process enable reliability and confidence when you score independently?	
What anchor papers have you collected to show levels of performance for specific skills in the rubric? How will you ensure each team member gets the anchor papers to use for scoring independently? How will you use the anchor papers within instruction to help students improve their writing skills?	
How are you tapping the expertise and input of colleagues? Do you need my support to help make this happen?	
What process do you have as a team to make changes to prompts or rubrics as needed? What changes need to be made and why?	

Figure 4.5: Leadership guiding questions for calibration-scoring checklists.

*Visit **go.SolutionTree.com/literacy** for a free reproducible version of this figure.*

what this work entails and why all educators focus on this endeavor. To articulate shared leadership in supporting teachers to develop and use rubrics and checklists, uniformly interpret rubrics, collect anchor papers, and involve students in their own learning, review figure 4.6.

Student Ownership of Learning

Teachers implement a variety of strategies to ensure students use rubrics and student checklists to understand proficiency and expectations. Students use these tools to explain their learning journey.

Lead Teachers and Instructional Coaches

Lead teachers and instructional coaches support collaborative teams to design rubrics and checklists that articulate proficiency expectations and task requirements. They also assist (facilitate) teams as they participate in collaborative-scoring sessions.

School Leaders

School leaders provide professional development opportunities and observe teams and classrooms to support deep understanding and implementation of rubrics and checklists, and to ensure consistent expectations for proficiency through collaborative scoring.

District Leaders

District leaders develop tight expectations for students to take ownership of their learning.

Figure 4.6: A district's shared-leadership culture.

Figure 4.6 represents a call to action for student ownership of learning, whereby students, teachers, and school and district leaders equally share responsibility. To achieve this, collaborative teams design lessons in which teachers use a rubric and checklist as instructional tools that enable students to keenly understand what they must do to be successful on a given task. Lead teachers—well-trained and supported by instructional coaches—assume the role as head of their respective collaborative teams. They spearhead rubric and checklist design. Plus, they facilitate collaborative-scoring sessions in which team members calibrate expectations of student work and determine anchor papers, including exemplars. At the next level, school leaders provide professional development and resources and observe and support teams as they collaboratively score using their common analytic rubric. Leaders at the district level establish tight expectations and mandate this work by providing policies and professional development to continuously support these expectations.

Shared leadership is critical work, both at the district and school levels. As we stated in chapter 1 (page 9), it isn't as simple as putting teachers together on teams and giving them time to work. What makes a difference is the ongoing training, support, coaching, and guidance to ensure each teacher understands the purpose that drives the collaborative work teams do together. Use figure 4.7 (page 100) to consider your next steps as a leader. What will you revise, eliminate, or include in your practices around transparent learning expectations and scoring consistency to ensure leadership at all levels, including from students? The inclusion of *students* requires special attention in this instance, so we added a column in figure 4.7 to clarify their role in shared leadership.

The Final Word

Author Timothy D. Kanold (2017) reminds all educators:

> There is nothing more important to the thought leadership and wisdom of our professional work than our ability to effectively monitor student learning, provide feedback for refinement during the learning process, and then expect our students to act on the feedback. (p. 221)

For you, as a leader, to ensure this happens, teachers must achieve clarity and agreement on the learning expectations for students. Providing the purpose and protocols, supporting the development of the tools, and holding teachers accountable to collaboratively score to calibrate and collect anchor papers are all effective contributing factors to student success.

Of course, sharing success criteria with students will accomplish optimal impact since doing so enables them to become leaders of their own learning. As part of this work, reflect on practices you wish to see and hear in classrooms and within collaborative teams to ensure this shared ownership of learning expectations. How will you support both teachers and students in knowing what proficiency means and the steps necessary to get there? What will you change or need to do as a leader to accomplish these goals? In the next chapter, we turn our attention to the evidence of learning through data and our response to student needs through intervention.

Leadership Area: Build Shared Leadership				
District Leader	School Administrator	Instructional Coach	Lead Teacher	Student
☐ Empower school leaders to develop shared-leadership models within their school to ensure and embed district expectations in daily practice. ☐ Support collaborative scoring as a tight expectation with ongoing professional development. ☐ Create a district culture that includes student ownership of their learning as a tight expectation.	☐ Build common understanding of why and how to determine learning expectations. ☐ Create tight expectations so collaborative teams develop tools such as rubrics and student checklists as part of their work and then share these tools with students and use them in classroom instruction. ☐ Provide professional development and support for lead teachers, instructional coaches, and teachers on the importance of learning expectations and the tools necessary to support this work. ☐ Observe and provide feedback to collaborative teams as they develop rubrics and checklists and collaboratively score student work. ☐ Observe classroom practice with an intentional focus on student ownership of learning. ☐ Create opportunities for students to explain their learning and share this with their parents or guardians.	☐ Develop your personal understanding of why and how to create tools that support the district's tight expectations so you can further the work of collaborative teams. ☐ Facilitate a collaborative-scoring session to train teams on how to conduct it on their own. Ensure they collect anchor papers, including exemplars, or research to find existing anchors for the task teams administered. ☐ Observe collaborative teams and classroom practices to provide feedback and coaching support so teachers and students design and use proficiency expectations more effectively.	☐ Learn to create rubrics, student checklists, and other tools that support the district's expectations that collaborative teams define proficiency expectations. ☐ Support and lead collaborative team conversations as they use anchor papers and exemplars to collaboratively score student work. ☐ Help other teachers deepen their understanding of the need to determine proficiency and to share this ownership of learning with students.	☐ Share learning goals with parents or guardians by explaining the rubric or checklist. ☐ Use checklists as a guide while writing or addressing any task to ensure requirements are met. ☐ Use rubrics to self-assess; determine areas of weakness that direct revisionary work for improvement. ☐ Use rubrics to critique published and student writing samples and to provide feedback to peers. ☐ When appropriate, cocreate rubrics and checklists with peers and the teacher.

Figure 4.7: Leadership area guidelines for collective understanding of learning expectations—Build shared leadership.

*Visit **go.SolutionTree.com/literacy** for a free reproducible version of this figure.*

CHAPTER 5

Respond to Student Data to Ensure All Students Learn

Maybe stories are just data with a soul.

—BRENÉ BROWN

As teachers learn and practice how to collaboratively score student work, the focus turns to acting on the results. Leaders and educators gain access to data from various checkpoints—classroom formative practices, collaborative team common assessments, student work, district benchmarks, and state or provincial and national assessments. Each of these checkpoints tells a story. Until educators understand the purpose and use data to take action, data are fairly meaningless and represent missed opportunities. In education, we often say we are "data rich and information poor." To avert this adage, your role as a leader necessitates you and your teachers capably use data to inform next steps in student learning. In other words, possessing an abundance of assessments displayed on extensive graphs and charts is purposeful only when data analysis leads to student-centered decisions.

In *Rising Strong*, professor, lecturer, author, and podcast host Brené Brown (2015) tells educators, "In the absence of data, we will always make up stories. . . . In fact, the need to make up a story, especially when we are hurt, is part of our most primitive survival wiring" (p. 79). When focusing on students' needs, leaders and educators work to discover concrete evidence among data to reveal an accurate picture of students' capabilities. Without the facts, the creation of a fictitious story can mislead teachers, which can result in false starts, incorrect actions, and the implementation of ineffective instructional strategies. Confronting the brutal reality challenges district and school leaders; however, when educators neglect using data to understand student needs and next steps, they run the risk of not realizing or comprehending a student's true narrative.

Leaders, teachers, coaches, and others who interface with students make decisions about curriculum, learning outcomes, instructional strategies, assessments, and interventions based on evidence, not opinion. How will you and your teachers recognize what students know and are able to do? What will determine instructional next steps or adjustments to curriculum and pacing calendars? What are the criteria for establishing interventions for those who struggle and those who need extensions? How do you, teachers, and other invested educators know which intervention strategy is best and progress monitor for results?

Think of the last time that you met with a doctor, lawyer, or building contractor. As each considered next steps, at any point, did you believe that he or she merely acted on an opinion, or were you confident that he or she gathered evidence and created a plan of action based on a collection of evidence? How comfortable would you be with a doctor who only listened to your self-appraisal of your symptoms and did not ask questions, order tests, or conduct any kind of an assessment to treat a problem? What would you think of a lawyer who pleaded on your behalf in court with only opinion rather than evidence to defend your case? Which builder would you prefer—one who measures to determine the next step or one who takes a quick look and then proceeds with sawing and nailing?

When leaders and teachers proceed to the next step with students without an understanding of the correct story that data provide, their actions can resemble the doctor who disregards tests or a lawyer who ignores evidence. When students fail to thrive or need extension opportunities, teachers must respond accordingly, and leaders must authentically know that they and teachers are appropriately responding to those needs. These tenets underpin the third and fourth critical questions of a PLC: *How will we respond when some students do not learn it?* and *How will we extend the learning for students who have demonstrated proficiency?* (DuFour et al., 2016). This chapter addresses compelling and difficult questions teachers and administrators should confront when using data to effectively respond to student needs. This includes establishing collective efficacy and considering tools and resources to support data inquiry. Together, these practices ensure and further students' learning progress with regard to literacy skill development. Success in this endeavor further requires a focus on two leadership areas: (1) achieve focus and stay intentional and (2) use evidence for decision making and action.

Collective Efficacy

Collective efficacy is both a perception and a data-driven reality that collective action and shared belief in that action have positive effects on students and learning (Goddard, Hoy, & Hoy, 2004). Researcher and author John Hattie (2016), through his extensive meta-analysis studies, identifies collective efficacy as a top influencer contributing to student achievement. Providing more insight into this imperative, education consultants Jenni Donohoo and Steven Katz (2017) contend:

> When teachers share the belief that, together, they can positively influence student learning over and above other factors and make an educational difference in the lives of students, they actually do. . . . In fact, collective efficacy is what matters most in improving student learning. (p. 21)

Therefore, as a leader, vigilantly create myriad situations that depend on the concerted efforts of collaborative teams to work together to overcome obstacles and attain intended results. Remember, the second big idea of a PLC requires that districts and schools establish a culture of collaboration in which teachers build common understanding based on collaborative inquiry (DuFour et al., 2016). When teachers examine data together, it positively impacts collective efficacy. Confidence expands their ability to service students optimally as, together, teams discover evidence of the accurate story of what students learn. When teachers experience the byproduct of their instructional impact, it reinforces their hard work and success as collaborative teams.

Data drive decisions about instruction *and* intervention, which specifically encompass remediating skill gaps for those who have yet to demonstrate proficiency and extending learning for those who show they've already achieved mastery of those skills. As a leader, you must stipulate and provide teams dedicated time to participate in collective-data inquiry to effectively analyze what the data reveal. Based on the information, teachers provide high-quality, timely, and systematic instruction that targets students' specific needs to move them along on their learning journey. Providing the time and expecting data-driven discussions, however, are not enough. As a leader, you must see to it that teachers recognize the link between collaborative instructional planning, assessment, and interventions and the evidence in student outcomes.

REFLECTION

As a leader, what messages can you send overtly or covertly to ensure all teachers assume the responsibility of shared ownership for all students? How do you build collective efficacy as a culture within the district, school, and collaborative teams?

For optimum results in achieving successful collective efficacy that inculcates a supportive environment for worthwhile data-analysis discussion, leaders must first play a key role in building and creating a trusting, safe, and professional environment. This climate invites teachers to freely work together in myriad ways—for example, to identify priority standards, design curriculum, or plan a school field trip. Frankly, teachers engage openly rather well to accomplish these tasks. The difficulty often lies in their ability to feel comfortable honestly sharing their students' results. In the absence of this comfort level, some teachers invent alibis akin to a student using the proverbial excuse that a dog ate his or her homework. For instance, teachers might say that they cannot find their students' data or delay meeting dates in an attempt to hide the scores. As a leader, instill in teachers the wherewithal to develop and interact in a trusting workplace, which enables them to embark on honest conversations about what their students know or don't know and can or cannot do.

Let's suppose you are a principal joining a collaborative team as teachers begin to examine student work and data from a recent common formative assessment. You notice one teacher, who is typically willing to share opinions and speak with confidence, quietly sitting at the table. She averts eye contact with the others, and although she appears to have her student work and data with her, she avoids participating in the discussion. Perplexed by this, following the collaborative meeting, you speak with the team leader and together agree that you will invite the teacher to your office for the three of you to talk.

At this meeting, the teacher immediately shares that her students performed rather poorly in comparison to her colleagues' data. These weak results left her extremely embarrassed. She explains that she implemented instructional strategies the collaborative team had agreed to use and felt the lesson went well; however, the data indicated this was not the case. She candidly admits her reluctance to reveal to her teammates how deficient her data are and how distressed she personally feels about her professional practice.

As a school leader, your role necessitates fostering a trusting culture for professional dialogue without fear of judgment, which takes time and effort. You feel you've accomplished this safe environment to a degree, since the teacher willingly reveals her feelings to you; however, her hesitancy in sharing openly with colleagues indicates an opportunity for improvement. In response, you confide in her that you also have struggled with the worry of what others might think when sharing your work, but you have learned over time that you need others to offer suggestions and support in order for you to be the best advocate for students. You explain that it takes courage to be vulnerable among colleagues and that honesty, collegial input, and collective action to respond to the unsatisfactory data will reap rewards for her and for students. You offer to attend an upcoming team meeting and suggest it would be important for her to share her feelings with her teammates. She agrees that, with you there, she will be more comfortable broaching the conversation. At the meeting, the teachers appreciate her candor and are quick to state (not surprisingly) that, at times, they have all felt the same way. They know this courageous conversation benefits students since inviting other members' help and tapping their expertise will advance learning. Collective efficacy requires courage, respect, trust, and a mutual commitment to make certain that teachers will continue to build these tenets. As a leader, it's your responsibility to ensure your school or district's culture makes this possible.

This example illustrates taking appropriate action to develop accountability. In *Help Your Team*, coauthors Michael D. Bayewitz, Scott A. Cunningham, Joseph A. Ianora, Brandon Jones, Maria Nielsen, Will Remmert, and their colleagues (2020) remind leaders about the importance of focus and accountability and that, unlike in a traditional system (where accountability moves up the chain of command), "a leader and team member in a PLC must engage in horizontal, or mutual, accountability" (p. 25). This begins with the teams' willingness and ability to describe the behaviors that honor their values and collective commitments. "Teams typically establish norms of acceptable behaviors at team meetings, but norms really apply to all interactions in which teams engage" (Bayewitz et al., 2020, p. 25).

In this section's scenario, based on the teacher's reticence to be vulnerable and share her concerns, the team revisited its norms and stated expected behaviors. In this case, it meant asking each and every team member to engage in open and honest discussions about student achievement to ensure trust and respect are mutually agreed on as part of the team's collective commitments. As a leader, you must gauge the pulse of the culture of each of your collaborative teams in general and do so when you ask them to share and discuss student data.

Donohoo (2017) identifies six enabling conditions that increase the likelihood for collective efficacy to thrive: (1) advanced teacher influence, (2) goal consensus, (3) teachers' knowledge about one another's work, (4) cohesive staff, (5) responsiveness of leadership, and (6) effective systems of intervention. Leaders are wise to infuse these conditions into the operation of their districts, schools, and teams. Use figure 5.1 as a guide to implement Donohoo's (2017) six conditions into your daily leadership practice.

Six Enabling Conditions (Donohoo, 2017)	What Does It Mean in Leadership?	Leader Self-Reflection Questions to Develop Collective Efficacy
1. Advanced teacher influence	When leaders trust and empower teachers to contribute and assume responsibility for important decisions, they form a stronger sense of efficacy.	How can I compel teachers to take leadership roles or create roles for them? How can I provide opportunities or empower teachers to make decisions on schoolwide issues, such as those involving curriculum design, assessment, and professional development?
2. Goal consensus	When collaborative teams establish SMART goals (Conzemius & O'Neill, 2014), teachers understand and aim for purposeful results. (See also Leadership Area: Use Evidence for Decision Making and Action, page 123.) Leadership teams at the school and district levels arrive at a consensus on SMART goals for the same reasons—to set direction and establish expected results.	How can I lead my staff to collaboratively develop, communicate, and achieve consensus on important school goals? What are examples of measurable and appropriately challenging SMART goals for my school that teachers will commit to supporting?
3. Teachers' knowledge about one another's work	As teachers collaborate to answer the four critical questions of a PLC, conversations about one another's instruction and assessment practices evolve, which builds professional capacity as they coconstruct next steps together.	In what ways can teachers learn about one another's instructional practices? How can I lead my staff or colleagues to learn more about one another's classrooms? What can I do to encourage the sharing of teacher expertise?
4. Cohesive staff	*Cohesion* represents the extent to which teachers agree with one another on fundamental and organizational issues. Through	How can I create a situation in which teachers agree on fundamental educational issues that support learning, creating a

	collaboration and opportunities to discuss mission, vision, and collective commitments, teachers begin to understand one another. Awareness of one another provides a framework to work together to meet the needs of students.	cohesive staff? What can I do to lead my district or school staff to further understand one another's beliefs and commitments to student learning?
5. Responsiveness of leadership	Leaders accept the responsibility to demonstrate an awareness of teachers' personal and professional needs and protect them from distractions. Teachers feel valued when leaders provide resources and learning opportunities, as well as when they hear and respond to teachers' concerns.	How can I support teachers in successfully doing their job? For example, what resources can I provide to promote and support their teaching? How might I insulate them from issues or influences that interfere with their teaching time or focus?
6. Effective systems of intervention	When teachers see students achieve success through their collective efforts, they feel a sense of collective efficacy. Leaders create this feeling of success by ensuring that effective systems of intervention are in place for students, using the expertise of all educators.	How can I ensure that three tiers of intervention are systematically available to all students in need? What can I do to use the expertise of the educators in my system to develop interventions for students? How can I lead collaborative conversations identifying what students need and how teachers can respond to these needs?

Figure 5.1: Leadership self-reflection questions for developing collective efficacy.

Data-Inquiry Guidelines and Processes

As stated often in our signature series books and in this leader's guide, the altogether vital work of collaborative teams in the PLC process is grounded in responding to the four critical questions. Teams represent much more than a group of people merely meeting together—they are composed of individuals who interact interdependently to ensure high levels of learning for *all* students (DuFour et al., 2016). To accomplish this, collaborative teams must engage openly about what the data reveal to ascertain precisely what students are learning or not learning. Then they plan and conduct lessons in a timely manner based on these findings to support continuous improvement. These actions require team members to understand *why* these conversations are crucial and *how* to participate in them effectively. By doing so, they feel more driven to be successful in their collaborative efforts.

Collective efficacy serves as the foundation of why teams examine data together. Students profit from the "many hands make light work" adage as teachers collectively dig deep to determine what prevents a student from mastering skills and acquiring knowledge and what needs to occur to positively change this faulty or stunted learning trajectory. When teams routinely engage in cycles of collaborative data inquiry, they continuously deepen their knowledge, improve their practice, and impact student success (Reeves & Eaker, 2019). With shared ownership of student learning, teachers consistently build their practice of analyzing student work and data so they can uncover meaningful opportunities to meet student needs (Buffum, Mattos, & Malone, 2018).

As a leader, it is incumbent on you to assist teams in adhering to a set of guidelines for using and discussing data. With inspiration from organizational leadership expert and author Thomas W. Many (n.d.), we recommend the following.

1. Data are accessible, easy to manage, and purposefully arranged.

2. Data are publicly discussed.

3. Data are action oriented.

The following sections address each of these recommendations.

Data Are Accessible, Easy to Manage, and Purposefully Arranged

Accessible, *manageable*, and *purposefully arranged data* help teachers maintain focus on student results and limit potential distractions from a faulty or complicated presentation format. This means teams must do the following.

▸ Choose and devise a data-collection tool for sharing and displaying students' results (for example, a print or computer-generated table, chart, graph, or spreadsheet).

▸ Purposefully arrange data in a complete, accurate, and straightforward format.

▸ Grant all members who interface with students access to the data-collection tool.

Most experts at analyzing student data recommend a school (or even better, an entire district) adopt common data protocols so educators collect and display data consistently throughout a system. Response to intervention (RTI) experts Austin Buffum, Mike Mattos, and Janet Malone (2018) recommend using a tool that reflects both individual student and classroom assessment results for learning targets. One such tool, a *data wall*, refers to a literal wall in a room away from public viewing—often called a *data room* or *collaborative team room*—dedicated to displaying data. Lacking space, some schools use a wall in the faculty lounge for this purpose. Additionally, a data wall might represent a metaphorical expression for results teachers share electronically—for example, on a spreadsheet accessible on a computer or hard-copy results in a folder.

To illustrate, teams might display results from a universal screener, such as using color-coded Standardized Testing and Reporting (STAR) data for ELA connected to proficiency levels—exceeding expectations (blue), meeting expectations (green), close to expectations (yellow), and far from expectations (red). See figure 5.2 for an example. In addition to common formative assessment data such as these, teams might simply print out and affix an electronic version of data on the walls.

STAR DATA: ELA

	Exceeding expectations (Blue)	Meeting expectations (Green)	Close to expectations (Yellow)	Far from expectations (Red)
Grade _____	_____%	_____%	_____%	_____%
Grade _____	_____%	_____%	_____%	_____%
Grade _____	_____%	_____%	_____%	_____%
Grade _____	_____%	_____%	_____%	_____%

Figure 5.2: Data wall example one—STAR data for ELA.

Figure 5.3 (page 110) depicts a data wall for a second-grade collaborative team focused on reading levels members measured during benchmark assessments. Posted to a wall in the team's meeting room, the data wall features each student's name on a colt-shaped cutout (the school's mascot) and positioned according to his or her progress: exceeded grade-level expectations (first row), met grade-level expectations (second row), close to grade-level expectations (third row), and needs support and corrective instruction to reach grade-level expectations (fourth row). With this visual, the team can quickly determine which students still need intensive interventions to move from the fourth row and those who are close and would benefit from additional support. The visual aids teachers in quickly viewing and remembering students' status toward grade-level learning targets as they continue to progress monitor. (See more about tiered intervention in Data Are Action Oriented, page 119.) Collaborative teams also use these data to set SMART goals (Conzemius & O'Neill, 2014). Prominently and conspicuously displaying student results serves to instill the notion of evidence-based decisions as a daily practice and a constant reminder of student progress and a team's agreed-on goals.

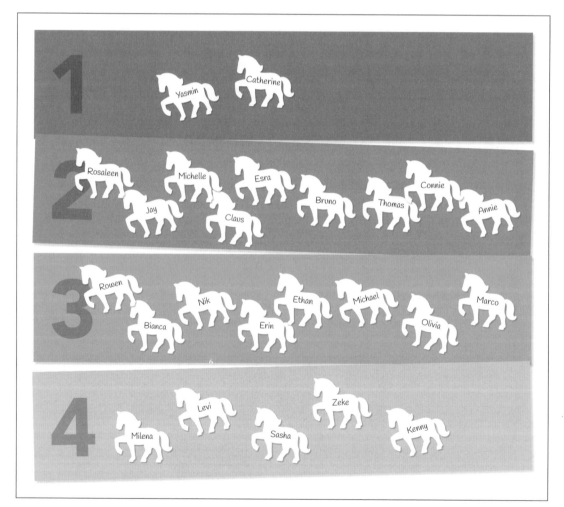

Figure 5.3: Data wall example two—Second-grade reading levels (by student by color).

Within the classroom, teachers can post evidence of student progress with regard to specific learning targets such as the example in figure 5.4 for a component of the Speaking and Listening strand in ELA. (Visit **go.SolutionTree.com /literacy** to see a full-color mathematics example of this figure.) In this regard, students realize their growth as a class and can champion and support each other to collectively achieve goals.

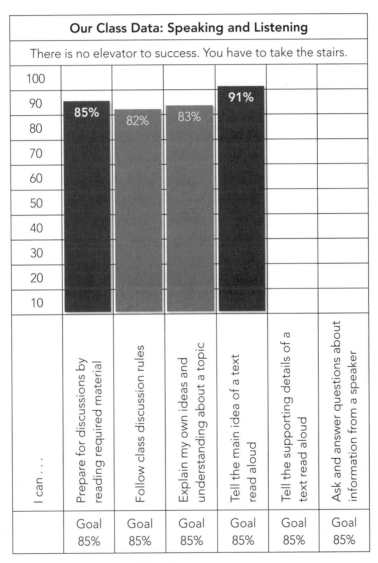

Figure 5.4: Data wall example three—Class formative assessment data.

In *The New Art and Science of Teaching*, Marzano (2017) articulates a framework for representing data that incorporates overarching categories, design questions, elements, and multiple instructional strategies that focus on student outcomes. Within the design area for this framework, he emphasizes two elements—(1) providing and communicating clear learning goals and (2) tracking student progress—which speak to students setting their own goals and tracking their scores on a proficiency scale as well as teachers tracking the progress of the entire class (Marzano, 2017). Figure 5.5 shows a delightful picture of a student with an entry from the data notebook she uses to self-monitor and explain her learning journey to others, including her parents. Each column on the bar graph reflects a learning target expressed as an *I can* statement within a learning progression, where reaching the top of the chart indicates mastery. In this classroom, the teacher allows students autonomy to choose their own colors to personalize their charts.

With your lead, as teachers develop a results-driven culture, students and parents become more accustomed to seeing data displayed individually, like in a notebook or sometimes on classroom walls. For the latter, teachers can post a learning target or goal and use a bar graph or other method to show the number of students (not their names) at different levels. Consider a collective approach, such as: *we did it, almost there*, and *not there yet*.

Data Are Publicly Discussed

During data analysis, public discussions occur within teams as teachers courageously share their data with one another. Publicly discussing data draws the teacher from an isolated classroom where only he or she knows how well students are achieving; hence, it becomes public to all team members. The norms teams develop allow for this open and honest dialogue.

Why is it important to insist collaborative teams participate in data discussions and share their results with others? How do these data conversations benefit students? Candidly, doing so allows teams to confront the reality their data uncover and eliminate any personal bias and vulnerabilities that might stand in the way of servicing students optimally. Overlooking the facts and ignoring what they can identify as the root cause of student needs impede and detrimentally interfere with school improvement. During data conversations, teams make noteworthy discoveries about instructional practices, effective resources, and curriculum adoption. For teachers to engage in discussions that garner intended results, they must set norms to foster open, honest communication and use protocols for examining data—both aspects at the heart of this guideline. (Refer to the signature series for

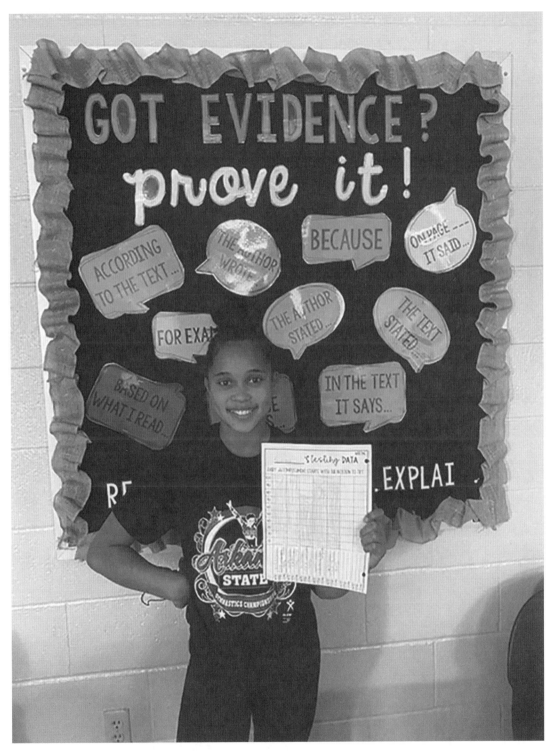

Source: © 2021 Morrilton Intermediate School, Arkansas.

Figure 5.5: Charting student progress.

how teams can determine a set of norms to engage thoughtfully and productively in a supportive environment.)

When analyzing data, teachers essentially identify trends, determine what led to the results, and ultimately develop an intervention plan to responsively teach particular students by providing corrective instruction for those struggling to meet standards or extension for those ready for more. To support teams to analyze data, the signature series books feature Kildeer Countryside Community Consolidated School District 96's *Here's What, So What?, Now What?* protocol, which is one choice among many that schools can employ. Another guide for analyzing common formative assessment data is Bailey and Jakicic's (2017) protocol for using common formative assessment data (figure 5.6). Additionally, consider perusing other options for your district or school, such as those from the National School Reform Faculty (https://nsrfharmony.org) and AllThingsPLC (https://bit.ly/2LrW8tC).

Whichever protocol a team selects, it is necessary to incorporate a step that compels teachers to engage in causal discussion. In figure 5.6, step 4 contextualizes this as "Determine student misconceptions and errors." In other words, teachers ask, "Why isn't _____ learning _____?" To answer this question, team members pose a series of questions (the first one beginning with *why*) until the collaborative team confidently determines the root cause of each student's deficits.

This exercise prompts teachers to look beyond the numbers in the data to the source of the problem. For example, suppose you observe a collaborative team data discussion and hear a teacher say, "Jamie cannot comprehend what he reads." You wait for the team to begin examining why Jamie fails to understand the text. You expect them to use the protocol you have provided, which guides members' thinking through a series of questions. Unfortunately, the members mistakenly record *cannot comprehend* as the root cause and proceed to investigate data for their next student.

Without employing a quality protocol that ultimately leads to pinpointing causes in addition to identifying overall deficits, the collaborative team is ill-equipped to engage in the deeper discussions necessary to impact learning. As a leader, you must provide more training to the lead teacher and the collaborative team by modeling a fruitful discussion to help them understand they must uncover what causes a student to miss a learning target. Using the example of Jamie, the team might pose the following questions while concurrently examining the student's work and data: "Why is Jamie unable to show comprehension? Why does the text seem challenging for him? Do we focus our support to bolster his reading

Steps	Team Notes
1. Set the stage. • Establish the purpose of the meeting. • Review norms (focusing on data norms).	Two minutes
2. Review the focus of the assessment. • Identify the essential learning targets we assessed and which questions we designed to assess each of them. • Review the expectations for proficiency (for example, two out of three correct on a multiple-choice assessment, or a level 3 on the rubric). • Discuss any questions we had when we scored student work.	Two minutes
3. Discuss the data. • For each target, identify how many students will need additional time and support.	Five minutes Each team member must participate in this discussion.
4. Determine student misconceptions and errors. • For each target, identify which students need help. • Once we've identified the students who need help, regroup them by specific need (for example, students who made a calculation error versus students who chose the wrong solution pathway).	Ten minutes Be careful to do this step one essential learning target at a time.
5. Determine instructional strategies. • Decide whether we will develop small groups for reteaching or if we will use a re-engagement lesson with the whole class. • Each teacher should share his or her original instructional strategy so that we can see if one strategy worked better for certain students. • For each target and for each mistake or misconception, develop a plan to help students move ahead on their learning of that target. • If necessary, go back to best practice information about how to teach the concept or about what strategies work best for struggling students. Consult instructional coaches or specialists if necessary.	Fifteen minutes Make sure that all team members have the same understanding of what this will look like.
6. Develop the items that we will use to monitor whether students met the learning target after this response. This will provide information about which students still need help on this essential target.	Ten minutes This reassessment may be done orally or may be a version of the original assessment.

Source: Bailey & Jakicic, 2017, p. 82.

Figure 5.6: Protocol for using common formative assessment data.

*Visit **go.SolutionTree.com/literacy** for a free reproducible version of this figure.*

accuracy, background knowledge, or vocabulary? What do the data reveal specifically? What evidence can we use to ensure our next steps reflect the correct course of action? What intentional planning, such as specific instructional strategies, will address Jamie's needs and boost his achievement? How will we know that we are succeeding with our plans for Jamie?"

REFLECTION

What guiding questions will you model for teams to assist them in discovering root causes of deficiencies? How will you support them to deeply understand the accurate story data can reveal?

By questioning and using student data, teams directly support each student on his or her learning journey. Therefore, steer your teams toward using a data protocol that incorporates a thorough investigation into the root causes that impede a student's learning. As a leader, make it clear that data drive the entire culture of the school—not just within teams. Explain that principals and other leaders review and analyze data for different purposes, such as for state tests, attendance, tardiness, reading levels, programs, and so on. Model how principals and leaders use and share these data authentically for public discussions. Ensuring guiding coalitions analyze data as part of regular meeting agendas, plus making decisions and taking action based on these data, will help exemplify the importance of a data-driven culture. Progress monitoring the actions educators take for effectiveness also guides them in understanding the accountability you, as a leader, expect from the next steps they determine for student learning or for other aspects of the school. In other words, that data-analysis process you expect collaborative teams to use can and should also be a regular practice within district and school leadership teams.

Another meaningful way you can strengthen teachers' expertise regarding an expectation for data-driven decisions is to host data conversations. For example, as a school principal, invite individual teachers or collaborative teams to meet with you on a rotating basis to discuss student data. Focus your guiding questions and feedback on seeking information on the learning progression for each individual student and what next steps the teacher or team deems necessary. These individual coaching conversations also provide an opportunity to learn more about the instructional needs of the teachers, teams, and students. Your intentional focus on data analysis will provide deeper understanding of the expectations and account-ability of evidence-based practices in your district or school.

Leaders may find, at first, the reluctance of some teachers to recognize the bene-fit of data discussions and what they can yield. These individuals will need contin-ued support and repeated effort to hone their data-analysis skills. Offer guidance to deepen their conversations until they truly and personally appreciate the value and relevance of the work and build confidence. Present expectations, including protocols, for their discussion, analysis, and next steps.

Building on their professional expertise and collective efficacy empowers teachers and collaborative teams to successfully meet students' needs. Hattie (2012) states:

> Teachers are adaptive learning experts who know where students are on the continuum from novice to capable to proficient, when students are and are not learning, and where to go next, and who can create a classroom climate to attain these learning goals. (p. 111)

This statement speaks to the heart of why it is critical that you pay attention to building teachers' professional capacity to understand the value of evidence-based decisions.

Regardless of the protocol teams choose to follow, figure 5.7 (page 118) features options for reflective questions that you can choose to use while observing and guiding collaborative teams in conversations around data analysis.

The questions in figure 5.7 also serve as a reminder of tight expectations district and school leaders can adopt to advance a data-driven culture for both leadership and collaborative teams. Consider the following actions you promote and expect by addressing the guiding questions.

1. Identify which assessment, student task, and common rubric teachers use as the basis for the meeting.

2. Ensure each team member administered the assessment in the appropri-ate time frame and scored the expected student work using the common rubric prior to the team meeting.

3. Guarantee all team members have access to and understand how to use the data-analysis protocol and tools.

4. Expect all team members to enter their data on the data-collection tool prior to the collaborative team meeting.

Leadership: Guiding Questions for Data-Analysis Meetings	Collaborative Team Notes and Next Steps
Identify the assessment and accompanying rubric. What formative or summative assessment task is the basis for this data-inquiry meeting? What rubric did your team use to score student work? Do line items on the rubric align to the learning targets teachers measure?	
Ensure team members administer and score all students' assessments in a logical and feasible time frame. What specific plans did your team agree to for administering the common assessment within a defined and agreed-on time frame? (Teammates administer within a day or two of one another.) How did each of you plan for scoring students' work in advance of the team meeting? How did your team build in a collaborative-scoring session to ensure scoring consistency before each of you scored your papers individually?	
Verify all team members come prepared to the meeting. What evidence can you share that shows you've come prepared to the team meeting? Specifically, where is the data-collection tool that shows scores that you each entered? How do they share student work (hard-copy or electronic links)? How will you address a situation in which someone on your team arrives unprepared?	
Ensure the team only determines action steps once members are confident they have reached consensus on the root cause or causes of student deficits. How are all team members willingly sharing student data and participating in the conversations? What protocol is your team following? What probing questions are team members asking one another that focus on understanding and agreeing on the root cause of student deficits? How do you address next steps in instruction based on data? What actions will you take if your team's conversations are not deeply examining student data and using them to plan future learning?	

Figure 5.7: Leadership guiding questions for data-analysis meetings.

Visit **go.SolutionTree.com/literacy** *for a free reproducible version of this figure.*

5. Ensure all team members bring their student-assessment task and scored writing samples or discuss plans for collaborative scoring.

6. Ensure team members engage in a discussion on student work and determine action steps once the team is confident they have reached a consensus on the root causes of student deficits.

Participating in these tight expectations as a district and school leader will help team leaders facilitate the team data analysis and provide more opportunities for teachers to share ownership of all students and their learning journeys.

Data Are Action Oriented

Once collaborative teams determine a method for organizing data, establish norms that foster a trusting culture, and engage in data conversations, they need your leadership to support them to act on what the data uncover, including identifying next steps and progress monitoring to ensure impact. According to Many (n.d.), this speaks to the third guideline—*the response to the data is action oriented.* In Bailey and Jakicic's (2017) protocol, it is steps 4, 5, and 6 (refer to figure 5.6, page 115). Consider what this involves based on each student's identified needs in a data-driven culture.

When educators begin to examine data, they initially identify specific skills individuals or groups of students struggle with or exhibit proficiency in based on grade-level learning targets. Next, collaborative teams analyze further to determine and clarify the root cause of those deficit skills and then create a plan of action to provide intervention. As mentioned, this means designing appropriate extension opportunities for those ready for more challenge and scaffolding for others in need of support. Some students require intensive and very targeted support to build background knowledge in foundational skills they lack. The information an individual teacher, a collaborative team, or a school leadership team gleans from student data must directly align with what they determine as the next course of action.

As a leader, to support collaborative teams and classroom teachers in building an understanding of how to systematically support student learning, we highly recommend implementing the three RTI tiers Buffum and his colleagues (2018) describe in *Taking Action: A Handbook for RTI at Work.* We also cite this text in chapter 9 (page 207) to articulate the link between equitable access to learning in a supportive system of intervention. What follows is a summary of how leaders and teachers can apply the three tiers of intervention as a response to data analysis.

Tier 1

The first tier of support for students occurs within core instruction. All students, no matter their existing proficiency level with standards, require the same access to high-quality grade-level instruction. Teachers typically collect data formatively within classroom practice for this tier and design and implement instruction in response to individual or small-group needs. For example, Tier 1 support can entail conducting running records, issuing exit slips, or taking observational notes on group discussions to quickly ascertain what must be done to differentiate instruction. Hattie (2012) advises leaders:

> For differentiation to be effective, teachers need to know, for each student, where that student begins and where he or she is in his or her journey towards meeting the success criteria of the lesson. Is that student a novice, somewhat capable, or proficient? What are his or her strengths and gaps in knowledge and understanding? What learning strategies does he or she have and how can we help him or her to develop other learning strategies that he or she needs? (p. 109)

Leaders create opportunities for teachers to understand and practice effective instructional strategies since all students address grade-level learning and have opportunities for success within Tier 1 (core) instruction. Ideally, it should only be necessary for approximately 20 percent of students to need Tier 2 and Tier 3 supports. In our experiences in low-performing schools, however, we witness a reverse of these percentages—80 percent of students require Tier 2 supplemental intervention and Tier 3 intensive supports, and only 20 percent show achievement from core instruction (Tier 1). This speaks to the very important role leaders have in ensuring teachers can capably deliver high-quality, effective instructional practices in the classroom.

See *Best Practices at Tier 1: Daily Differentiation for Effective Instruction, Elementary* (Gregory, Kaufeldt, & Mattos, 2016) for more information about this intervention level.

Tier 2

Teams identify students in need of Tier 2 supplemental inventions as those who struggle to master grade-level skills. In response, teachers allow extra time and scaffold instruction to assist them in acquiring these skills. (Our signature series provides various scaffolding strategies teachers can implement to support student needs.) For instance, as teachers discuss root causes of student deficits, they work together to determine how to find additional time and regroup students to provide necessary support to address specific learning targets or progressions. Tier 2 also accounts for providing extension learning opportunities for students who already demonstrate proficiency.

Consider the following team example: a literacy collaborative team has done an excellent job of analyzing its data using the leadership-provided data protocol. As a leader, you are pleased with the root-cause analysis and next steps, which involve all teachers regrouping students based on the data to provide support and extensions for thirty minutes for the next four days. The teachers agree they will reassess the students who need more time and support on day five and then meet again to analyze the new data. One teacher, whose students exhibit strong results, offers to work with students who scored the lowest on this assessment. The team agrees that her instructional strategies proved very effective, so she offers to reteach those students who require more intensive support with this essential learning progression. Other students are assigned to the remaining teachers who provide interventions geared to the learning deficits revealed in assessments. And students who showed mastery with core instruction worked with yet another teacher to extend their capabilities.

As a team, members remind one another that when providing extension opportunities to this latter group, instruction must be within the existing learning targets rather than exposing students to new standards. For example, if some students prove they can determine a theme in a grade-level text, teachers can instruct them to identify more sophisticated themes from across two or three works in more challenging literature. In this way, they deepen their experience with the learning target on which they demonstrated proficiency as opposed to advancing to other targets. This cycle of data analysis, intervention, and reassessment provides accountability for which learning experiences the team decided would best move students' learning forward.

See *Best Practices at Tier 2: Supplemental Interventions for Additional Student Support, Elementary* (Kramer, Sonju, Mattos, & Buffum, 2021) for more information about this intervention level.

Tier 3

The third tier provides intensive remediation for specific skills students lack. These are typically foundational skills students failed to master in previous grades, and a schoolwide intervention team most often determines them. Leaders must include a district- and schoolwide process for using universal screeners and other diagnostic tools to identify and address specific deficits that impede grade-level learning. The district- or schoolwide team studies the data to create the necessary supports for individual students. Well-trained interventionists and other educators who specifically focus on remediating targeted foundational skills usually deliver Tier 3 interventions.

See *Best Practices at Tier 3: Intensive Interventions for Remediation, Elementary* (Rogers, Smith, Buffum, & Mattos, 2020) for more information about this intervention level.

Leadership Area: Achieve Focus and Stay Intentional

As a leader, no doubt your inbox and desk fill up with data charts and vast quantities of reports and documents that provide you with evidence of practice, some encouraging and others disheartening. Despite the results, whether positive or negative, you must stay focused and intentional. Effective use of data, or any other aspect of leadership, depends on your ability to focus on what the evidence reveals and be intentional about subsequent steps. In our experience, it is common to enter a principal or district leader's office to find an overwhelming amount of data. At times, it feels endless and overwhelming, which can create anxiety. In this situation, you face difficult questions: What will you find in the data, and how equipped are you to face the hardcore facts of perhaps disappointing results and current reality? How will you know what to do with what you find? What messages do you send when you avoid spending time in data conversations or neglect creating an intentional focus on evidence-based practices?

Addressing information through a lens of intentionality will aid your use of the evidence data provide. Prior to beginning analysis, clarify what information you want to collect so you are clear about your focus when confronting data. For example, suppose you receive a large document containing reading data for each student in your district. Scanning the pages, you see low numbers within many strands and topics. Not surprisingly, you struggle to find focus and an intentional use for these data. You take a minute to write down the first and second factors that seem important for you to know, such as one or two particular strands your district has grappled with and that perhaps have been a recent focus for professional development. Would it be beneficial to look at the data from those strands to determine whether or not the training helped teachers improve their practice? Is there one grade level that's been of particular concern and, as a consequence, you directed instructional coaches to work closely with teachers there to support curriculum implementation? Is there one school with an influx of students who performed poorly on reading and caused you to recently create a stronger coaching model so you want to ascertain the impact of this use of resources? Deliberately digging into the data with specific outcomes in mind will prevent the daunting and exhausting feeling that often presents itself when you are confronted with data overload.

Once you identify the purpose for perusing data and uncover the evidence they reveal, you can begin to create clear action plans. Yet, the mistake leaders often make is the inability to stay focused on the intended actions. Committing resources, modifying curriculum expectations, developing time and resources for collaborative teams to answer the four critical questions of a PLC, providing training and support to improve instructional practices, expecting interventions in every school, and progress monitoring for improvement are all intentional and focused steps as a response to data analysis. However, in addition to recording next steps and committing to the plans, you must endeavor to stay the course and avoid distractors that can derail your purpose or avert your direction (knowingly or unknowingly).

Spiller and Power (2019) remind leaders:

> Clarifying your intentions and priorities so others understand them, focusing on a few goals, minimizing distractions, establishing *systemness* (by aligning these elements through what you say and do), and working to maintain a positive mindset about the work support a cohesive culture in your school. (p. 22)

Leaders who intentionally focus on the purpose for reviewing specific data, data-driven conversations, expectations, and evidence-based decisions as part of the overall organizational culture enable a more laser-like focus on improving student learning. After reading the next leadership-focus area, we provide various suggestions to reflect on actions you can immediately implement to improve your intentional focus on data analysis as well as use evidence in a judicious way.

Leadership Area: Use Evidence for Decision Making and Action

The second leadership area for this chapter must undoubtedly address using evidence for decision making and action. Spiller and Power (2019) tell leaders that no matter how they attain a leadership role, their experiences will influence how they make decisions. This can certainly be helpful when tackling challenging problems and issues, but leaders must ensure evidence is the main driver of their decisions. Reeves (2016) supports this view, noting it is human nature to use background knowledge, lean on past experiences, and influence others from our comfort zone: "However clear the evidence, personal experience remains triumphant in too many discussions of education policy" (p. 6).

Leaders should avoid relying only on experience; rather, they must analyze data to reveal accurate stories that explicitly ascertain the needs of each student. Your awareness about the learning students have mastered and any potential gaps will contribute to a more successful partnership with teachers to improve achievement. Only through a data-driven culture can you provide direction and support in the much-needed next steps.

As collaborative teams discover the root causes of student deficits through the use of their data-analysis protocol, they will establish goals for continuous improvement. To do so, they create SMART goals, which is an acronym for goals that are strategic and specific, measurable, attainable, results oriented, and time bound (Conzemius & O'Neill, 2014). These goals provide leaders and educators with direction and focus. Progress monitoring SMART goals creates an opportunity to celebrate even the smallest of wins and identify effective interventions and instructional strategies or those needing adjustments. These sage words of hockey legend Wayne Gretzky (BrainyQuote, n.d.) aptly apply to the need to use data to inform all leadership practices: "A good hockey player plays where the puck is. A great hockey player plays where the puck is going to be." Use figure 5.8 to set a focused direction for purposeful use of data for district and school decision making.

The Final Word

Teams review and analyze data from a common assessment to find trends in students' performance. With this information, they capitalize on the findings and one another's expertise to devise ways to support struggling learners and extend the capacity of those who have achieved mastery.

In *Concise Answers to Frequently Asked Questions About Professional Learning Communities at Work*, PLC experts and architects Mike Mattos, Richard DuFour, Rebecca DuFour, Robert Eaker, and Thomas W. Many (2016) write:

> Until educators are using evidence of student learning generated from team-developed common formative assessments to inform and improve their individual and collective practice, they are not fully engaged in the PLC process. This collective analysis to better meet the individual needs of students

Leadership Areas: Achieve Focus, Stay Intentional, and Use Evidence for Decision Making and Action			
District Leader	**School Administrator**	**Instructional Coach**	**Lead Teacher**
☐ Support school leaders in creating the conditions for collaborative data-driven discussions so they stay focused on cultures that foster trust and respect. ☐ Ensure district policies and practices intentionally align to an expectation for data-driven use and accountability. ☐ Use time wisely to intentionally analyze data to glean evidence necessary for immediate decisions in support of student success. ☐ Create accountability expectations (including SMART goals) for progress monitoring all actions taken to support students based on data. ☐ Visit schools and intentionally observe and provide support and feedback on the use of data to inform next steps for student achievement.	☐ Ask guiding questions during data analysis that focus collaborative team discussions on the root cause of student deficits. ☐ Model evidence-based expectations by intentionally hosting data conversations with teachers and collaborative teams with the purpose of improving student achievement. ☐ Ensure leadership team (guiding coalition) meetings focus on data analysis, setting SMART goals, monitoring progress, and determining next steps based on evidence. ☐ Provide professional development resources (such as funding, release time, tools, and training) to all educators to build their capacity in analyzing data to collect evidence and plan next steps. ☐ Visit classrooms, intentionally observe, and provide feedback on the use of data to inform next steps for student achievement.	☐ Provide guidance and support to teachers and collaborative teams struggling with how to intentionally meet the needs of students based on their data. ☐ Intentionally guide data conversations to root-cause analysis as teachers build efficacy and ownership of data-driven practices. ☐ Ensure teachers input data correctly prior to meeting so that meeting discussions center on data analysis. ☐ Observe and support classroom instruction with an intentional focus on how teachers respond to evidence and meet the needs of their students.	☐ Ensure collaborative team meeting agendas stay focused on addressing the four critical questions of a PLC, particularly the third and fourth questions, during data analysis. ☐ Use data-analysis protocols (see Data Are Publicly Discussed, page 112) to focus collaborative team discussions on evidence-based decisions. ☐ Facilitate data conversations, and ensure teams conduct a root-cause analysis to determine next steps. ☐ Ensure the team creates SMART goals based on data analysis and progress monitors the effectiveness of their next steps.

Figure 5.8: Leadership area guidelines for student data—Achieve focus, stay intentional, and use evidence for decision making and action.

*Visit **go.SolutionTree.com/literacy** for a free reproducible version of this figure.*

and to improve instructional practice represents the very heart of the PLC process. (p. 109)

By operating from a position of recognizing students' learning needs, teachers are well positioned to design sound, quality instruction and develop progress-monitoring tools to ensure learning occurs. Through *gradual release of responsibility*, a research-based instructional framework explained in chapter 6 (page 127), teachers can deliver the effective learning all students deserve.

Design Lessons Using the Gradual Release of Responsibility Instructional Framework

Tell me, I forget. Show me, I remember. Involve me, I understand.

—CONFUCIUS

In the previous chapters, we discussed how to determine priority standards, develop a literacy-focused learning progression with accompanying assessments, establish learning expectations, and implement a process to gather and collaboratively assess data. We also focused on how teachers must use the data they collect to inform their classroom instruction each day to ensure all students learn. These are all undoubtedly critical aspects in teaching. So, too, is how teachers design and deliver instruction—specifically, the methodology (pedagogy) of that instruction.

Fundamentally, the purpose of a collaborative team responding to the four critical questions of a PLC necessitates solid classroom instruction that meets students' needs. When teachers leave a team meeting and return to their classrooms, the cycle of standards-based planning, including developing assessments to collect data, must directly impact instruction. For it's the evidence from data that pinpoints where instruction is working or lacking in its intended effect. In fact, direct your attention to figure 6.1 (page 128), which positions instruction as the focal point of the four critical questions. The answer to these queries impacts instruction—the *how* of teaching and responding—which connects the dots and provides alignment for *what* to teach and use to provide the necessary support and extension to each student based on needs.

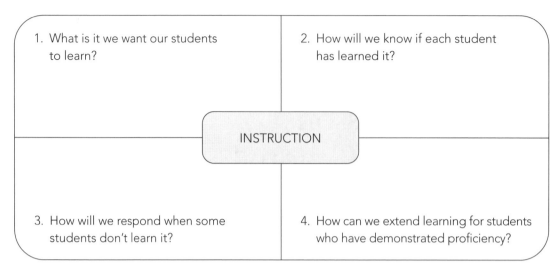

Source: Adapted from DuFour et al., 2016.

Figure 6.1: Connect the dots—Instruction and the four critical questions of a PLC.

As a leader, devote time and intentional focus to what happens after collaborative teams meet and each individual teacher begins to teach. How are teachers addressing the standards in the classroom? Is there evidence that the learning progressions steer lesson development? What can you do as a leader to ensure teachers create or find well-designed lessons and appropriately implement them in the classroom?

This chapter is the first of three (along with chapter 7, page 149, and chapter 8, page 177) that focus on how teams and individual teachers use their assessment data to plan instruction and address critical questions 3 and 4. How teachers approach instruction by using their standards-based planning and incorporating learning progressions requires careful thinking about organization, time management, and student involvement. In *Architects of Deeper Learning*, author, coach, and leadership expert Lissa Pijanowski (2018) reminds educators:

> Not every student learns at the same rate or at the same time. We know that. All students have different gifts and strengths. We know that, too. Our charge is to be intentional about our instructional design while letting go so our learners are empowered to take responsibility for their learning. Empowering our students to believe they can do anything is the greatest gift that we can give them. (pp. 95-96)

One effective way to do this is to design lessons using *gradual release of responsibility*—an ideal framework for appropriately providing differentiated instruction that enhances students' growth when acquiring any new skill, strategy, or procedure. In this chapter, we detail this instructional framework, show you how to teach it to your collaborative teams, demonstrate how teams can design lessons using it that foster deeper learning, and establish how you can observe teachers' use of the framework and provide feedback. We conclude by examining the leadership areas of establishing and maintaining organization and leading instruction.

The Gradual Release of Responsibility Framework

To create and execute effective lessons, we recommend teams use the gradual release of responsibility instructional framework (*gradual release* for shorthand), which enlists students in the learning process. Gradual release entails an orchestrated, graduated cognitive shift from teacher-directed modeling and guided practice of new learning to students ultimately employing the framework independently. San Diego State University educational leadership professors Douglas Fisher and Nancy Frey (2014), who took inspiration from coauthors P. David Pearson and Margaret C. Gallagher's (1983) model, identify the following four phases of gradual release.

1. Focused instruction ("I do it.")

2. Guided instruction ("We do it.")

3. Collaborative learning ("You do it together.")

4. Independent learning ("You do it alone.")

Consider the following scenario: you purchase a home that needs multiple renovations. You decide to take on these projects yourself and begin the first one—updating the windows. Although you lack construction experience, you feel confident you can figure this out by yourself. After ordering new windows and waiting for their arrival, your excitement mounts as the delivery truck finally backs into your driveway with them. You declare demolition day on the first old window and begin! Not long into your day, you realize the hole you managed to sledgehammer is not perfectly square to accommodate the dimensions of the new window, so it doesn't seem to exactly fit the now-empty space. Contemplating your strategy to enlarge the hole slightly, you realize that you lack the wherewithal and expertise to proceed in order to position the window correctly. In effect, you recognize you require some *direct instruction before independent practice*. The next day, you visit your local hardware store to seek advice. Coincidentally, you notice a posting for a window installation mini-course one night that week designed as an opportunity to practice installing a window with guided support. You eagerly sign up, knowing you need both the direct instruction and guided practice before returning to your own project.

Similar to the novice-carpenter vignette, sometimes in the classroom, teachers unintentionally assign students to work independently without first providing direct instruction and collaborative-work opportunities. This leaves students ill-equipped to fully grasp skills. As we discussed in chapter 4 (page 83), teachers determine success criteria for students through rubrics and aligned checklists. This ensures students know the teachers' expectations and requirements of a task and what proficiency looks like. However, to achieve the articulated outcomes effectively, teachers must conduct sound lessons, which the gradual release of responsibility framework can offer.

As with our DIY window project, once you know what the installation looks like, the steps for success, and, ideally, the advantage of collaborating with someone to install a window before doing one yourself, you feel adept and confident to do this work alone. This scenario mirrors all four steps of gradual release— (1) focused instruction (you watch and learn from an expert), (2) guided instruction (you practice at the hardware store with the class), (3) collaborative learning (you and another person agree to help each other install the first window), and (4) independent learning (you install it alone).

Gradual Release of Responsibility in Professional Development

As a leader, make instruction a priority in your organization. Creating a tight expectation for well-planned lessons using gradual release requires guidance and support that new and seasoned teachers will surely appreciate. Model it for organizing and delivering professional development and coaching to teachers. For example, use the process steps in a professional development session that focus on how to create quality constructed-response questions for common formative assessments. Explain to teachers you are purposely modeling how to use gradual release to bolster their understanding of the steps in the framework, as well as to teach them specific skills they can apply in their classrooms. Thoroughly modeling the process you expect them to incorporate into their teaching repertoire helps avoid the common leadership mistake we often see in schools and in districts: *assumptions*.

Never assume teachers understand what you are doing or why you are doing it. Rather, if your tight expectation demands they employ this framework, communicate your intention—in this case, using gradual release of responsibility—so they pay more attention to the structure and content of this worthwhile professional learning experience.

The following steps summarize how you might model each part of gradual release.

1. **Focused instruction:** To begin, the cognitive load rests on you as you model and use a think-aloud with teacher teams. You, as a teacher to your collaborative teams, accept all responsibility for this step in the instructional framework. While teaching, you feature the process for devising a constructed-response question to address a standards-based learning target, setting the purpose and benefit of using this type of format on an assessment. Concurrently, you explain your thinking while working through how to create the question. You may share a handout of the process for developing this assessment format so teachers can annotate on it or follow along as you model and use the think-aloud strategy. For this initial step of the framework, you solicit limited participation from the teachers.

2. **Guided instruction:** Next, you purposefully group teachers into pairs or triads to develop a constructed-response question for a different learning target than the one you featured so they can practice this skill. You circulate the room, offering guidance, and then ask groups to share their work with everyone. You offer feedback on the level of rigor and alignment to the standard and correct any misconceptions, as necessary. Additionally, you may choose to differentiate the learning, providing an extension for a group that is easily able to create their question or offering scaffolds for a group in need of more guidance.

3. **Collaborative learning:** You ask teachers to meet with their collaborative teams and begin working together to create an assessment using constructed-response questions. Each team works interdependently with relevant grade-level learning targets. You visit each team and listen to the discussions to verify and ascertain teachers' ability to create constructed-response questions, then determine your instructional next steps accordingly. Follow up with the whole group to debrief the lesson. Again, give feedback on the quality of their questions before moving the teams to the next step.

4. **Independent learning:** Instruct teachers to independently create constructed-response questions for students in their classroom to use as bell ringers during their next day of instruction. You may find the need to return to whole-group, focused instruction if all or most teachers show an inability to work independently at creating sound constructed-response questions. You should also ask teachers to bring these questions to their next collaborative team meeting to share with members as they begin to create their next common formative assessment. When you join these meetings, provide input to the teams on the efficacy and rigor of the questions and their alignment to the grade-level standards. At this time, you may need to offer more instruction to a teacher or collaborative team, depending on the quality of the work and level of understanding in how they would implement this skill.

Although the gradual release framework is flexible, as a leader, impress on teachers that when presenting new content, they must incorporate all four phases into the lesson. (When subsequently reviewing information, they can omit some steps.) This, however, doesn't necessarily mean they must teach each step in order. To this point, consider how you might reorder the steps for your teachers when modeling the previous professional development example. For instance, you ask them to come prepared to the session with sample constructed-response questions they create. You invite them to meet with their collaborative teams to share and discuss their questions to learn from one another. When circulating the room, notice the quality of the questions and the content of team discussions. Next, purposefully combine two collaborative teams to share their questions and insights with one another. Again, visit the groups and listen to their comments, provide feedback, and redirect any misconceptions. Finish the professional learning with focused instruction, providing clarity on the purpose of constructed-response questions as an assessment tool and how to align the rigor of the question to the standards-based learning target. You provide further guidance based on the teacher-generated questions you read and the group conversations you heard.

In this reverse application of the framework, you use steps 1–3 as a preassessment, which offers evidence of teachers' progress on their learning journey. Leaders find reordering the steps most helpful when they recognize teams already have some common understanding of the content they will teach or when teachers practice a skill but fail to demonstrate complete mastery without any direct instruction. Now that you're familiar with ways to teach gradual release, use the reflection questions for review before moving to the next section.

> ### REFLECTION
>
> What are your tight expectations for instructional practice? How do teachers currently build common understanding of these practices? How can you use the gradual release framework as an effective instructional practice in your school or district? What next steps will you conduct to accomplish this?

Deep Learning Through Gradual Release of Responsibility

Much focus in academic literature centers on ensuring *deep learning* for students. Veteran educators, authors, and consultants Jay McTighe and Harvey F. Silver (2020) describe what it means to learn something in this way:

> We propose that deep learning results in enduring understanding of important ideas and processes. However, we also contend that understanding must be 'earned' by the learner. In other words, understanding is not something that teachers can transmit simply by telling. Although we can directly teach facts and procedures, understanding of conceptually larger ideas and abstract processes must be constructed in the mind of the learner. Students earn understanding through the active mental manipulation of content via higher-order thinking skills. . . .
>
> When deep learning and understanding are the goals, the teacher's role expands from that of primarily a dispenser of information or modeler of a skill (the sage on the stage) to a facilitator of meaning making (a guide on the side). (pp. 1–2)

For students to examine, analyze, and critique lofty ideas and concepts and ultimately grasp their essence, teachers must first be clear minded about a unit's standards and goals; hence, the critical nature of completing the PREP process and learning progressions. Teachers then must devise gradual release lessons to position students for this kind of profound thinking, as well as foundational basics.

White paper coauthors Michael Fullan and Geoff Scott (2014) link deep learning to the six core competencies of 21st century skills or *six Cs*: (1) character,

(2) citizenship, (3) collaboration, (4) communication, (5) creativity, and (6) critical thinking. They state, "There are some slight variations on the theme when people refer to the deep learning or 21st century skills but the best ones involve a small number of academic and personal/interpersonal qualities and capabilities" (Fullan & Scott, 2014, p. 6). Instructional leadership requires a desire to develop these six core competencies in all students in your school and district, and purposeful attention to teaching practices that create engaging opportunities for students to develop these skills.

Teachers can design and lead gradual release lessons to teach the four phases we detail in the following sections to address targeted standards. In our example, teacher Mrs. James centers instruction on a first- or second-grade standard: *Describe the connection between two individuals, events, ideas, or pieces of information in a text* (CCSS RI.1.3) or *Describe the connection between a series of historical events* (CCSS RI.2.3; NGA & CCSSO, 2010). Throughout the lesson, she weaves in opportunities for infusing the 21st century skills. More specifically, students collaborate to learn from and contribute to each other's learning, communicate orally and in writing, and think critically about the connections they can make between pictures and historical events featured in texts and to current events. Situations from the texts highlight qualities of individuals worth examining, prompt students to think about issues and their effects on their communities, and consider the role of leaders.

Focused Instruction

Mrs. James, a K–2 teacher, establishes a goal for her students to explore the philosophy of nonviolence. Focusing on the first- or second-grade standards listed in the previous section, she accesses Stanford University's *The Martin Luther King, Jr. Research and Education Institute* website (https://kinginstitute.stanford.edu) and finds a lesson plan on how to teach nonviolent direct action. The basis for this lesson includes two texts: *A Sweet Smell of Roses* by Angela Johnson (2007) and *Freedom on the Menu: The Greensboro Sit-Ins* by Carole Boston Weatherford (2007), which Mrs. James will use within instruction to address the targeted standards. Each story depicts historical examples of nonviolent direct action during the African American freedom struggle during the 1960s, and Mrs. James will use the events within the complex texts to identify issues in the school and community. Mrs. James might also ask students to formulate a plan for addressing current injustice.

This extended lesson spans several days and incorporates most of the six Cs of Fullan & Scott's (2014) 21st century skills to some degree. Before students experience both texts, she shares the following *I can* statement to set the purpose for learning: *I can describe connections between two events.* She also poses the following guiding questions: "After studying the pictures and words in both stories, what can you tell us about a similar event that takes place?" and "Can you connect what is happening in the stories to anything going on today?"

She models and uses think-alouds to show how students can make connections among visuals from the beginning of the texts while inviting minimal participation to check for understanding. Throughout the lesson, she adds text-dependent questions, such as: What does *nonviolence* mean? and What words and pictures from the stories show nonviolence?

Guided Instruction

Mrs. James purposefully groups students in pairs based on what she noticed during focused instruction and her knowledge of her students. She asks the partners to identify more connections between the two texts besides the one she modeled so they arrive at new insights. She gives students the following instructions: "Find pictures and words in both stories that show a similar event is happening. Share with your partner what is the same and explain your thinking. Can you connect what is happening in the stories to anything going on today?"

She circulates the room while listening and observing to gauge levels of understanding, then coaches students based on what each pair needs to successfully find connections. Mrs. James might provide more scaffolding support to some pairs who might struggle while extending learning to others by asking probing questions to call their attention to more sophisticated details in the stories. She brings the class back together to clarify any misconceptions on the targeted skills and to invite students to ask questions or share highlights of their peer conversations with the class.

Collaborative Learning

Mrs. James reviews the learning target with students, so they continue to focus on making connections. Once she regroups students in triads, she asks them to return to the two texts and discuss with one another how a picture and a sentence (or phrase) in one story can be placed in the other text because the connection is clear. Students must be prepared to justify their thinking. Mrs. James augments the activity instructions by asking the following questions to probe their thinking: "What details in a picture make it fit well in the other story? Are there words you can use in both stories? Why do you think this?" She combines two groups to share their transferrable pictures and sentences along with their rationale.

Independent Learning

Mrs. James asks students to link what they noticed in the two texts—*A Sweet Smell of Roses* (Johnson, 2007) and *Freedom on the Menu* (Weatherford, 2007)—with present-day examples. To this end, she distributes photos of more recent marches and demonstrations. She poses this prompt that students can respond to in writing or by dictation: "How do any of the photographs or captions connect to the events in the two texts we read?"

District and school leaders can create a common understanding of the purpose of the gradual release of responsibility framework by associating its use to a need to deepen learning and engage students in the six 21st century competencies (six Cs). To do so, teams use their collective expertise to identify an appropriate complex text with associated guiding questions, tasks, and formative assessments that will engage students. Let's now turn our attention to classroom observations of the lesson framework and how to give constructive feedback to teachers.

Focused Instructional Observations

In *Rethinking Teacher Supervision and Evaluation*, former teacher, administrator, and principal Kim Marshall (2013) identifies seven deficiencies in common supervision-evaluation models (see the left-hand column of table 6.1). He asserts that these deficiencies might provide an explanation for leaders' difficulty in accurately assessing teacher performance and determining appropriate steps to assist teachers in improving their practice. Marshall (2013) conversely cites ideal situations for classroom observation that can mitigate any shortcomings (see the right-hand column of table 6.1).

Principals conduct formal evaluations as a matter of commonly required practice. In addition, we recommend principals lead observations in a purposeful manner by deliberately considering the strategy or lesson outcome that frames the classroom visit. As we consider classroom observations of instruction in this and the following two chapters, heed Marshall's (2013) list of factors that promote or prevent administrators from providing effective constructive feedback that generates instructional improvement.

Envision a time that you recently visited a classroom. With honest reflection, were any or all of the seven factors present during your observation? Did you spend a fraction of the time in the room, allowing you only a partial understanding of the lesson plan? Did the teacher appear to be performing for your benefit (the

Table 6.1: Supervision and Evaluation—Avoid and Adopt

Shortcomings of Current Supervision-Evaluation Models	Ideal Situations for Supervision-Evaluation
1. There isn't a shared definition of *good teaching*.	1. Principals and teachers have a shared understanding of what *good teaching* looks like.
2. The principal sees only a tiny fraction of teachers' work.	2. Principals get into classrooms and see typical teaching in action.
3. The principals' presence changes what's going on in the classroom—what the teacher does (the *dog-and-pony show*) and how students behave.	3. Principals capture and remember key points from their classroom visits.
4. The teacher's full-lesson write-ups rarely change anything.	4. Principals give teachers feedback on what's effective and what needs to improve.
5. The extremely time-consuming process keeps principals out of classrooms.	5. Teachers understand and accept the feedback.
6. Teachers are passive recipients of evaluations the principal conducts in isolation from the teacher's colleagues.	6. Teachers use the feedback to improve their classroom practice.
7. Student learning is not part of the process.	7. As a result, student achievement improves.

Source: Adapted from Marshall, 2013.

dog-and-pony show)? Or did you spend sufficient time to see authentic teaching in action? Did you use a generic checklist that lacked an opportunity for helpful feedback? Did you observe an ineffective lesson but not address it with the teacher? Or did you provide useful feedback specifically targeting key points about the lesson and what the teacher can do to improve his or her practice?

Instructional leadership demands knowing and positively impacting the teaching students receive on a daily basis. Principals, as well as instructional coaches and even trained peers, can aim to accomplish this by conducting classroom observations that incorporate feedback with the intentional focus of improving practice. Marshall (2013) recommends conducting short, frequent, and unannounced mini-conferences, which we endorse as well. We also advocate a more structured observation preplanned with teachers, which enables them to hone their ability to implement an instructional framework—in this case, gradual release of responsibility. For this observation type, leaders must spend dedicated time to conduct a lengthier classroom observation to more keenly witness all facets of the learning experience.

The following example applies Marshall's (2013) seven suggestions of ideal conditions for observing and providing feedback on instruction to the gradual release of responsibility framework.

1. **Principals and teachers have a shared understanding of what *good teaching* looks like:** Ms. Williams, a principal, provides professional development on the gradual release of responsibility framework. She clearly articulates her expectations that teachers will employ this approach during instruction and offers additional support beyond the professional development sessions to those in need of further training. She informs all teachers of her plans to conduct observations for the next two weeks, specifically focusing on this model. Ms. Williams asks teachers to submit a schedule of times that they will be using the model, and she plans her time accordingly.

2. **Principals get into classrooms and see typical teaching in action:** Based on the schedule, Ms. Williams visits classrooms for the entire lesson to observe the steps of the gradual release of responsibility framework. She is mindful that for more rigorous skills, a teacher likely does not conduct all four steps in one class period. Rather, Ms. Williams might observe a thorough treatment of one to three steps. By devoting a dedicated chunk of time, she honors a teacher's lesson preparation and can collect substantial information and provide quality feedback. She knows there is also a need to perform quick visits or observations to be visible and notice student behaviors and learning; however, to give valuable feedback to teachers on the implementation of gradual release, she must observe enough of a lesson to truly see the strategy in action.

3. **Principals capture and remember key points from their classroom visits:** Ms. Williams uses a graphic organizer for cataloging personalized observation notes from each teacher on his or her use of the gradual release (see figure 6.2, page 140). As stated previously, it may not be prudent for a teacher to teach a lesson that includes all four steps if he or she addresses a more sophisticated learning target that spans several days. As a leader, note this might occur so you avoid unnecessary and inaccurate observations. By the same token, make sure you relay to teachers that when you observe, you understand the lesson may not include all four steps. However, as part of the observation, if the administrator notices

a better use of gradual release, he or she will take notes to discuss any issues with the teacher during debriefing. For example, maybe a teacher spends too much time on one or two steps when moving on seems more engaging and warranted based on a missed opportunity for informal formative assessment.

4. **Principals give teachers feedback on what's effective and what needs to improve:** Principal Williams leaves a note for Ms. Ward, a third-grade teacher. In it, Ms. Williams thanks her for the lesson and shares an observational detail she thought was particularly strong, as well as suggests available times to debrief with her. The note serves to reduce any stress a teacher might experience since some find waiting for the debriefing meeting rather challenging and anxiety provoking. All teachers, though, welcome immediate feedback, although it may be cursory at this point. When the principal and teacher meet to debrief, it ideally occurs in a teacher's classroom during a period when students are not present. This disarms teachers and helps them feel more comfortable on their home turf. At this meeting, Principal Williams reviews the stages of gradual release of responsibility she observed and offers her recommendations for improvement.

5. **Teachers understand and accept the feedback:** Ms. Ward appreciates the feedback and states she experiences some struggle with implementing parts of the model. She wonders if the instructional coach can work with her to improve her expertise. Principal Williams briefs the coach on the teacher's request and sets a follow-up time with Ms. Ward to observe her again after she works with the instructional coach.

6. **Teachers use the feedback to improve their classroom practice:** Ms. Ward reviews the principal's observation notes with the instructional coach. They agree the coach will model for Ms. Ward's students the steps in the gradual release framework that she needs support in honing. Then, the coach will observe a lesson Ms. Ward conducts and debrief with her in preparation for the principal's return observational visit.

7. **As a result, student achievement improves:** Ms. Ward continues to focus on using the gradual release of responsibility framework with fidelity, accepting coaching and feedback for improvement. She knows as students become the cognitive owners of their learning, their engagement and learning will increase.

Gradual Release of Responsibility Phases and Descriptions	Observation Notes
Focused Instruction—"I Do It" ☐ Teacher sets the purpose for learning. *(Does the teacher clearly state and display the skill or learning target? Is the skill appropriately rigorous for the grade level? Is the purpose of the lesson evident and based on what students are doing?)* ☐ Teacher models or demonstrates and thinks aloud. *(Does the teacher model the skill and simultaneously use a think-aloud to explain his or her internal thoughts of how to implement the skill? Does he or she include any common mistakes or misconceptions students might make when applying this skill, as appropriate?)* ☐ Teacher invites students to minimally participate, such as turn and talk, thumbs up or down. *(Do students participate in some way so the teacher can informally formatively assess?)*	
Guided Instruction—"We Do It" ☐ Students practice the skill. *(Does the teacher purposefully pair or group students based on similar needs? Does the activity align to the learning target?)* ☐ Teacher circulates among the class, providing feedback. *(Is the teacher questioning, prompting, and discussing the skill with students?)* ☐ Teacher differentiates instruction. *(Is the teacher redirecting, remediating, or repeating information or extending instruction? In other words, is the teacher scaffolding instruction for those who struggle and extending instruction for those needing more challenge? How will the teacher assess learning?)*	

Collaborative Learning—"You Do It Together" ☐ Students engage and collaborate with partners or small groups on the learning target. *(Does the teacher purposefully pair or group students? Does the activity include the right cognitive demand? Is there time on task? Are students engaged? How will the teacher assess learning?)* ☐ Teacher engages in guided practice with pairs or groups needing this support. *(Does the teacher circulate around the room to formatively assess by listening in and observing each group? Does he or she then determine next instructional moves and actively offer necessary support?)* ☐ Teacher plans for individual accountability. *(Are students prepared for independent practice? What evidence does each student show to demonstrate understanding? What does this assessment entail?)*	
Independent Learning—"You Do It Alone" ☐ Teacher assigns an independent task that aligns to the learning target. *(Does the teacher write the task clearly? Is it purposeful and aligned to the rigor of the learning target? Are students aware of the requirements and success criteria by using a student checklist and rubric?)* ☐ Students work independently to apply the skill in a novel way. *(Does the task ask students to apply the skill in a different way than the teacher modeled? Is there time on task? If some students exhibit difficulty, does the teacher reteach phases of gradual release of responsibility or group students together to provide differentiated support?)* ☐ Teacher provides feedback. *(Does the teacher check in on students, as needed, to ensure they can move forward independently?)*	

Figure 6.2: Gradual release of responsibility observation form.

*Visit **go.SolutionTree.com/literacy** for a free reproducible version of this figure.*

As a leader, when you observe and provide feedback on the gradual release of responsibility (and any other instructional strategy), communicate your tight and loose expectations. Specifically, you must clearly relay the tight requirement that teachers employ this strategy. As well, ensure they understand loose aspects, such as when teachers flexibly implement the model while retaining the appropriate rigor. Emphasize each teacher can use the lesson framework to address the same or different learning targets in ways conducive to his or her learning style or creative energy, or to appeal to students' characteristics. For example, one team focuses on a standard related to a writer's purpose. All teachers work together to find writing excerpts to use in an activity. Some are excerpts of story passages, indicating the purpose is *to entertain*; others detail the directions for playing a game or loading a dishwasher to represent a writer's intent *to explain*; still other excerpts show examples for the following purposes: *to describe*, *to persuade*, and *to inform*.

In this example, one teacher on the team prepares cards with an excerpt on each. She distributes a set of cards to each small group of trios and asks them to participate in a tactile activity in which they sort the cards according to the author's purpose. Another teacher conducts a museum walk exercise. In this classroom, the teacher posts the excerpts on poster or chart paper and affixes them on different walls. She asks groups to examine each passage and write the author's purpose on a sticky note. As students work together, teachers circulate around the room to visit each group while they are sorting cards or as they examine excerpts posted on the walls to formatively assess and question, prompt, and discuss to assist students with a modified guided practice. When students finish, teachers focus instruction to establish learning targets, provide context, and show what the skill entails. Then teachers return to the activity to offer more saturated guided instruction and proceed with collaborative and independent learning. Teachers might certainly repeat steps as well. In fact, they should if students' performance necessitates a review of information or reteaching.

As you observe the lesson, pay attention to how a teacher uses gradual release to address students' needs. Recognize the teacher's application of the framework and appreciate his or her adaptation for the lesson, or take note of how he or she might improve it. As mentioned earlier, some lessons that address particularly challenging skills might require extended time for students to learn beyond one class period, so refrain from taking inaccurate observational notes. Shanahan (2018) realistically relays the iterative nature of this framework:

Those decisions are hard because they need to be made on the spot. And, when they are wrong—that is, when it turns out that the kids can't take the reins successfully—the teacher has to take back the responsibility, for the time being, that is.

That's why I think of gradual release as: I do it, we do it, I do it again, we try to do it again but this time a little differently, we do it, we do it, oops, I have to do some of it with more explanation, you do it (no, not quite like that), you do it, we do it again, okay now you can do it. (I know it isn't catchy, but it is more descriptive of how the process really tends to work.)

For concrete grade-level lesson examples of the four phases of the framework in action, you might point teachers to chapter 6 in each book of the signature series. Remember, each lesson teachers design and conduct must align with a learning progression, so be sure to show this connection. As a leader, you want to see evidence of teachers employing this or a similar instructional framework. For this purpose, revisit figure 6.2 (page 140) to articulate the expectations for each step and questions you can pose to students (in modified form) or yourself as you observe and debrief with teachers.

Leadership Areas: Establish and Maintain Organization and Lead Instruction

In the second chapter of *Leading With Intention*, Spiller and Power (2019) take readers on a virtual journey to two concert experiences—one well organized and seemingly safe and another chaotic and unsafe. In the former concert venue, people can easily enjoy their time, whereas in the latter they clamber to leave. The difference in the experiences rests squarely on the organizers' ability to institute sound procedures that contribute to a successful event, such as sensible traffic flow, various and culturally diverse food options, adequate and knowledgeable security and staff, and so on. Leading schools and districts requires careful attention to details as well. Procedures that bring a sense of purpose to daily practices provide the structure both staff and students need to be successful. This includes instructional planning. How can you establish and maintain school organizational structures that connect and impact classroom practices? How does an organizational plan provide support and coaching for teachers within a collaborative team to improve student learning?

Districts and schools not only need prudent instructional practices but also organizational systems that everyone uses. Leaders can apply organizational structure to expectations for instruction, such as the gradual release of responsibility framework—an effective district- or schoolwide example that leaders might choose as a mandated tight expectation—or other proven strategies. As stated earlier, model classroom implementation during professional learning to provide clarification. Creating collaborative cultures of learning requires leaders to institute the necessary practices and systems and demonstrate consistent application and expectations. For example, consider building an accountability tool for yourself, similar to the one in figure 6.3, to identify necessary steps, follow up, and provide feedback on instructional expectations to reaffirm the message. For each instructional tight expectation you deem necessary, you can create a consistent step-by-step plan for implementation using figure 6.3 as a guide.

Leaders create a culture for quality instruction with an organizational focus that develops and increases teachers' professional capacity and capabilities. Districts and schools that pay attention to this dynamic successfully build teachers' collective efficacy, which, in turn, enables them to meet students' needs. Coauthors Andy Hargreaves and Michael Fullan (2012) reference it this way:

Capabilities—skills and qualities that lead to accomplishment—build confidence. When you know you are truly capable of performing better, and when you have the knowledge and skill to reach your students and develop their own capabilities far beyond what anyone first expected, then this is invigorating. (p. 55)

When leaders support teachers in discerning effective from ineffective instruction and position teachers for success, teachers' confidence and capabilities soar. Supplement this with intentional observations and feedback, and the sky is the limit!

Use figure 6.4 (page 146) to review practices that can improve instructional leadership within your organization as it primarily relates to implementing the gradual release of responsibility framework.

Steps for Instructional Improvement	Action Required for Implementation	Additional Notes
1. Clarify tight expectations for instruction.		
2. Devise and implement a professional learning plan focused on tight expectations.		
3. Provide coaching and classroom support.		
4. Observe classrooms with an intentional focus on tight expectations for instruction.		
5. Provide specific feedback on the instructional tight expectations.		
6. Revisit classrooms to observe how teachers incorporate the feedback.		

Figure 6.3: Organizational structure for improving and implementing effective instructional strategies.

*Visit **go.SolutionTree.com/literacy** for a free reproducible version of this figure.*

Leadership Area: Establish and Maintain Organization and Lead Instruction			
District Leader	**School Administrator**	**Instructional Coach**	**Lead Teacher**
☐ Develop tight expectations within the district that teachers will implement the gradual release of responsibility instructional framework. ☐ Create an organizational structure that provides a professional development plan to build leadership and professional instructional capacity. ☐ Provide ongoing support and progress-monitoring tools to principals and others in leadership positions to observe and provide coaching and feedback to ensure deep implementation of the gradual release of responsibility framework.	☐ Establish organizational structures within the school culture (such as a leadership team and collaborative teams) that communicate tight expectations for instructional effectiveness. ☐ Ensure an organizational plan for professional development to model and build instructional capacity, including the implementation of the gradual release of responsibility framework. ☐ Identify expectations and support instructional coaches and lead teachers as critical members who guide and assist collaborative teams to plan and implement the gradual release of responsibility framework. ☐ Observe and provide intentional feedback on instructional implementation of the gradual release of responsibility framework.	☐ Lead professional development, modeling, and building understanding of the gradual release of responsibility framework. ☐ Coach collaborative teams as they plan instruction. ☐ Model the gradual release of responsibility lessons in classrooms. ☐ Observe teachers as they implement a lesson using the gradual release of responsibility framework, intentionally providing feedback and coaching strategies. ☐ Participate in organizational discussions with the goal of increasing overall instructional effectiveness in the district and school.	☐ Ensure teachers understand the benefits of the gradual release of responsibility framework in meeting students' needs. ☐ Invite team members to watch you teach a gradual release lesson to facilitate deeper understanding of this framework. ☐ Identify teachers, perhaps new or less-experienced teachers, who need more support in understanding the value of and implementing the gradual release of responsibility framework.

Figure 6.4: Leadership area guidelines for gradual release of responsibility—Establish and maintain organization and lead instruction.

*Visit **go.SolutionTree.com/literacy** for a free reproducible version of this figure.*

The Final Word

Douglas Fisher, Nancy Frey, and John Hattie (2016) write, "Every student deserves a great teacher, not by chance, but by design" (p. 2). Instructional leadership demands that any who serve in a leadership capacity, beginning with district leaders then transitioning to school leaders, pay acute attention to bolstering the teaching capacity of teachers. When acquiring a new skill, strategy, or procedure, teachers maximize the potential for students to learn by employing a direct-instruction framework such as gradual release of responsibility. This framework is predicated on four phases teachers use to plan lessons to promote successful mastery. As a leader, institute the expectation that teachers across content areas apply and perfect this or another direct-instruction framework and provide the necessary training and support to make this a reality. Ensure teachers plan and implement lessons with fidelity so fruitful learning takes hold in each classroom. In subsequent chapters, readers will increase their competencies to lead literacy instruction with a collection of effective ways to instruct and assess. You can use what you learn in these upcoming chapters to lead, coach, and support the design of solid, cohesive gradual release lessons that address learning targets.

CHAPTER 7

Plan for
High-Quality
Instruction in Literacy

Literacy is a bridge from misery to hope.

—KOFI ANNAN

Quality *and* quantity. It is not about one or the other. Leaders should protect and provide both. In chapter 6 (page 127), we asked you to support teachers as they develop a lesson using the gradual release of responsibility framework in their classrooms. Now, your leadership role centers on supporting teachers in their understanding and application of a structured, well-planned segment of the school day devoted to literacy. Typically schools refer to this segment as a *literacy block*, *English language arts*, or something similar. During this time, teachers conduct high-quality and comprehensive instruction that interweaves the domains of reading, writing, speaking, and listening. In developing essential skills relative to these strands, teachers guide students in making natural connections among them.

In this chapter, you will read about the specific components for teaching literacy and why and how you must create tight expectations for deep implementation of each component. You will consider ways teachers structure their time and configure student groups as you learn more about your role as a leader in this area. Doing so enables you to think about what teachers need to build expertise in the planning and delivery of highly impactful literacy instruction. This chapter addresses the following and other related questions: What are the structural and contextual components of teaching literacy effectively? How do teachers group students and structure lessons? How do you ensure sufficient time is built into the school's daily schedule for literacy? How do you protect time each day for literacy instruction?

To address these questions, this chapter explores the components of literacy instruction, plus ample time for and shared ownership of literacy-focused instruction. We conclude by examining two specific leadership areas related to these topics: (1) how you establish and maintain organization and (2) how to effectively lead instruction. In addressing these topics to ensure delivery of sound literacy instruction, your teams extend and deepen their response to the third and fourth critical questions of a PLC: *How will we respond when some students don't learn it?* and *How will we extend and enrich the learning for students who have demonstrated proficiency?*

The Components of Literacy Instruction

As a leader focused on improving literacy instruction school- and districtwide, you and other school administrators or leaders should visit elementary classrooms throughout the school or district to conduct observations. As a prerequisite for this work, it's optimal that you and your leadership or administrative team review the components of literacy instruction that you expect teachers to utilize when designing valuable literacy learning experiences. This ensures you all operate with the same expectations prior to visiting the classrooms.

Structural and contextual components geared to literacy instruction each serve a different purpose. Classrooms, schools, and districts each vary in how they utilize them; however, the commonality is strengthening skills within and beyond the classroom to produce skilled, independent readers and writers. Teachers implement structural components when building a well-balanced, equitable approach to literacy by using different grouping configurations to meet the needs of a diverse range of elementary-age students. Within groups, teachers afford students a rich learning experience by considering contextual components (or facets of literacy). Figure 7.1 features grouping configurations and suggestions for the contextual aspects of literacy instruction within this structure.

Figure 7.2 (page 152) lists some contextual components and recommendations for literacy instruction. We suggest you peruse the signature series books for more widespread discussion and treatment of each of these topics. The recommendations for reading instruction are featured in *Reading Next* (Biancarosa & Snow, 2004) and the ones for writing in *Writing Next* (Graham & Perrin, 2007). Although the research-based findings in these documents offer strategies for grades 4–12 students, they also have implications for primary grades. Furthermore, teams shouldn't use these suggestions in isolation but rather weave them together within

Whole-Group Reading

- Shared texts
- Modeled fluent reading
- Think alouds
- Choral, echo, and partner reading
- Student discourse and engagement
- Explicit instruction related to:
  - Reading standards
  - Comprehension strategies
  - Vocabulary and word work
  - Foundational skills

Whole-Group Writing

- Modeled write-alouds
- Mentor texts
- Student discourse and engagement
- Explicit instruction related to:
  - Writing standards
  - Writing skills and strategies
  - Spelling and conventions
  - Vocabulary and word work
  - Foundational skills

Small-Group Writing

- Guided modeling and student practice
- Differentiated supports and scaffolds
- Student discourse and engagement
- Explicit differentiated instruction and guided practice with:
  - Writing standards
  - Writing skills and strategies
  - Spelling and conventions
  - Vocabulary and word work
  - Foundational skills

Literacy-Skill Application

- Independent and cooperative practice
- Reading-skill application
- Writing-skill application
- Standards-aligned practice
- Hands-on learning
- Individual accountability
- Vocabulary and word work
- Foundational skills

Small-Group Reading

- Carefully selected texts
- Students grouped according to skill needs
- Differentiated supports and scaffolds
- Student discourse and engagement
- Explicit differentiated instruction and guided practice with:
  - Reading standards
  - Specific strategies
  - Comprehension skills
  - Vocabulary and word work
  - Foundational skills

Source: Onuscheck, Spiller, Gord, & Sheridan, 2020, p. 170.

Figure 7.1: Components of literacy instruction.

Reading Instruction Recommendations	Close Reading of Complex Texts	Writing Instruction Recommendations	Feedback	Mentor Texts	Spelling	Vocabulary
• Direct, explicit comprehension instruction • Embed effective instructional principles in content. • Motivation and self-directed learning • Text-based collaborative learning • Strategic tutoring • Diverse texts representing a wide range of topics at a variety of reading levels • Intensive writing to improve written skills and to deepen understanding of reading content • A technology component • Ongoing formative assessment of students	• Determine the text complexity level using the three-part measurement model (see chapter 3, Text Complexity, page 72). • Return to the text multiple times with a clear purpose for each reading encounter. • Chunk the text into manageable passages. • Develop and use text-dependent questions. • Ensure a unit connection.	• Writing strategies • Summarization • Collaborative writing • Specific product goals • Word processing • Sentence combining • Prewriting • Inquiry activities to develop ideas and content for a writing task • Process-writing approach • Study of models • Writing for content learning	• Goal referenced • Tangible and transparent • Actionable • User friendly • Timely • Ongoing • Consistent	• Align with learning targets • Are used during instruction as teaching tools in reading and writing • Serve as models of what students can produce • Can be complex text at the center of instruction	• Appears in most educational standards • Improves reading • Requires understanding of the relationship between letters, sounds, and word parts • Enhances writing • Connects spelling with vocabulary instruction	• Use direct instruction to teach key vocabulary. • Provide multiple exposures to new words. • Teach word parts. • Use examples and explanations rather than definitions. • Ask students to represent word knowledge in linguistic and nonlinguistic ways.

Source: Adapted from Biancarosa & Snow, 2004; Graham & Perrin, 2007; Wiggins, 2012.

Figure 7.2: Contextual components and recommendations for literacy instruction.

a rich curriculum to meet students' needs. The key elements for feedback shown in figure 7.2 are from Grant Wiggins (2012).

Successful use of the components in figure 7.2 requires teachers to emphasize two critical areas that support literacy growth: (1) foundational literacy skills and comprehension and (2) reading and writing development. Your knowledge of these areas ensures you can subsequently conduct productive observations and evaluations of the literacy teaching in your school or district.

Foundational Literacy Skills and Comprehension

Success in teaching literacy requires students to have proficiency on a series of foundational skills. In *Phonics from A to Z: A Practical Guide*, early reading specialist and children's book author Wiley Blevins (2017) writes on the importance of foundational skills to literacy:

> Two powerful predictors of early reading success are *alphabet recognition* (knowing the names of the letters and the sounds they represent) and *phonemic awareness* (understanding that a word is made up of sounds and the ability to manipulate sounds in spoken words). In essence, these two skills open the gate for early reading. Without a thorough knowledge of letters and an understanding that words are made up of sounds, children cannot learn to read. (p. 28)

Success with alphabet recognition and phonemic awareness ensures students have a foundation for immediate, effortless word retrieval. Some students can develop into readers even without specific training in phonemic awareness. However, for many students, without specific and methodical training in these areas, they will have difficulty learning to read. Proficiency in these areas requires that early elementary educators, in particular, place a high priority on students mastering specific foundational skills—print concepts, phonological awareness, phonics and word recognition, and fluency. Therefore, they engage students in explicit and systematic instruction in these skills, as well as in vocabulary acquisition, comprehension, writing, and building content knowledge. The following explains each of the foundational skills.

>   ▸ *Print concepts* encompass basic features of print, such as following words from left to right, top to bottom, and page to page; understanding that spaces separate words; identifying and naming upper- and lowercase letters of the alphabet; and recognizing sentence qualities like capitalization and end punctuation.

▸ *Phonological awareness* is an individual's cognizance of the sound properties of spoken words, like segmenting sentences into words and words into syllables and sounds.

▸ *Phonics and word recognition* instruction teaches students to engage with print by decoding words, thus focusing on the acquisition of letter-sound connections and their application to reading and spelling. By doing so, students make the connection between letters or letter combinations with sounds they represent, blending those sounds into spoken words to access meaning.

▸ *Fluency* refers to the ability to read text accurately, with *automaticity* (reading quickly without a focus on the process of reading), and *prosody* (appropriate expression, intonation, and phrasing).

As part of a comprehensive literacy program, foundational skills are taught in conjunction with comprehension, which is a reader's or listener's ability to understand and access meaning of oral or written text. Students first develop comprehension skills through listening—which makes the case for incorporating read alouds into classroom instruction—then transfer what they learn to reading. Among these skills is a specific connection between fluency and comprehension. When responding to a recipient's query about this link, Shanahan (2020a) states:

> We need to emphasize explicit daily teaching of comprehension and fluency (along with work on word knowledge—decoding and morphology, and writing). . . .
>
> The research on this is clear: (1) we should teach text reading fluency—in the classroom, in interventions, and in special education programs; (2) the teaching of fluency doesn't take the place of phonemic awareness, phonics, vocabulary, comprehension, or writing instruction—it is just one, along with those others, of the important things that needs to be taught; and (3) students' text reading fluency needs to be accurately estimated—considering accuracy, automaticity, and expression simultaneously.

To fully grasp an author's work is the quintessential goal of comprehension. When students have a solid footing in the foundational skills, they make strides in meaning-making and can tackle increasingly difficult texts. It might be noteworthy to consider a distinction of these skills as constrained and unconstrained (Paris, 2005; Paris, Carpenter, Paris, & Hamilton, 2005; Snow & Matthews, 2016). *Constrained skills* constitute those skills students readily master during their development, usually in a short or finite period of time, such as common spelling rules or capital letters. *Unconstrained* refers to those skills students continue to grow over time and with experience or from the duration of learning. These latter skills have potential unharnessed growth (as in vocabulary acquisition, building schema, or reading comprehension). As students master the foundational constrained skills of literacy, they can make headway in deepening unconstrained skills to more fully appreciate rich content.

Reading and Writing Development

In the comprehensive resource *Guiding Readers and Writers, Grades 3–6*, authors Irene Fountas and Gay Su Pinnell (2001) feature two continua—one for writing and another for reading. Each continuum lists various characteristics students exhibit throughout the elementary grades as they progress across five levels of reading and writing development: (1) emergent, (2) early, (3) transitional, (4) self-extending, and (5) advanced. The following summarizes just some of the aspects Fountas and Pinnell (2001) describe for writers.

▶ **Emergent writers:** Writers at this level display characteristics such as accurately writing alphabet letters, using letter names while constructing words, recognizing relationships between print and pictures, and communicating meaning through drawings. Written products at this level include labeling drawings, writing words phonetically, and even writing some relatively easy words correctly.

▶ **Early writers:** Examples of what writers exhibit at this level include using phonetics to spell words, being able to write from left to right across lines (as much as two or three short sentences about a topic or idea), and replicating writing concepts and techniques they see from authors. Written products at this level feature a few sentences based on a single idea with at least some accurately spelled words.

▶ **Transitional writers:** At this level, students can call on multiple strategies to spell words; develop ideas with growing confidence; and expand writing to different genres plus add dialogue, beginnings, and endings. Products transitional writers generate are longer and a bit more developed, plus reflect command of basic punctuation and capitalization.

▶ **Self-extending writers:** Here students exhibit traits such as spelling most words accurately with automaticity, editing their drafts to identify and implement improvements, providing peer feedback, using more advanced techniques to organize writing (compare and contrast, cause and effect, and so on), expanding their use of vocabulary, and accessing resources to advance their own writing including using mentor texts. Written products at this level show a more complex sentence structure with increasingly well-organized and well-developed ideas in both fiction and nonfiction.

▸ **Advanced writers:** Writers at this level demonstrate characteristics such as writing more rapidly and doing so with accuracy and fluency, using multiple resources (a dictionary, thesaurus, source texts, and so on) to plan and revise written products, and transferring a large speaking and listening vocabulary to written products. Students write a variety of long and short compositions for distinct purposes such as poetry, multiple fiction genres, and different modes of nonfiction. They inform their writing by noticing an author's craft and applying what they learn.

For reading, Fountas and Pinnell (2001) identify traits such as the following.

▸ **Emergent readers:** Readers at this level display characteristics such as gaining an awareness of print, hearing sounds in words and connecting words with names, reading simple words out loud left to right, and understanding some letter-sound relationships. Texts at this level convey simple stories with one or two lines of text at a time.

▸ **Early readers:** Students at this level, for example, begin to know the names of alphabet letters, use letter-sound information to solve words, start to read silently without pointing at text, recognize fairly simplistic and high-frequency words, and rely on details in pictures to augment what they read. Ideal texts at this level include long books that contain many high-frequency words and supportive illustrations.

▸ **Transitional readers:** These students demonstrate characteristics such as knowing a large core of words automatically; accessing multiple sources for information; lessening reliance on illustrations; and combining information like letter-sound relationships, text meaning, and language structures. They read texts organized into short chapters with many lines of print and increased genre diversity.

▸ **Self-extending readers:** As students blossom into more confident readers, they exhibit actions such as being fully comfortable reading silently and reading orally in a fluent fashion, which are characteristics for advanced readers, as well. Other examples include sustaining focus while reading long texts (including across days or weeks), increasing comfort analyzing and interpreting complex multi-syllable words, and advancing skills for building background knowledge, identifying and empathizing with characters, and forming connections between multiple texts. They read a variety of long and short texts across multiple genres.

▸ **Advanced readers:** When functioning at this level, student readers display characteristics such as using context clues (for example, breaking apart words, using analogies, and so forth) to define unknown words, acquiring new vocabulary and content-area knowledge through reading, forming attachments to favorite authors and topics that will extend to lifelong reading, and making connections between multiple texts for greater understanding and critical analysis. Students read more extensively and continue to grow in terms of breadth of genre and purpose.

It is unlikely students will demonstrate all characteristics for a particular category. For instance, a student might be *advanced* with using resources and *transitional* with possessing the stamina to work on writing over several days to produce a longer, more complex text. As a leader, we suggest accessing and sharing with teachers the full continua from Fountas and Pinnell (2001), which appear on pages 7 and 8 of that text, and using them for your own understanding of the progress students must make in these two critical areas of literacy.

A term circulating in education time and again is the *science of reading*, which the International Literacy Association (n.d.) defines as "a corpus of objective investigation and accumulation of reliable evidence about how humans learn to read and how reading should be taught." Rather than dedicate space to this pervasive topic, it is best that you peruse material (perhaps as a team, school, or district) and arrive at your own conclusions to determine how you might proceed given the information you learn. To this end, leaders might increase their understanding through *Reading Research Quarterly's* special issue: "The Science of Reading: Supports, Critiques, and Questions" (International Literacy Association, 2020b). In it, the coeditors compile over two dozen articles by more than seventy authors utilizing their collective experience to reframe the debate over the science of reading. They present myriad definitions and seek to illuminate or validate interpretations of the science of reading and present key findings.

Literacy Instruction Observations and Evaluations

With this grounding on the tenets of sound literacy instruction, consider how you might conduct a classroom observation to assess literacy instruction within your school or district. For this scenario, imagine you are a district-level administrator; you and your administrative team are tasked with conducting districtwide observations with a specific focus on literacy instruction. Prior to you and your colleagues' visit at the first school, the principal forewarns you that she has not yet had much time to observe classrooms. Therefore, she cannot guarantee teachers meet the district expectations for devoting a consistent and concentrated block of time each day to literacy instruction nor clearly grasp the components relative to this area. As your team of administrators observes classrooms in her school, the principal's assumption of a lackluster literacy program becomes apparent to you. In fact, you are inwardly chagrined for teachers and even students at the inconsistent, unplanned lessons that occupy precious time. Furthermore, in some classrooms, you see a daily schedule posted. One reflects a general line item indicating sixty minutes for literacy. In another classroom, you see a daily schedule that shows forty minutes for reading, but the specific goals remain unclear. You leave the school contemplating what actions you might recommend district and school leaders take to ensure deep understanding and implementation of consistent and well-planned literacy in all classrooms.

At the next school, in stark contrast to the first, the principal clearly prepared for your team's visit and presents his master schedule, which reflects a daily ninety-minute literacy block for all classrooms. He uses a template that includes the components of literacy (similar to figure 7.1, page 151) and adds a spot to identify the learning target of each classroom. He then circles and annotates what he observes and connects his notes to the learning target. As you walk the school halls, moving from classroom to classroom, an apparent pattern emerges—a definite focus on intentional, well-planned literacy instruction with a collaborative approach. The evidence confirms this truth—teachers configure student groupings similarly, use the same or similar complex texts during instruction, and engage students in comparable reading and writing activities. As you speak to students, they clearly understand expectations as they transition from one component to another.

When your team reconvenes to debrief with the host principal, he explains that at the end of each week, he sends his teachers a summary of his observations, avoiding naming specific teachers. In it, he indicates how many classrooms he visited and which components he observed. He also provides general, overarching comments and positive highlights of implementation at the school, plus constructive feedback for improvement. For example, he might write:

This week, I was able to visit twenty-two classrooms during literacy instruction. During these visits, I observed five strong examples of small-group instruction, where students used annotation for the learning target of identifying a main idea. I also noticed twelve effective instances when teachers used hand signals during whole-group reading to informally check that students could identify explicit details in a story. From my observations, next week I will look for more ways and opportunities that we are able to use formative assessments for reading instruction.

On Wednesday, our literacy coach will conduct a short presentation after school on various ways to informally assess using examples of complex text just to make sure we all take every advantage to check in on student learning. Anyone needing assistance or wanting to further his or her expertise on this component is welcome to attend.

Using his sample as a guide, he invites your team to compile observations and prepare a summary of collective observations for his teachers as well.

REFLECTION

Would an observation tool that specifically describes the look-fors be helpful? How could you incorporate something like this into your daily practice, using figure 7.1 as a starting point to design your own template?

As you drive away from the second school, you consider the differences in what you observed in both schools. At the second school, you reflect on the sense of clarity and accountability of literacy-instruction expectations. In his bestselling book, *Focus: Elevating the Essentials to Radically Improve Student Learning*, Schmoker (2018) states:

Educators yearn to be told something like this:

We are declaring a moratorium on new initiatives—at least for a time. Instead, we will focus *only* on what will have the most immediate and dramatic effect on learning in your classrooms. (p. 2)

In the case of literacy instruction, leaders must place a priority focus on well-planned and deliberate implementation of structural and contextual components in both schools and districts. Schmoker (2004) is also notable for his simple but critically important statement, "Clarity precedes competence" (p. 85).

As you observed in the first school, teachers and perhaps the administrator showed ambiguity in applying the required components as well as inconsistency in the amount of time dedicated to this instruction—both prime opportunities for leaders to pursue improvement. Were you to visit a school like the first one in this example, consider addressing a starting point for a customized professional development plan to address the issues. How would you build a common understanding of the literacy components? What literacy skills and knowledge might teachers need to learn? What would you require teachers to dispense with because it hinders or stagnates learning? As a school and district leader, what resources would you need to suggest to leaders, teachers, or other staff or acquire for them? What action steps would you suggest the leaders strategize and initiate?

To help determine your next steps, use figure 7.3. However, be cognizant that, during one classroom visit, you'll likely observe only certain components. For example, administrators in this section's scenario likely did not see both whole-group reading and small-group reading or writing during their tour; therefore, narrow the scope of comments in your use of this figure to those structural and contextual components that were present (or perhaps noticeably missing) in the time allotted for your observation.

The Value of Ample Literacy Time

We are not aware of many schools or districts overwhelmingly excited about the results of their students' reading scores (yet). This is typically a "work in progress" for all and requires leaders to continuously examine and ensure resources and support are in place for solid literacy instruction. This includes prioritizing time in a master schedule for this instruction and an emphasis on effective daily lesson design to offer students maximum opportunities to learn to read, read to learn, and write competently. Leading quality instruction requires an understanding of many factors, such as deep knowledge of the core content (contextual components), ways to group students for express purposes (structural components), and the precious commodity of time required to ensure learning for all students. As a leader, it is necessary that you have tight expectations for the use of instructional

Classroom Teacher: _____	Grade Level: _____
Room Number: _____ Date: _____ Time: _____	

Leadership: Literacy-Component Observation Questions	**Notes and Suggestions for Next Steps**
Based on classroom observations, what specific structural and contextual components of literacy did you observe that went particularly well? In what way? What evidence supports this assertion?	
Based on classroom observations, what components of literacy instruction were weak or absent that could have improved learning for students? Did you notice this was an isolated situation or consistent across classrooms?	
What first steps would you initiate to develop the missing components? Consider the causal (for example, a lack of resources, a need to change the master schedule, or a missed opportunity for professional development training).	
How will you monitor progress for changes in structural or contextual components?	

Figure 7.3: Leadership guiding questions for building tight expectations for literacy components.

*Visit **go.SolutionTree.com/literacy** for a free reproducible version of this figure.*

time and convey to teachers the critical importance of dedicating sufficient time to the teaching of literacy.

Coeditors Austin Buffum and Mike Mattos (2015) highlight the significance of time in students' education:

> In the United States, the average student spends thirteen years and approx-imately fifteen thousand hours of time at school from kindergarten through high school—a boatload of time. Yet, with the staggering amount of required curriculum that must be taught each year, teachers are faced with a daunting reality; so much to teach, so little time. (p. 1)

Buffum and Mattos (2015) use a mathematical statement to show the correlation of time to learning: *targeted instruction + time = learning*.

So, how much time should educators dedicate to literacy? Shanahan (2019b) recommends 120–180 minutes per day of reading and writing instruction, which aligns with the findings of Buffum and Mattos (2015). He concludes teachers must determine whether to grant less or more time within this spectrum based on students' needs (those who struggle require more time) and the strides teachers attempt to make. Shanahan (2019b) writes:

> Given the ambitious learning goals that we are striving for, I see no way of accomplishing them with fewer than 2 hours per day (or 360 hours per year). And, no matter how great the needs, I can think of no situation where I would devote more than 3 hours per day to these goals because of the importance of math, science, social studies, the arts, etc.

Not surprisingly, Shanahan (2019a) encourages integrating reading and writing across the content areas, which he finds results in a multiplier effect that furthers literacy learning. Also, he makes a valid point that in some classrooms, teachers compromise block time, so leaders might be alert to possible situations that can erode time intended for literacy instruction (Shanahan, 2019a). For example, a teacher might slate reading instruction to begin at the start of the school day when, in fact, school announcements, the community circle, or other morning routines monopolize the first fifteen minutes.

The amount of time solely devoted to literacy instruction may vary by grade level across your district. For example, some districts structure their kindergarten sched-ule to accommodate two-and-a-half hours of this instruction each day, while upper-elementary students receive sixty minutes of ELA with the expectation that teachers also infuse literacy into other subject areas throughout the day. Science and social studies teachers, for instance, design rich reading and writing learning experiences around grade-level nonfiction and informational complex text. The integration of literacy skills is supported by researchers Gina Biancarosa and Catherine E. Snow (2004), who recommend "extended time for literacy, which includes approximately two to four hours of literacy instruction and practice that takes place in language arts and content-area classes" (p. 20). They recognize reading and writing occur within language arts but are careful to note that teachers can fulfill literacy-instruction requirements in an interdisciplinary way by using texts from science, history, and other subject areas to both convey disciplinary content and to practice and improve literacy skills. Although the Biancarosa and Snow (2004) report is geared to students in grades 4–12, these findings have implications for teachers in self-contained elementary classrooms who teach various disciplines using pertinent text.

Literacy instruction may entail reading and writing within one successive time frame and treated in a more integrated fashion, or teachers may teach them separately at different times within the school day. However, teaching these critical areas of literacy concurrently is more prudent and efficacious. When providing high-quality literacy instruction, educators should teach reading and writing together with an interdisciplinary mindset. There is an interconnectedness between the two that supports literacy development in students, and it is present not just in ELA but in every academic content area.

In *Writing to Read*, writing instruction experts Steve Graham and Michael Hebert (2010) affirm the findings of multiple research-backed resources on the interrelated benefits of reading and writing. The report articulates the significant ways that writing has the propensity to boost students' reading (Graham & Hebert, 2010). Further, the report "Research Advisory: Teaching Writing to Improve Reading Skills" (International Literacy Association, 2020a) states:

> Reading contributes to learning how to write. Scientific evidence provides ample support for this vital contention. Elementary and secondary students become better writers by reading as well as by analyzing text. . . . Collectively, writing and the teaching of writing enhance not only students' comprehension and fluency when reading but also their recognition and decoding of words in text. (p. 2)

It is critically important for leaders to continue examining the way in which the master schedule reflects time for literacy instruction and how this time is allocated in the classrooms. As a leader, you must define and support deep understanding of the non-negotiable expectations surrounding literacy across the district and school.

A noteworthy example originates from author and educator Brian K. Butler, a former principal of Mason Crest Elementary School in Annandale, Virginia, from 2012 to 2017. He considered creating the school's master schedule a top priority (Buffum & Mattos, 2015). In *It's About Time*, Butler (2015) explains his approach to planning interventions and extensions at the elementary level:

> Before we began the work, we outlined some non-negotiable components. These non-negotiables have their foundation in district requirements for instructional time but were enhanced for our school and the needs of our students and staff. All grade levels *must* have the following.
>
> • Two hours of daily uninterrupted language arts instruction
>
> • Ninety minutes of daily mathematics instruction
>
> • One hour of common planning time at least four days a week (p. 53)

Read the suggested exercise in the reflection box to examine how time is allocated to literacy in your district or school. Prioritize this review in order to understand both the quantity of time and how it is being used to enhance literacy skills.

REFLECTION

Consider conducting a *time audit* of your literacy instruction across your school or district. Record the time that is allocated in a master schedule and that you observe in a classroom. Is the time indicated on the master schedule happening in actuality? Notice the quantity and quality. Have you scheduled enough literacy time? Are you seeing literacy instruction across the curriculum? Are reading and writing skills integrated in practice? What could be the next steps to improve the use of time for literacy instruction?

In reality, we know that some students need additional time to succeed. Therefore, leaders must secure a structure that grants educators the necessary time to accommodate each student's unique needs. As shared in chapter 5 (page 101), understanding data and determining next steps for students create an opportunity to understand the corrective instruction and extensions needed to answer the third and fourth critical questions of a PLC. Once the structure is in place, teachers can map out learning to maximize every instructional minute to aim for success. When teachers assess and analyze the results, they can pinpoint instruction accordingly. In chapter 5, review the three intervention tiers and consider how your school or district is giving permission to teachers to add necessary time to support and extend student learning.

As a district or school leader, work together with colleagues to create a workable structure that accommodates ample time for interventions (both corrective instruction and extension). Reeves (2020b) notes:

> Schools serving students who come to class with reading skills years below grade level must be willing to acknowledge that their traditional schedules, designed to provide one year's progress in reading, are insufficient. In some school systems, I have found the variation in reading time to be wildly erratic, with some schools giving three hours every day to literacy instruction and other schools claiming to address the same curriculum in 45 minutes every day. . . . The best curriculum and pedagogy will have minimal impact if teachers are not given the time necessary to address student needs. (p. 61)

For example, if some students in fifth grade read at a second-grade level, they require more time than a single literacy period a day to achieve grade-level reading goals. When teachers and teams are diligent about conducting in-class and common formative assessments, they can detect students who are struggling and expeditiously tend to their needs during time set aside for intervention. As a leader, it is imperative that you consider time—used wisely and with teachers who implement sound practice—as a pivotal and critical variable that contributes to student success for those most in need of interventions.

The imperative obligation that emerges from all of these research-backed conclusions is that leaders must create schedules that designate *specific and sacred time* for literacy instruction and make a concerted effort to do so in an integrated fashion if literacy instruction is currently not configured this way. *Specific* implies that this particular chunk of time is intentionally devoted to the teaching, refinement, and practice of literacy skills and standards. *Sacred* refers to the utmost priority assigned to this endeavor, and as such, remains safeguarded as a fundamental part of a student's day like mathematics and other disciplines. As a leader, it will be your responsibility to remove any distractors and interruptions to sacred literacy instruction and make certain teachers implement its specific components in all classrooms.

Shared Ownership

It warrants repeating that leadership in the PLC process requires a commitment to ensuring dedicated, weekly time for teams to collaborate (DuFour et al., 2016). This requires all collaborative team members to share ownership of students' learning, including and especially their literacy growth. As teams address each of the four critical questions of a PLC, they are deliberate about what they will teach and how they will deliver quality instruction. Shared ownership and responsibility of teachers contribute substantially to effective planning and delivery of sound instruction, and many opportunities for doing so exist. It is not about "my students, my results" but rather "our students" and how "we all collaborate to meet the needs of all students." As leaders develop a culture based on the PLC process, they expect teachers to share their expertise and collective commitment to ensuring all students learn at high levels. For example, when primary students are just learning to read, teams discuss and choose decodable texts they use to target specific phonics skills. Also, teachers work together to apply the three-part complexity model to judiciously choose complex text for each instructional unit. (See Text Complexity, page 72.) This applies to students of all ages since primary-level teachers feature read-aloud texts to foster a love of reading, build background knowledge, and for other purposes. In guidance on ELA instruction in the Common Core, the NGA & CCSSO (2010) state:

> Children in the upper elementary grades will generally be expected to read these texts independently and reflect on them in writing. However, children in the early grades (particularly K–2) should participate in rich, structured conversations with an adult in response to the written texts that are read aloud, orally comparing and contrasting as well as analyzing and synthesizing, in the manner called for by the *Standards*. . . .
>
> Having students listen to informational read-alouds in the early grades helps lay the necessary foundation for students' reading and understanding of increasingly complex texts on their own in subsequent grades. (p. 33)

This means within each text, teams identify particular passages that will lead to authentic teachable moments in developing reading, writing, vocabulary, and foundational skills. They also carefully select or design close-reading activities and writing prompts; discuss plans for explicit teaching, modeling, differentiating, and assessing; and ensure opportunities for student engagement. With consideration of structural and contextual components of literacy, teachers create plans together to ensure common understanding and quality instruction of each component. In other words, teammates guarantee laser-focused learning experiences in all classrooms and draw on one another as valuable resources to optimize learning for their students—a prime opportunity for shared ownership. Although teachers will undoubtedly apply unique teaching styles within their individual classrooms and adapt instruction to meet the diverse needs of their specific students (a loose aspect of PLC culture), working as a team allows teachers to profit from their collective expertise and plan high-quality literacy instruction.

To take the notion of shared ownership further, consider the work of coauthors Michael Fullan and Mark A. Edwards (2017), who explain that professional capital comprises these three types: (1) human, (2) social, and (3) decisional.

> *Human capital* refers to knowledge and skills of a job. For teachers, this means skills like knowing how to write lesson plans, building a strong learning environment, or implementing prudent instructional strategies.

> *Social capital* relies on collective efficacy and collaborative teams developing shared responsibility by establishing mutual commitments, or more specifically, planning together, designing common formative assessments, and interpreting a rubric to collect anchor papers. It also means being able to trust and rely on one another, even to tactfully confront a colleague if he or she is not servicing students well.

> *Decisional capital* suggests using professional judgment in various circumstances that require making choices. By virtue of years of practice, experienced teachers are more adept at decision making; however, newer teachers can derive decisional capital by observing and consulting veteran teachers, an instance of social capital at play.

Shared ownership is embedded in social capital; however, all three forms are intrinsically linked. Hargreaves and Fullan (2012) contend that, together, these forms of capital amplify one another across the whole teaching profession:

[Professional capital] is about what you know and can do individually [human capital], with whom you know it and do it collectively [social capital], and how long you have known it and done it and deliberately gotten better at doing it [decisional capital] over time. (p. 102)

Because social capital produces increasing volumes of human capital, in addition to fostering collective efficacy, as a leader, you can be a driving force in promoting social capital (along with the others). Pay attention to the stated intentions teams devise so they achieve interdependence when planning instruction. Teachers hold one another accountable to these commitments, and leaders can follow up with teams to ensure these statements are actionable and concretely materialize through their work together.

Additionally, design opportunities for structured peer observations to increase human and social capital by asking teachers to reflect on their own teaching as a form of self-assessment, as well as tap the expertise of their team members. This also supports one of Hattie's (2012) eight mind frames in *Visible Learning for Teachers*—that teachers and leaders treat assessment as feedback about the effect of their instruction. Hattie (2012) also states, "those teachers who are students of their own impact are the teachers who are the most influential in raising students' achievement" (p. 17).

To assist teachers with self-critiquing and capitalizing on collegial input and expertise, use or adapt figure 7.4, which includes guiding questions for the teacher who will be observed during literacy instruction and a companion set of questions for the team observer.

Guiding Questions	Teacher Self-Reflective Notes and Leader Observations
Skill *Teacher:* What skill is the focus for your lesson? How do students know what it is? *Peer:* What skill is the teacher's focus for this lesson? How did he or she make students aware of it?	
Grouping *Teacher:* How did you determine the student grouping? *Peer:* How suitable did the student grouping seem, based on the lesson goal?	
Text *Teacher:* Which complex or mentor text did you use during instruction? What was your rationale for choosing this text? How appropriate was this text selection? *Peer:* Which complex or mentor text did the teacher use during instruction? How appropriate was this text selection?	

Modeling *Teacher:* How did you conduct modeling? How effective was it? *Peer:* How did the teacher model the skill? How well was the think aloud strategy used with modeling?	
Guided practice *Teacher:* How did you lead guided practice? How effective was it? *Peer:* What guided practice did the teacher conduct? How did it support the learning target?	
Differentiation *Teacher:* How did you differentiate instruction? How might you incorporate other differentiation strategies next time? *Peer:* How did the teacher differentiate instruction? What other differentiation strategies might he or she have used?	
Engagement and interaction *Teacher:* What do you perceive was your students' level of engagement and interaction? What other strategies might you incorporate next time? *Peer:* How engaged and interactive were students? What other strategies might the teacher have incorporated?	
Evidence of learning *Teacher:* How did you assess learning? What evidence did you collect? *Peer:* How did the teacher assess learning? What evidence did he or she collect? How did it aptly measure proficiency for the learning target?	

Figure 7.4: Small-group reading or writing teacher self-reflection and peer-observation tool.

Visit **go.SolutionTree.com/literacy** *for a free reproducible version of this figure.*

In figure 7.4 (page 168), complex text for elementary refers to a read-aloud teachers introduce to perhaps focus on comprehension skills or vocabulary acquisition. Teachers who use this figure may choose to add a row for decodable texts, which students read to apply newly learned phonics skills. Furthermore, all cells may not apply during peer observation. Teachers would complete this or a similar template after they conduct a lesson; a team member or members respond through their lens as observers of the same instruction. Shortly afterward, the group convenes so the teacher can share his or her reflections and insights and listen and compare team members' observations. Together, the team determines ways the teacher can develop more expertise, including relying on colleagues to participate in the responsibility of improvement. This might include, for example, sharing resources, revisiting the classroom to conduct another peer observation, suggesting an online class or webinar, or engaging in a professional book club discussion.

REFLECTION

Consider how you can provide guidance to a collaborative team. What questions might you ask to deepen conversations to reveal the root causes of struggle among students or address students who need more challenge? How can you create additional time to target specific students' needs? How can you offer feedback on the current use of literacy time by conducting classroom observations with a specific, intentional focus?

As teachers become more evidence based in their practices (see chapter 5, page 101), they work together to create literacy instruction and assessment plans, including corrective instruction and extensions for students. They should consider how they utilize their time at both the collaborative team and individual classroom–teacher level. For example, from analyzing common formative assessment data, a team identifies significant learning gaps in reading. They feel they planned both whole-group and small-group reading instruction well; however, the data compel them to confront the reality of deficiencies in student performance. In particular, students in one classroom show greater inadequacies than students in other classrooms. In response, the team begins to discuss concrete ways to work with students who need additional support with specific skills during small-group reading instruction. How can they best use their time as a team to address these students' shortcomings? What can the individual classroom teacher whose students struggled most in literacy do differently? How can the team support this teacher and his or her students?

As a leader, consider how you can offer direction to this team. What probing questions might you ask members to deepen their conversations so they arrive at the root cause of students' needs? Use the reflection box in this section to consider how you might pose such questions.

Leadership Area: Establish and Maintain Organization

Spiller and Power (2019) state, "In our experience, when leaders create a culture with very clear expectations and students and staff understand and take ownership of their learning and actions, there are higher levels of engagement and motivation" (p. 37). They assert that this applies to the overall organization of a school and school day, and perhaps even more important, the organization of instruction for students (Spiller & Power, 2019). To mindfully lead by maintaining and establishing organization, this leadership lens centers on these guiding questions: How do you, as a school or district leader, begin to create systems and protocols to promote a well-organized, consistent culture versus a chaotic and inconsistent instructional experience? How can you establish and maintain school organizational structures that connect to effective classroom practices? How does the organizational plan provide support and coaching for collaborative teams to improve student learning? Throughout our signature series and in this book, we establish systems, protocols, and practices that positively impact overall instruction for students.

To implement this work well, you must design an instructional improvement system that includes clarifying expectations, devising a professional development plan, and providing coaching and ongoing support. In fact, you should use professional development in conjunction with coaching and dedicated ongoing support for it to prove useful. Hargreaves and Fullan (2012) note professional development that relies on individual learning does not have the impact of collaborative efforts, stating:

What is crucial is what happens between the workshops. Who tries things out? Who supports you? Who gives you feedback? Who picks you up when you make a mistake the first time? Who else can you learn from? How can you take responsibility for change together? . . . Learning is the work, and social capital is the fuel. If social capital is weak, everything else is destined for failure. (p. 92)

Those who ascribe to and implement the PLC process and culture know with certainty the preceding quote is a ringing endorsement for an organizational structure that incorporates collaborative teamwork and collective efficacy throughout many aspects of a system. By leading and supporting teachers through the work this chapter details, you establish instructional organization and clarity for teachers, as they consider the following guiding questions.

▶ What are components of sound literacy instruction, and why are they important?

▶ What are the clear, non-negotiable tight expectations?

When doing your job, avoid inadvertently falling into the trap of sending mixed messages. Spiller and Power (2019) indicate, "One of the most typical situations we see in relation to mixed messages is when teachers are inconsistent in applying expectations" (p. 47). Consider the scenario from this chapter of a district administrative team visiting two schools to observe literacy instruction. (See Literacy Instruction Observations and Evaluations, page 158). In the first school, you observed and traced the evidence of mediocre instructional practices back to less-than-optimal leadership—inconsistent expectations and mixed messages (or no messages) regarding literacy instruction, its structural components, and the critical connection between allocated time for literacy and student success. If leaders fail to communicate clearly and neglect to offer guidance and support, it is hardly surprising that teachers fail to implement consistent and quality-driven literacy learning.

Reflect on your job as a leader. What do you see as your role in planning and implementing literacy components? As an instructional coach, how do you act as the bridge across grade levels and content areas to provide consistency in the approach to literacy instruction? What are your expectations as a school administrator, and how do you communicate them? What time do you allocate for literacy instruction and for teams to engage in collaborative planning? As a district leader, what do you need to consider in planning and implementing a literacy segment in the school day across all grade levels in every school? What decisions should specific schools and grade-level teams make? After you read about the next leadership area, you can pause to consider what actions you can take organizationally and to lead instruction within literacy.

Leadership Area: Lead Instruction

Sometimes teachers feel overwhelmed with their collaborative planning and instruction. As Spiller and Power (2019) write:

> The complexity of instruction can be dizzying; differentiating lessons, grouping and regrouping students based on learning needs, providing additional time for learning, reteaching when necessary, and knowing exactly what a student needs to move to the next level of learning are non-negotiable expectations in schools today. (p. 117)

Teachers will experience more confidence and assurance if those serving in a leadership capacity take active roles to support them in leading instruction. In your current role, how might you provide support to teams when planning lessons, for example? How can you take an active role to lead effective literacy instruction?

As previously stated, of primary importance in literacy instruction are the specifics of *what* is taught and the *sacred* use of time. Consider which of the following questions, and others you envision, relate to ways you can assist teachers: How can you structure time in the school day for literacy instruction so teachers can deliver effective lessons? How can you help teachers determine which structural components are appropriate for a learning target? What contextual components can you suggest teachers implement during whole-group instruction for a specific learning task? Based on data, how might teachers plan a small-group lesson? What professional development can you conduct or suggest around literacy? What current research and resources can you share with teams in connection with lesson planning that will improve their practice? How can you collaborate with teams as they plan lessons?

To augment these questions and those posed in the preceding leadership area, review figure 7.5 (page 174) for specific suggestions on ways you can further the development of literacy instruction in your school or district pertinent to your personal leadership role.

The Final Word

Responsible leadership is multifaceted. For literacy, focus on leading quality instruction and establishing and maintaining an organizational structure. To accomplish these lofty goals, work with teachers directly, arrange professional

Leadership Areas: Establish and Maintain Organization and Lead Instruction			
District Leader	**School Administrator**	**Instructional Coach**	**Lead Teacher**
☐ Develop tight expectations within the district that teachers collaborate to plan using the specific literacy components and implement them with fidelity.	☐ Provide adequate time for both collaborative planning and literacy instruction at all grade levels, ensuring you protect that time.	☐ Ensure you understand *what* each literacy component entails and *how* each is used to lead and support collaborative teams as they plan literacy instruction.	☐ Model and facilitate a deeper understanding of each literacy component through team discussions.
☐ Support principals by providing expectations and guidelines on how to create a master schedule with ample time for literacy instruction and collaborative team meetings.	☐ Support and participate with collaborative teams as they plan and implement literacy instruction, assessments, and interventions (that is, corrective instruction and extension).	☐ Model and demonstrate classroom instruction specifically using the literacy components.	☐ Promote team commitment to shared ownership of student learning through collaboration and the use of data to determine next steps answering the four critical PLC questions.
☐ Create a professional development plan that supports teacher effectiveness in all literacy components, including ways to integrate reading and writing instruction across content areas.	☐ Identify expectations and support of team leaders and instructional coaches in leading literacy planning and instruction.	☐ Collect observational data in classrooms and team meetings you can use to design professional learning or coaching opportunities to refine the consistent implementation of literacy components.	☐ Identify teachers, perhaps new or less-experienced, who need more support in understanding and applying literacy components.
☐ Discuss ways to integrate reading and writing instruction to support research in this regard (see The Value of Ample Literacy Time, page 160).	☐ Monitor instructional planning and implementation through observations and feedback for teachers on specific literacy components.	☐ Support teachers in understanding how to use time for literacy instruction and in differentiated ways to support student learning as identified through evidence.	☐ Support collaborative teams as they plan their instruction, ensuring they consider time as a variable.
☐ Provide ongoing support and progress-monitoring tools to principals and other leaders for observing and providing coaching and feedback to increase instructional effectiveness.	☐ Provide professional development and feedback that guide and redirect (if necessary) literacy instruction.	☐ Support collaborative team discussions as members use evidence to ensure they allocate ample time for literacy instruction and interventions (corrective instruction and interventions) to meet students' needs.	☐ Communicate with other lead teachers, coaches, and administrators (as part of the school's guiding coalition) to share and promote ways to further support literacy instruction across content areas.

Figure 7.5: Leadership area guidelines for literacy components—Establish and maintain organization and lead instruction.

*Visit **go.SolutionTree.com/literacy** for a free reproducible version of this figure.*

development, or secure resources so they deeply understand each specific component of literacy. Furthermore, make sure teachers grasp how components interact and interrelate to create engaging, effective, and challenging learning opportunities for students. Lastly, dedicate adequate time, or even more than enough time, so teachers can effectively do their jobs and stay squarely centered on planning and delivering the effective instruction all students rightfully deserve.

Creating collaborative cultures of learning requires leaders determine and model the necessary systems and practices and demonstrate consistent application and expectations to optimize teachers' literacy expertise. The next chapter will bring you closer to effective collaborative team and classroom practices as we select appropriate instructional strategies to facilitate high-quality literacy instruction.

CHAPTER 8

Select Appropriate Instructional Strategies

No matter how brilliant your mind or strategy, if you are playing a solo game you will always lose out to a team.

—REID HOFFMAN

A new school year begins. As a novice principal, you eagerly look forward to seeing your teachers in action. You have met with each teacher to cultivate a relationship and understand his or her beliefs and values. With staff, you created collective commitments to delineate the behaviors that adults agree will create success for students, and your collaborative teams worked together to plan their first two units of study. The building sparkles with cleanliness, and as the buses roll in, you take a deep breath and hope for an amazing year for each of your students. Deep down, you understand the reality that success for students hinges on how well collaborative teams plan and deliver instruction. How will teachers capitalize on valuable instructional time? What formative practices will provide them with timely information about each student's learning journey? How will they use data to instruct, as well as scaffold or extend? Will they have a strong understanding of an instructional framework, literacy components, and strategies to engage students? What will be their coaching and professional development needs? How will you know the extent of each teacher's capabilities and shortcomings?

Although these questions swirl in your head, you feel prepared and know that you can capably support your staff for areas of growth opportunities. In addition to your training and experiences you've amassed, you recall what you've learned within these pages. In chapters 6 (page 127) and 7 (page 149), we focused on building your understanding of the benefit and structure of the gradual release of responsibility framework and the components of literacy lessons. While reading prior chapters, in your leadership capacity, you've learned about ways to enhance effective teaching by asking collaborative teams to identify and unpack essential standards and build learning progressions, which direct a pathway for instruction. You've also assisted teams to identify appropriate assessments along with clarity about learning expectations, evaluate student work, and analyze data.

Now, we hone in on specific instructional practices to positively impact your ability to ensure successful classroom experiences for students in your school and district. To this point, Marzano (2017) reminds leaders:

> Teachers function within the context of at least two systems: (1) the school and (2) the district. Those systems enhance individual teachers' effectiveness and contribute to the ineffectiveness of individual teachers, usually simultaneously. While schools and districts certainly have policies that help classroom teachers, they also have policies (some long-standing) that are glaring impediments to effective teaching. These impediments can and should be addressed. (p. 103)

Two examples of policies that thwart learning are an unawareness of expectations and inexperience with knowing and implementing effective instructional strategies.

As featured across our signature series, this chapter discusses the following teaching strategies that support students on their learning paths with regard to literacy-skill development. In addition, we examine the leadership area of using evidence for decision making and action.

- *Annotation* is a strategy students employ while interacting with reading material to deepen their understanding of content, but can also be used as a peer review tool for writing.

- *Vocabulary acquisition* provides access to reading and enhances writing skills and projects.

- *Graphic organizers* enable students to process what they read to enhance meaning, and students can use them as a writing tool to plan and organize their ideas.

- *Concept attainment* is a strategy designed for students to uncover attributes and definitions of concepts or skills so they can aptly apply them.

- *Cooperative and collaborative learning*, two grouping strategies, further the goals of many learning activities.

Each of these approaches is effective for literacy instruction within ELA. Furthermore, they are transferable, meaning that teachers can alter and employ these strategies to teach other skills in a variety of contexts across content areas. For instance, concept attainment is an effective strategy teachers can use to help students differentiate between and identify types of sentence structures, engagement strategies to hook readers, renewable and nonrenewable resources, or approaches to solving mathematics problems. Although annotation and graphic organizers in particular already appear widely in many teachers' toolbox, we'll discuss ways to use them optimally and perhaps expand the purposes for how teachers currently implement them.

Lay the Groundwork

To help you properly contextualize this chapter's content, it's important to clarify certain terminology. When delivering lessons, teachers pair instructional strategies with learning activities since the two go hand in hand. *Instructional strategies* (also called *teaching strategies* or *teaching methods*) are the techniques teachers use throughout instruction—whether it be a structure, procedure, or process—to make learning attainable for all students. *Learning activities* are the tasks students engage in to practice and demonstrate their learning, which results in some form of assessment.

As a leader, you might observe teachers using an instructional strategy also as a learning activity or assessment. For example, think about a graphic organizer. As an instructional or teaching strategy, the teacher models how to compare and contrast two characters using a Venn diagram or three-column chart. Afterward, he or she distributes a blank diagram for students to complete as an activity during collaborative learning. During independent learning, students complete a Venn diagram on their own which the teacher collects as a tool to formatively assess students' learning. Emphasize to teachers that each time students use the organizer, they should focus on a different reading passage than what the teacher modeled or when students worked together so they avoid regurgitating the same information. This way, the teacher can accurately assess how well students can apply the new skill.

As you consider the instructional strategies we offer in this chapter, reflect on ways you can aid teachers in understanding how to use them within tasks for students to practice skills and sometimes to demonstrate their learning, too. In each of the two previous chapters, we shared myriad tools to help you assist teams and increase their efficacy, and for you to conduct classroom observations to improve instruction.

For example, table 6.1 (page 137) details what Marshall (2013) determines as causes for the failure of conventional supervision and evaluation as well as the following seven factors that foster an ideal situation for classroom observation.

1. Principals and teachers have a shared understanding of what *good teaching* looks like.

2. Principals get into classrooms and see typical teaching in action.

3. Principals capture and remember key points from their classroom visits.

4. Principals give teachers feedback on what's effective and what needs to improve.

5. Teachers understand and accept the feedback.

6. Teachers use the feedback to improve their classroom practice.

7. As a result, student achievement improves.

You can apply these conditions as you learn about specific instructional strategies highlighted in this chapter that you can develop in your school or district. In particular, heed the first step, which contributes notably to effective instructional leadership. We include district leaders along with principals and teachers since they, too, play a prominent role in this step. As with each of the seven factors, leaders apply intentional actions to deepen collaborative teams' understanding and implementation of instructional strategies.

Deep Reading Through Annotation

Imagine as a superintendent, an end-of-year data report sits on your desk. You open it and turn to the summary for your district. A glaring statement confronts you: 75 percent of the students in your district read below grade level. The summary also reveals many students lack comprehension skills. When you were a teacher, you were not trained to teach reading. Rather, you spent your career teaching science and mathematics and now feel hard-pressed to know where to even begin assisting teachers to improve their students' comprehension skills. Upon honest reflection, you are aware that those who struggled to read in your class were at a disadvantage to learn the subject-matter content. However, you were never quite sure how to help them. You taught long before collaborative teams worked together to meet students' needs and certainly before school administrators expected every teacher to infuse the teaching of literacy skills within their content areas. Reading and writing were skills taught in isolation in an ELA classroom.

You know teachers in your district have significantly improved their practice and abilities to act collaboratively; however, the data clearly indicate they still either avoid teaching essential skills, students fail to learn them, or a combination of both. You invite literacy instructional coaches from across the district to meet with you to discuss this pressing issue.

As a team, you agree with the need to establish tight expectations on a few strategies to help students read and comprehend text (Gehr, 2019). Teachers expect students to read widely; therefore, their responsibility dictates they teach students how to grapple with complex fiction, nonfiction, and informational texts and address learning targets in service of these texts. For example, a standard indicates that students make inferences, so teachers choose an appropriate complex text to provide an opportunity for them to learn and apply this skill.

The instructional coaches suggest all teachers receive professional development on annotation, a beneficial strategy that will support reading for meaning. The coaches help you understand that teachers ask students to dive into a complex text, sometimes multiple times. Each encounter with the text serves a different purpose, and the teacher uses prompts and guiding questions to establish the goal of each reading experience across content areas. Goals can vary; for example, in ELA, teachers may require students to compare and contrast characters' points of view in a novel or establish the main idea of an informational text. During a social studies lesson, collaborative teams may use text to help students understand the significance of a historical moment, instructing students to look for clues as to the causes of the event. A science team may expose students to complex text that addresses the function of the Earth's atmosphere and ask them to identify how it protects people.

The coaches explain to you when teachers assign an annotation task, the question or prompt they pose aligns to a learning target. Students annotate the text by taking two interrelated actions: (1) mark pertinent words and phrases (such as by underlining, highlighting, or circling) in response to the purpose of the task, then (2) comment about the marked parts—which serve as textual evidence—such as by explaining, elaborating, analyzing, or drawing an inference. If students cannot write in a text, they can draw arrows on a sticky note to point to words or phrases they would mark and use another sticky note to explain the meaning. Students can also annotate electronically. The instructional coaches create examples of annotation tasks and accompanying student actions, like the options presented in figure 8.1 (page 182), to share with teachers.

Skill	What Students Underline, Circle, or Highlight	What Students Record	Annotation Task
Identify dialogue that develops events or shows responses of characters.	Meaningful parts of the dialogue	The purpose of dialogue exchange	Underline words and phrases in dialogue passages you think are important. Then, in the margin, respond to these questions: Why do you think what you underlined is important? What does it reveal to the reader?
Use context clues to determine the meaning of unknown words.	Unknown vocabulary words or terms and surrounding clues	Definition, example, or symbol	Circle words you do not know. Underline any nearby text that gives you clues to what the words mean. Then, in the margin, write a definition, example, or symbol to show what the word means.
Ask and answer questions to demonstrate understanding of a text, referring explicitly to the text as the basis for the answers.	Details or information that incite thinking, wonderment, confusion, or questions	A question about the text	Mark particular details that make you wonder about the text or confuse you in some way. Then write any questions you have about the text in the margin.
Describe characters by their traits, motivations, and feelings.	Words and phrases that give clues to a protagonist's character traits	A character trait	Underline any words and phrases that help you understand a character's trait. In the margin, write the trait that you feel describes this character.

Source: Adapted from Onuscheck, Spiller, & Glass, 2020; Onuscheck, Spiller, Gord, & Sheridan, 2020.

Figure 8.1: Annotation examples.

*Visit **go.SolutionTree.com/literacy** for a free reproducible version of this figure.*

In lieu of writing, sometimes teachers ask students to draw a symbol, picture, or emoji, which can be effective for primary students, as well as students in grades 4 and 5 when they first encounter a text. For primary-level students, teachers can prepare symbols, pictures, or emojis on cards for students to place next to text (that teachers might read aloud) or affix to popsicle sticks students hold up as they listen. Figure 8.2 shows a clarifying chart to help teachers consider symbols students could

Symbol	What It Can Mean
✳ **(or !)**	• This is something that I want to remember. • These words (or phrases) are very important. • This shows the main idea or premise of the text. • I feel a strong emotion connected to these words, phrases, or this sentence (such as anger, fear, happiness, surprise).
+	• I agree with this idea. • I like this idea. • This is new information or a new idea I just learned. • This is strong evidence or support for the main idea or theme.
—	• I disagree with this. • I know this is not true. • There is no evidence or support for this part.
?	• This part confuses me, and I need clarification or an explanation. • I don't know what to think about this yet. • I am unsure if this is valid, substantiated, or true.

Source: Adapted from Glass, 2015.

Figure 8.2: Options for symbol annotation.

*Visit **go.SolutionTree.com/literacy** for a free reproducible version of this figure.*

use when annotating. It serves as a resource for teachers rather than a handout they distribute to students. Teachers select certain line items geared specifically for a text at the center of instruction to create an annotation task.

Driving home, you reflect on the fact that the annotation strategy represents a lifelong skill. For example, you consider how often you read policies, articles, and even books you know contain salient information, but you sometimes have difficulty capturing the meaning of certain words or passages. For example, annotating often helps lawyers better comprehend court orders, acts, or new laws put into practice. As a mechanic or even as a car owner, being able to annotate the details from a maintenance-and-repair manual helps you understand the material better in order to make the car run more efficiently. Consider the benefits of annotating fine print in a rental agreement for an apartment or the contract for a car lease you must read and sign. People rely on printed text as well as digital material. For the latter, sometimes annotating using an electronic tool is an option, or people print a hard-copy version and make notations. This strategy can help students learn to decipher difficult print and digital media just as it might for many adults. Thankfully, you are pleased your instructional coach can capably build common understanding of the purpose and strategy of annotation with teachers.

As a leader, consider how you can model annotation during professional development sessions. What brief but pertinent article can you find for teachers to read and annotate that imparts information you want them to learn? Will you use the gradual release framework discussed in chapter 6 (page 127) to provide focused and guided instruction, plus collaborative and independent learning to target the skill of teaching annotation? Instructional coaching expert Jim Knight (2011) asserts:

> Leaders who walk the talk have a deep knowledge of the work done by people in the field. In schools, this means that principals understand good instruction and support and lead learning that makes an impact. . . .
>
> All forms of professional learning are integrated, so teachers can master and implement the practices. (p. 49)

Knight (2011) also asserts a primary task of principals is to ensure teachers engage in professional learning that impacts how they teach and, by extension, how students learn. Modeling annotation and expecting its implementation across all content areas is one way you, as a leader, can impact instruction. As you develop tight expectations for teachers to use annotation in classrooms—as well as other instructional strategies within this chapter that you deem imperative—consider using the template we featured in figure 6.3 (page 145) to assist you in helping teachers maximize their instructional potential.

Teachers aren't the only ones who must understand the importance of reading deeply for comprehension. If a parent inquires why teachers expect his or her child to use a highlighter, sticky notes, and symbols while reading a science text at home, what would you say? How would you explain that the student must read thoughtfully and reflectively to grasp meaning? In what ways have you communicated to students, parents, and even teachers the critical nature of this work?

Arriving at answers to these questions isn't just worthwhile for communicating with parents or other community stakeholders. ELA teachers understand how annotation supports comprehension; however, it may not resonate with mathematics, science, or social studies teachers how and why annotation builds comprehension skills. In *Falling in Love with Close Reading*, educational consultants Christopher Lehman and Kate Roberts (2014) state:

Structure can lead to habits, and habits can lead to independence. Our ritual for teaching students to read closely developed into three steps . . . :

1) First, read through *lenses*; Decide what you will be paying attention to while reading and collect those details.

2) Next, use lenses to find *patterns*: Look across all of the details you have collected and find patterns. . . .

3) Finally, use the patterns to *develop a new understanding of the text*. (p. 7)

Teachers provide clarity on the lenses by articulating the purpose of the reading so students approach a given annotation task with focus and intentionality. To this point, teachers should judiciously and deliberately assign such tasks. Leading deep understanding and usage of annotation across your school or district requires ensuring teachers do not overload students with too many prompts as they annotate. If teachers distribute an extensive list of options, like those in figure 8.1 (page 182) and figure 8.2 (page 183), it can overwhelm students and result in them missing the opportunity to actually use annotation to understand their reading, instead of focusing only on completing a litany of tasks. Therefore, encourage teachers to create explicit directions for the task based on a learning target and geared to the type of text and genre students read. Suggest teachers review the knowledge items and skills on their learning progressions and create different annotation activities and assessments since students return to the text several times for different purposes (as stated earlier). Also, provide differentiation suggestions that enable teachers to vary tasks as well as the complex text students annotate so both assignments and texts foster challenge.

Implementing a close-reading strategy such as annotation offers students one more valuable tool. This enables them to transfer practical meaning-making skills for accessing difficult text to comprehend material in other content areas and, in fact, all walks of life.

Success With Vocabulary

Undeniably, vocabulary acquisition presents innumerable benefits: "A child's vocabulary is part of his or her brain's toolkit for learning, memory and cognition. Words help children present, manipulate, and reframe information" (Jensen, 2013, p. 11). When asked where vocabulary instruction best fits within content areas, the answer is *everywhere*. Vocabulary is the gateway for accessing and comprehending a wide range of text types and genres as well as increasing oral and written discourse.

Marzano (2020) cites various research studies that catalog the expansive benefits of vocabulary development. He's not alone. With regard to vocabulary development's implication for reading, this finding will likely not come as a surprise: "There is much evidence—strong correlations, several causal studies, as well as rich theoretical orientations—that shows that vocabulary is tightly related to reading comprehension across the age span" (Beck, McKeown, & Kucan, 2013, p. 1). Leaders, therefore, must develop a learning culture that includes a focus on vocabulary throughout the school or district. To further this effort, couple the discussion in this section with the vocabulary-focused content in the signature series, specifically in chapters 7 (on high-quality literacy instruction) or 8 (on instructional strategies), or both. Then, together with other leaders, provide collaborative teams across content areas with existing knowledge about vocabulary research and aligned instructional approaches. Teams can then build a common understanding of how to teach and create opportunities to expand student vocabulary.

Undoubtedly, teaching vocabulary proves essential. However, what method yields optimal results for learning new words? Marzano (2020) asserts that direct instruction proves more impactful than extensive reading for students to acquire and apply new words:

> While wide reading is always a good idea, the logic of relying on wide reading in lieu of direct vocabulary instruction does not hold up under close scrutiny. . . . In effect, wide reading is not going to adequately address students' need to develop extensive vocabularies, especially at the lower grade levels. . . . Studies on direct vocabulary instruction have consistently shown positive effects. (p. 2)

Teaching through direct instruction has a higher likelihood that students learn new words than if they relied on contextual clues, which presents difficulty for some students. Vocabulary instruction experts Isabel L. Beck, Margaret G. McKeown, and Linda Kucan (2013) provide the rationale, stating when using context clues, students must already be proficient at decoding, recognize that there's actually an unknown word in the passage, and possess an inventory of tools for using context clues. For instance, an author might define, restate, or provide an example of the word in surrounding text. Additionally, a student's ability and grade level, plus the complexity of the text, dictate the chances of him or her learning a word in context.

Carving out time for direct instruction presents an issue for introducing the many words students must learn. So, what must teachers know? In the following sections, we examine several aspects of leading vocabulary instruction. This includes an introduction to a three-tiered system for vocabulary, suggestions for reinforcing tier two vocabulary in a concerted effort across the school, and a best practice process for teaching new words.

Understanding the Three Vocabulary Tiers

All leaders and teachers should be familiar with the three-tier system of categorizing words (Beck & McKeown, 1985; Beck et al., 2013).

▸ **Tier one:** This tier includes basic words people use frequently in conversation. Students acquire these words in everyday life; therefore, explicit instruction is usually unnecessary for native English speakers. Examples include sight words and other common words like *boy*, *chair*, *pretty*, *red*, and *hand*.

▸ **Tier two:** This tier includes words that mature language users commonly use. They are words, also called *academic vocabulary*, that often appear in texts but not as frequently in conversation. Examples include *investigate*, *determine*, *claim*, and *infer*. These words change meaning based on the context in which people use them. For example, a music teacher might *direct* the school chorus, whereas a teacher teaching a science unit might *direct* students to view a demonstration, and in a literacy unit, a teacher might have students study *direct* characterization.

▸ **Tier three:** Often called *domain-specific words*, this tier refers to words that appear most often in a specific discipline and are associated with a particular topic. Although they appear infrequently, these terms are critical to achieve understanding when learning about content tied to subject matter. Examples include *nucleus*, *genes*, *treaty*, and *electoral*.

With an inordinate number of vocabulary words teachers feel compelled to teach, which words should they concentrate on for direct instruction? Marzano (2020) states:

With tier one and some of the tier two terms, educators can rely on incidental learning because students will encounter these terms so frequently. . . . However, with tier three terms and the less-frequent tier two terms, the teacher cannot rely on incidental learning. Rather, the teacher must explicitly teach and reinforce these terms. (p. 38)

Marzano (2020) recommends a systematic approach for teaching some tier two words and only those tier three words that allow students access to content knowledge and concepts. However, he asserts that students growing up in poverty or nonnative language speakers will require more individualized support to learn tier one and some tier two words than other students. Marzano (2020) also delineates a comprehensive vocabulary program for elementary-age students a school or district can implement to lay the foundation for strong literacy development and academic achievement. This resource—replete with carefully and systemically researched tiers one, two, and three words—is designed for teachers to bolster K–5 students' word competencies so they enter secondary grades better prepared.

Beck and her colleagues (2013) also have guidelines teachers can use to carefully select vocabulary, such as the following four criteria (adapted from Glass, 2015).

1. **The word is useful and appears across texts:** Is the word tier two, and is it useful enough to warrant attention and teach students? Will students encounter the word in many texts in other domains, and is it indicative of words mature language users use?

2. **The word increases sophisticated word choices:** Are there words familiar to students similar to the target word? In this case, it is beneficial for students to learn the new word because it extends their inventory of vocabulary to include more expressive and specific words. This does not include adding synonyms to words already in their lexicon; rather, it provides students with new words that are more precise and complex versions of the familiar words they already use.

3. **The word aids in comprehension:** Does knowing the word enhance comprehension, and does it serve an important function in the context of the text? Does the word contribute to students' meaning making? If students don't know the word, will they not understand important concepts or find the text confusing?

4. **The word connects to other learning:** Does the word relate to other concepts students are studying? This might include other subject-matter texts or content areas. Does the word have the potential for students to build representations of it and connect to other words and concepts?

As a leader, guide teachers to reflect on these criteria; in doing so, teachers determine which chosen vocabulary words are worthwhile to teach and candidates for direct instruction.

Reinforcing Tier Two Vocabulary Across the School or District

Leaders might also initiate a district- or schoolwide initiative to concentrate on reinforcing selected academic tier two words that teachers might introduce. All content-area teachers should identify words within units of instruction so students experience them within the context of the subject matter and text they are using. To start, teams review their PREP templates and identify the tier two words within the unwrapped standards for each unit. These words might already be listed in the knowledge items, along with tier three words. Teams generate a chart for their units, like the one featured in figure 8.3 (page 190), for any tier two academic terms. Once complete, each team compares its chart with other collaborative teams vertically and horizontally across content areas. After cross-referencing, the school or district arrives at a list of tier two words that require direct instruction at particular grade levels. Teaching these words in various settings shows how they each change meaning, plus it serves to expose students to these words multiple times. Together, these contribute to students' meaning making.

Figure 8.4 (page 190) features mostly tier two general academic vocabulary from standards, learning outcomes, and various end-of-year assessments. Similar words appear in rows close together, for example, *analyze*, *evaluate*, and *explain*; *retell*, *summarize*, and *paraphrase*.

With this approach, rather than teams devising their own word list from units of study, the leader can present the list of words at a faculty meeting. Teams peruse the list to identify which words they teach within their content areas and the associated units and timeframes. The brief definitions in the figure may be limiting and do not necessarily represent all explanations of a given word, so teachers revise further, as needed. Once finished, they share the words they teach with staff. Being armed with the knowledge of when colleagues in other subject areas will or have introduced certain words (and in what context) allows teachers to intentionally make connections to the varied usages in other disciplines. This increases students' exposure to the words and more expansive ways to apply them.

Standard	Vocabulary Words	Explanation	Synonyms
RL.3.3 (A): Describe characters in a story.	Describe	Depict in your own words.	Portray, tell, report
RL.3.3 (B): Explain how characters' actions contribute to the sequence of events.	Explain	Write or tell details about something; make plain or clear.	Clarify, demonstrate, interpret, describe in detail
	Sequence	Arrange in the order of time.	In order, progressive
RL.3.9: Compare and contrast the themes, settings, and plots of stories written by the same author about similar characters (e.g., in books from a series).	• Compare • Contrast	• Find similarities and differences between two or more things. (Although many consider *compare* to only look at likenesses, the word is meant to examine both what is alike *and* different.) • Show differences between two or more things.	• Analyze, match, liken • Contradict, disagree, differentiate

Source for standards: NGA & CCSSO, 2010.

Figure 8.3: Tier two words—unit example.

Vocabulary Word	Common Definition	Synonyms
Analyze	Examine something carefully and in detail; break something down into parts or features.	Examine, study, scrutinize, explore
Evaluate	Determine or set the value or amount of; form a critical opinion of something.	Assess, decide, figure out, value, judge
Explain	Define, show, or tell how something works in detail; make plain or clear.	Clarify, demonstrate, interpret, describe
Clarify	Make clear, comprehensible, and understandable; clear up any confusion.	Interpret, analyze, simplify, clear up
Describe	Depict or report details in your own words.	Portray, tell, report, depict

Define	State or describe completely the nature, scope, or meaning of something; show the outline, limits, or form of.	Explain, interpret, describe, decide, determine
Demonstrate	Describe or explain by showing or giving examples.	Display, show, explain, instruct, express
Determine	Figure something out; draw a conclusion based on information.	Decide, ascertain, check, discover
Identify	Recognize the identity of someone or something.	Determine, recognize, label
Recognize	Identify something or someone known or familiar; acknowledge something exists.	Know, acknowledge, see, identify
Develop	Elaborate or expand on; grow or change over time to become more advanced or complete.	Explain, elaborate, grow, expand, progress
Support	Bear weight or load; agree with someone or their ideas; provide help and assistance; explain something is true or correct.	Hold up, reinforce; defend, endorse; aid, assist; justify, defend
Compare	Examine two or more things and find what is similar or different between them.	Analyze, equate, liken, connect
Contrast	Show differences between two or more things.	Contradict, disagree, differentiate
Distinguish	Recognize or understand how one thing is different from another.	Differentiate, separate, classify, categorize, discern
Recall	Remember something and tell others about it.	Recollect, remember, cite
Retell	Reiterate or tell something again in your own words or in a different way from the original form.	Restate, recall, reiterate, repeat
Summarize	Briefly state the main points and most significant details in your own words using the same text structure and order of the original text.	Review, condense, sum up, recap
Paraphrase	Restate author's words in your own words to make them easier to understand; express what someone has said or written in a different way.	Rephrase, interpret, reword, restate
Weigh	Evaluate by considering facts about a situation carefully before making a decision or giving an opinion.	Consider, contemplate, ponder, examine

Figure 8.4: Academic vocabulary as a schoolwide focus.

continued →

Infer	Use prior knowledge to make educated guesses about what is true.	Assume, speculate, deduce, gather, conclude
Draw	Collect information for a particular purpose.	Formulate, collect, gather, deduce
Draw Conclusion	Collect information to determine and explain an outcome or end result or the truth about something.	Deduce, surmise, determine
Interpret	Describe what you find to be the meaning and significance of something.	Define, decode, explain, clarify
Organize	Systematically put something in a particular order or structure; arrange something like an activity or event.	Arrange, classify, order, consolidate, systematize
Sequence	Place a set of related events, movements, or objects that follow one another in a particular order.	Arrange, order, place
Chronological	Arrange events in consecutive order of when they occur in time.	In order, sequential, progressive
Factor	A circumstance, fact, or influence that contributes to a result or outcome.	Element, part, component, facet, detail
Introduce	Bring something into use or enter into a situation for the first time.	Announce, originate, propose, establish
Locate	Find the place where someone or something is.	Find, trace, discover, uncover
Suggest	Make a proposal or declare a plan for something.	Advise, recommend, propose
Refer	Mention or direct for information; talk about or mention a subject or person.	Name, cite, consult, mention, recommend
Integrate	Merge, combine, or closely link together parts to form a whole idea or system.	Unify, unite, mix, merge, assimilate, blend, combine
Comprehend	Understand the meaning of something.	Grasp, catch on, perceive
Understand	Grasp the idea to know why or how something happens.	Figure out, comprehend
Generate	Cause something to begin or develop.	Produce, create, make, form
Confirm	Establish the truth or correctness of something stated or suggested.	Verify, approve, support, endorse
Hypothesize	Use various facts to consider whether something will happen.	Guess, conjecture, speculate

Synthesize	Combine ideas, facts, or experiences to form one idea or impression.	Integrate, manufacture, combine, incorporate
Observe	Notice or perceive something as being significant.	Detect, discover, watch, inspect, notice
Explore	Travel or traverse across a place for the purpose of discovery; think about or examine an idea or suggestion in detail to assess it carefully.	Investigate, examine, probe, seek, research
Cause-Effect	• Identify: The relationship between actions or events (causes) that produces a result (effect) • Cause: Actions or events that produce something • Effect: The result of an action or event that previously occurred	• Cause: Originator, reason, motivation • Effect: Consequence, outcome, result

Teaching New Words

Facilitating effective vocabulary instruction requires teachers to purposefully afford students multiple exposures to words so they each become part of students' working vocabularies. Assuredly, teachers incorporate many ideas and rules into their vocabulary program, such as generating word walls, introducing words of the day or week, modeling vocabulary through conversations with students, and supporting the use of digital platforms like Google Docs to share vocabulary among colleagues across content areas to further students' word exposure and knowledge. As a leader, participate and encourage a rich vocabulary culture, but create tight expectations using a research-based method for vocabulary instruction across all content areas. We suggest strategically structuring direct instruction for vocabulary using the following six-step process Marzano (2020) and his colleagues recommend for teaching each new word (Marzano, 2004, 2010; Marzano & Pickering, 2005; Marzano & Simms, 2013):

1. Provide a description, an explanation, or an example of the new term.

2. Ask students to restate the description, explanation, or example in their own words.

3. Ask students to construct a picture, symbol, or graphic representing the term or phrase.

4. Periodically engage students in activities that help them add to their knowledge of the terms to which they have previously been exposed.

5.   Periodically ask students to discuss the terms with one another.

6.   Periodically involve students in games that allow them to play with terms. (p. 38)

Teachers conduct the first three steps in succession on day one of instruction. The remaining steps occur throughout several days as teachers conduct various activities in an effort for students to learn and apply the words in speaking and writing. Of particular note, teams use step 4 to teach students affixes (prefixes, suffixes) and root words. Table 8.1 features prefixes and suffixes that appear most often, so teachers should focus their teaching energies on them. Notice the top three rows of table 8.1 represent the highest percentage of usage. Specifically, *un-*, *re-*, *in-*, *im-*, *ir-*, and *il-* indicate collectively that 51 percent of the time, these prefixes appear in words that include this affix. Although many authors compile lists of Greek and Latin roots, which are present in many tier three words, Marzano (2020) maintains there has been no rigorous study to identify which ones are most prevalent.

As teams collaborate around their understanding of the six steps (with your guidance) refer teachers to chapter 7 in the grades 4–5 signature series and chapter 8 of the preK–1 and grades 2–3 books for detailed guidance and examples of each step.

As a final point of emphasis, and to augment processes for direct instruction, Shanahan (2019a) asserts that teaching vocabulary effectively must include four principles.

1.   Rich meanings rather than just dictionary definitions

2.   Word connections

3.   Usage and review of words

4.   Student involvement in identifying some of the words they will study

We recommend two resources for using examples and explanations in lieu of sterile dictionary definitions: Vocabulary.com (https://vocabulary.com) and Collins Dictionary (https://collinsdictionary.com). Plan your observations and helpful feedback based on an intentional focus on vocabulary instruction.

Consider your next steps as a leader to increase a focus on vocabulary instruction. What professional development might teacher teams need? How can you support collaborative teams and teachers in ensuring vocabulary is a mainstay within your system? What district- or schoolwide initiative might you enact? How can

Table 8.1: Frequently Occurring Prefixes and Suffixes

Prefix	Percentage of All Prefixed Words	Suffix	Percentage of All Suffixed Words
un-	26	*-s, -es*	31
re-	14	*-ed*	20
in-, im-, ir-, il- (meaning "not")	11	*-ing*	14
dis-	7	*-ly*	7
en-, em-	4	*-er, -or* (indicating agency)	4
non-	4	*-ion, -tion, -ation, -ition*	4
in-, im- (meaning "in" or "into")	4	*-ible, -able*	2
over- (meaning "too much")	3	*-al, -ial*	1
mis-	3	*-y*	1
sub-	3	*-ness*	1
pre-	3	*-ity, -ty*	1
inter-	3	*-ment*	1
fore-	3	*-ic*	1
de-	2	*-ous, -eous, -ious*	1
trans-	2	*-en*	1
super-	1	*-er* (indicating comparison)	1
semi-	1	*-ive, -ative, -itive*	1
anti-	1	*-ful*	1
mid-	1	*-less*	1
under- (meaning "too little")	1	*-est*	1

Source: Marzano, 2020, p. 52; adapted from Marzano, Rogers, & Simms, 2015; White, Sowell, & Yanagihara, 1989.

you support teachers in implementing the six-step direct-instruction process for teaching new words?

By providing students with rich opportunities to understand the meaning of words and gain exposure and confidence in using more extensive vocabulary, you will help them create lifelong skills.

Graphic Organizers

Like annotation, graphic organizers commonly include teachers' repertoire of instructional strategies across grade levels and content areas. Throughout this book, we strategically insert figures with graphic organizers because they provide a content summary and a place for you to organize and solidify your thoughts and create a plan of action. When completed, they have likely served to enhance the meaning of the material in this book, which affords you a visual, holistic representation to clarify and review material. As a leader, you will assist teachers to increase the ways they can effectively use organizers in their classrooms, again, through professional learning, modeling, and creating an expectation of effective implementation during instruction. McTighe and Silver (2020) remind educators that graphic organizers demonstrate how to visually arrange information in ways that help students see the big picture, including the connections between different content blocks:

> Humans understand and retain important information by forming mental models that capture the gist of that information. That's why visualizing is so powerful in the classroom: it capitalizes on what the brain does uncannily well—and how the brain makes meaning. (p. 82)

Students can generate graphic organizers electronically or by hand, and they can include words, phrases, symbols, and pictures. Consider how you can support teachers to use graphic organizers to aid literacy skills by imparting the following and other purposes for using this strategy.

- ▶ Identify and activate prior knowledge.
- ▶ Demonstrate comprehension and facilitate recall.
- ▶ Organize information and ideas, recognize patterns, and show connections among ideas.
- ▶ Identify and explain the structure of a text—compare and contrast, problem and solution, cause and effect, sequence, or description.
- ▶ Plan for a writing task by brainstorming and collecting ideas.

▸ Prepare for a group or class discussion.

▸ Self-assess and peer-edit drafts to improve writing.

▸ Learn new words and terms.

Additionally, ensure teachers understand they can present *advance organizers* to students as a vehicle to introduce new content and show how it connects to what students previously learned. For example, teachers can explain and show the structure and elements of an opinion essay that students will write—opinion statement, reasons, supporting details (evidence)—and how this genre compares to other forms of writing.

Although people use various terms for graphic organizers, such as flow charts, timelines, webs, or Venn diagrams, there are four basic patterns.

1. *Hierarchical*, as the term denotes, shows higher-order thinking and its subordinating parts, such as the main idea with key details, concepts with subconcepts, or the genres and subgenres of writing.

2. *Conceptual* patterns center on a concept, category, or idea with supporting details, such as facts, examples, or characteristics. Web, cluster diagram, T-chart, and Venn diagram typify some options related to this pattern.

3. *Sequential* patterns show items in a linear or chronological order with identifiable beginning and end points; these patterns can help students identify causes and effects, problems and solutions, or a sequence of fictitious or historical events. A learning progression exemplifies a sequential pattern since it begins with rudimentary knowledge and skills and increases in complexity or is organized in some other way that reflects a specific order of teaching lessons in service of a priority standard.

4. *Cyclical* patterns reflect just what the name indicates—items in a series or cycle with no discernible start or end point. Figure 8.5 (page 198) shows a Plan, Do, Study, Act (PDSA) cycle Bailey and Jakicic (2012) align to each of the four critical questions of a PLC and in concert with the tenets of this book series. Although collaborative teams first engage in planning to identify what students should know and do, teams continuously cycle through all phases from pre-unit planning to post-summative, as needed.

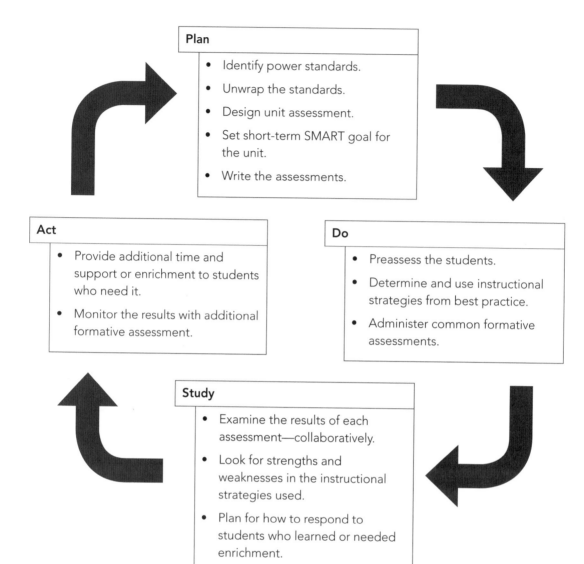

Plan
- Identify power standards.
- Unwrap the standards.
- Design unit assessment.
- Set short-term SMART goal for the unit.
- Write the assessments.

Act
- Provide additional time and support or enrichment to students who need it.
- Monitor the results with additional formative assessment.

Do
- Preassess the students.
- Determine and use instructional strategies from best practice.
- Administer common formative assessments.

Study
- Examine the results of each assessment—collaboratively.
- Look for strengths and weaknesses in the instructional strategies used.
- Plan for how to respond to students who learned or needed enrichment.

Source: Bailey & Jakicic, 2012, p. 117.

Figure 8.5: Short-term PDSA cycle for instruction.

As a leader, assist teachers in finding or devising graphic organizers and ways to use them effectively within instruction and assessment. (Refer to the signature series for lists of websites to access.) Suggest ways they can differentiate. For instance, teachers might provide students a choice in the type of organizer for a task (a Venn diagram versus a three-column chart, or a timeline with pictures and symbols versus one with words) to appeal to their individual learning styles. Allow students to select the delivery method for acquiring information they record on an organizer; for example, students can read text, watch a video or presentation, or listen to audio. Or add a kinesthetic option as Glass and Marzano (2018) write:

> [Students] can also create human graphic organizers to show relationships among characters or the sequence of events. For example, they can sit, crouch, or stand to represent a hierarchical struggle among characters or to reflect parent and offspring relationships. As well, movement can augment their physical positions as they might show interaction of causes and effects with a push and pull of their bodies. Any of these ideas can precede an electronic or hand-crafted graphic organizer that serves as a prewriting exercise. (p. 123)

To differentiate by readiness, teachers work more directly with those who struggle and scaffold instruction for them, as well as further challenge candidates requiring extension opportunities. For example, teachers can partially complete the organizer and give students a word bank of words, pictures, or phrases on cards for struggling learners to use as aids. For those ready, teachers ask students to generate their own graphic organizer to determine their ability to present information or ideas in an orderly manner based on the task.

Once you feel assured teachers understand and use graphic organizers effectively as an instructional strategy and task for students, determine what you will intentionally look for during classroom observations. Or focus on what teachers should avoid. What common errors or misconceptions do teachers mistakenly adopt as they use this instructional strategy or assign an activity? Do teachers overuse a particular graphic organizer as a teaching tool? Is this the only instructional tool you notice a particular teacher using to support visual learning? Are teachers assigning students the organizer without any focused instruction to identify the purpose of the task? Do students struggle beyond what would be considered productive?

In your leadership role, carefully consider balancing tight expectations with loose expectations. Be cognizant of avoiding overusing a single strategy inadvertently. For example, you provide professional learning on the use of graphic organizers and state you intend to observe how teachers implement this strategy in classrooms. Teachers misunderstand your request, thinking they should only utilize this one instructional strategy the week following the professional development session. It may not even be the most prudent strategy based on the learning goals the following week; however, teachers feel it is compulsory to utilize organizers. Furthermore, students become inundated with graphic organizers and soon become bored and frustrated by this sole instructional tool teachers assigned across all classes.

This scenario illustrates a cautionary tale, so make sure teachers realize your purpose and intention. Support tight expectations about selected effective strategies with an articulated understanding that teachers tap their own and collective professional expertise to know when and how to incorporate prudent strategies into lesson design. Therefore, communicate your expectations carefully. Consider engaging in the activity in the reflection box to support your staff in this area.

REFLECTION

How can you help teachers understand the purpose of the instructional strategies in this chapter (or other ones)? How can you ensure they select a strategy that effectively addresses the learning target? What can you do to guide their thinking of when and how to use a particular strategy?

Concept Attainment

As discussed in chapter 6 (page 127), the six competencies of 21st century learners include critical-thinking skills (Fullan & Scott, 2014). To help instill these skills, it is incumbent on teachers to provide the methods and resources for students to work independently and with peers through productive struggle. International speaker and education consultant Barbara Blackburn (2018) describes this teacher-orchestrated situation:

> Productive struggle is what I call the "sweet spot" in between scaffolding and support. Rather than immediately helping students at the first sign of trouble, we should allow them to work through struggles independently before we offer assistance. That may sound counterintuitive, since many of us assume that helping students learn means protecting them from negative feelings of frustration. But for students to become independent learners, they must learn to persist in the face of challenge.

Blackburn (2018) posits four criteria for productive struggle.

1. Productive struggle should challenge students' or student groups' specific weaknesses without overwhelming them.

2. Productive struggle should occur as part of challenging activities and assignments.

3. Productive struggle should be *productive* while still avoiding frustration. Think of how a novice chess player might learn more by playing an intermediate-level opponent as opposed to an international grandmaster.

4. Productive struggle should let students use metacognition to reflect on their approaches and thinking. Teachers can learn much more about teaching students a metacognitive strategy for challenging academic, social, and emotional problems in *The Metacognitive Student* (Cohen, Opatosky, Savage, Stevens, & Darrah, 2021).

As students engage in a learning experience, teachers usher them through the challenge by asking questions, redirecting, giving hints, or offering other supports that allow individuals and groups to proceed with the task and arrive at heightened awareness.

To help teachers set up situations for productive struggle, we recommend you model and coach them how to conduct a *concept-attainment exercise*, which fosters critical thinking and decision making as students work to grapple with and understand concepts. This strategy leads students through a process of analysis, including comparing and contrasting items to sort, then determining the attributes of a particular concept. Teachers can use concept attainment to help students build background knowledge as an introduction to a concept or skill, or perhaps teachers employ this strategy for collaborative learning while conducting a gradual release of responsibility lesson (see the next section). The following steps outline how students participate in this instructional strategy (Glass, 2018).

1. Examine and group a set of items according to their commonalities.

2. Identify the specific attributes of this grouped set, and name the set (if known).

3. Provide a definition.

4. Find and critique examples.

5. Create examples.

6. Apply the skill.

For step 1, teachers can provide students with pictures, words, sentences, paragraphs, or essays to group together in some fashion and articulate a rationale for their thinking. They sort items into either two or several defined groups. In the case of two groups, the first group aligns with the focus (examples) and the second does not (nonexamples)—for instance, sentences that are similes and others that are random sentences, or paragraphs rife with imagery and others that are bland. Defined groups might consist of various words organized by parts of speech or sentences organized into types (simple, compound, and complex). Once students sort these items, they critically examine them as they proceed with steps 2–6 and apply the new learning.

As a leader, consider how you can devise and conduct a concept-attainment activity for professional development during a staff or collaborative team meeting. For example, focus on understanding proficiency by asking teachers to sort a collection of rubrics into two groups—analytic and holistic (see chapter 4, page 83)—or by strong and weak examples. Or, have teachers critique a collection of lessons to differentiate between effective and ineffective examples of gradual release. As well, teachers can examine various assessments to discern formative from summative examples. All these examples serve as ways you can model step one of concept attainment, a critical-thinking strategy. Continue to develop the activity by leading teachers through all of the steps so they experience this strategy firsthand. For a more comprehensive explanation and specific examples of conducting a lesson that incorporates the concept attainment strategy, refer to the signature series books.

Cooperative and Collaborative Learning

Consider the continuous development of learning strategies that revolve around grouping. Throughout this book, *collaboration* appears repeatedly because leadership in a PLC culture necessitates building highly effective collaborative teams and sharing leadership responsibilities (DuFour et al., 2016). Teachers work collaboratively, take collective responsibility for student success, and share expertise through reflective, thoughtful examination of standards, assessments, data, student work, and instruction—all actions that require an interdependence among colleagues.

Within the gradual release of responsibility framework, collaborative learning signifies an important phase in which students work together to apply what they learn. Furthermore, teachers can use grouping strategies to intentionally develop the 21st century skill of collaboration, along with the other Cs: character, citizenship, communication, creativity, and critical thinking (Fullan & Scott, 2014).

The genesis of collaboration emanates from *cooperative learning*, which professors David W. Johnson, Roger T. Johnson, and Karl A. Smith (2006) identify as containing the following five key principles.

1. Positive interdependence

2. Face-to-face interaction

3. Individual and group accountability

4. Interpersonal and small-group skills

5. Group processing

Fisher and Frey (2014) explain how *collaborative learning* differs from *cooperative learning* in two discerning ways. First, teachers can assign a task with parameters but it can be more generally defined, such as one assigned in problem-based learning. Second, the teacher plays a different role in each construct. In cooperative learning, the teacher ensures groups are on task and the classroom is well organized and managed, which focuses more on a group's social processes. In collaborative learning, however, the teacher conducts guided instruction to each group periodically, as needed, and develops how members of the group learn together cognitively and metacognitively. When doing so, teachers can implement myriad instructional strategies, such as jigsaw, concept attainment, reciprocal teaching, literature circles, and book clubs (Fisher & Frey, 2014).

Leadership Area: Use Evidence for Decision Making and Action

As you create, communicate, and model tight instructional expectations for collaborative teams, also establish leadership habits that will yield evidence of executing quality instructional practices. How can you be confident students are the beneficiaries of research-based effective instructional strategies in classrooms? How can you provide professional development, conduct observations, and offer feedback to support deep implementation? What evidence will you collect to determine with certainty the instructional strategy teachers select actually impacts student learning?

To address such questions, for example, you can collect data (or evidence) by observing classroom practice, listening to student discussions, analyzing student work or collected data, or meeting with teachers and collaborative teams to discuss student results. Put simply, merely collecting evidence means little if teachers neglect to use evidence to facilitate change that increases student learning. Coauthors and consultants Anthony Muhammad and Luis F. Cruz (2019) urge, "A leader has to create a compelling, fact-based case for change, and then use his or her ability to convince people to make the organizational challenge their personal challenge" (p. 25). For positive, transformational change to occur, leaders must know what is and is not working. What will you do if evidence fails to show incremental improvement? Use figure 8.6 (page 204) to review leadership actions that support evidence-based decision making about instruction.

Leadership Area: Use Evidence for Decision Making and Action			
District Leader	**School Administrator**	**Instructional Coach**	**Lead Teacher**
☐ Develop district tight expectations so principals and teachers have a common understanding of the various types of effective instructional strategies and ways to implement them.	☐ Communicate tight expectations of both team leaders and instructional coaches to analyze data to collect and use evidence of instructional effectiveness.	☐ Ensure teachers use formative and summative assessment data to inform instructional planning and practice.	☐ Facilitate evidence-based discussions to ensure effective instructional planning occurs in response to students' needs.
☐ Model how to use evidence of effective instructional practice to increase understanding among school leaders throughout the district.	☐ Ensure collaborative teams understand how to use data to reflect whether or not (or to what degree) an instructional practice proved effective.	☐ Assist teams to identify the root causes of underperformance, and help them align the strategies they use with these root causes of students failing to meet learning targets.	☐ Participate in peer-to-peer classroom observation and feedback with the intent of improving instruction based on evidence of student performance.
☐ Lead the practice on using evidence to determine the instructional impact of teacher implementation of specific strategies.	☐ Lead change, as needed, based on evidence of ineffective instructional strategies.	☐ Lead or suggest professional development and resources to bolster teachers' use of effective instructional strategies.	☐ Share effective instructional strategies with team members, building common understanding of the various types and implementation of effective instructional strategies.
☐ Create accountability expectations (including SMART goals) for progress-monitoring implementation of effective instructional strategies throughout the district.	☐ Provide professional development resources (such as funding, release time, tools, and training) for all educators to build capacity in research-based instructional strategies.	☐ Conduct lesson demonstrations, arrange peer observations, and provide other support to increase teachers' expertise of effective instructional strategies.	☐ Lead data analysis to understand the evidence of effective and ineffective instructional practices and their impact on student learning.
	☐ Model the use of data at the leadership team and guiding coalition meetings to establish next steps, SMART goals, and progress-monitoring tools based on evidence of instructional effectiveness.	☐ Observe classrooms and provide feedback based on evidence of practice.	☐ Model a student-centered focus as the primary benefit of effective instructional strategies.
	☐ Observe and provide feedback to collaborative teams, classroom teachers, and interventionists on effective instructional strategies and how they impact student learning.		

Figure 8.6: Leadership area guidelines for instructional strategies—Use evidence for decision making and action.

*Visit **go.SolutionTree.com/literacy** for a free reproducible version of this figure.*

The Final Word

Instructional leadership requires a strong commitment to and understanding of effective instructional strategies since classroom practice cannot be left to chance. Rather, leaders must vigilantly and continuously devote rigorous attention to ensuring teachers plan instruction well, including selecting and implementing appropriate strategies to address specific learning targets. Furthermore, part of your instructional responsibility entails determining with certainty that teachers collect evidence of effectiveness and know when and how to create necessary changes to assist students in grasping intended learning. In fact, "one of your primary responsibilities is to develop and enforce an enduring, unending cycle of continuous improvement" (Kanold, 2011, p. 52). This is built on strong instructional leadership, which manifests opportunities for leaders and teachers to work collaboratively in service to students. Quality classroom experiences grounded in solid instruction open doors for students to learn. In the next chapter, we will continue this focus on *open doors for students* as we close our book with an imperative focus of equitable practices in leading districts and schools.

CHAPTER 9

Consider Equity in Literacy

While poverty persists, there is no true freedom.

—NELSON MANDELA

As teams thoughtfully plan instructional strategies to meet the needs of students, this final chapter represents a call to action requiring you, as a leader, to carefully consider your role in creating equity in your districts, schools, and classrooms. In this context, *equity* refers to how educators ensure all students have access to the learning and supports necessary to help them thrive in school, regardless of any situation that might put them at a disadvantage outside the classroom. About *equity*, Muhammad (2015) writes:

> In a society that prides itself on being fair and just, providing every child with a solid educational foundation should not be controversial. Superiority and equality cannot exist at the same time. Students, families, and schools who are at the bottom of the achievement gap have to reflect on their own perceptions and behaviors to try to improve their own station. Closing the achievement gap has to evolve from patronizing talk to real action and sacrifice by all parties. (p. 9)

Leading this work demands courageous conversations and critical decisions. Each student of a different gender, race, ethnic background, language ability, disability, or other quality contributes uniqueness to the collective classroom, school, and community.

The connection between literacy and equity may not appear evident to everyone; however, there's an undeniable causal relationship. Since our society strives to honor the fundamental tenet that all are created equal, it must ensure equitable access to the necessary skills for everyone to aim for success. And it is through literacy that teachers can orchestrate learning experiences for students to engage in diverse texts and thoughtful discussion that highlight and celebrate what each student brings to the classroom and world. As a leader, what conversations and decisions will be important for you in considering equity and honoring diversity in literacy? What will you examine and adjust to change current practices? How will you know if you are successfully creating equitable situations for all students to learn? This chapter addresses compelling and difficult questions teachers and administrators should confront concerning equitable school practices.

Stop and consider the many actions you take in a given day that require literacy skills. Perhaps you read an email from a friend, write a response to a colleague, reply to an invitation, research a recipe to make for dinner, sign a contract or consent form, or consult maps to navigate your way on uncharted roads. Since people rely on literacy skills pervasively on a daily basis, teachers must provide *all* students a literacy advantage that positions them to function fully and effectively in school and in society now and in the future. Use the following statistics to deepen educators' understanding of the importance of education in daily life.

▸ In the United States, over fifty percent of preK–12 students in public schools come from homes of poverty (Walker, 2015).

▸ Nearly 1.2 million Canadian children younger than the age of eighteen live in poverty (Statistics Canada, 2017).

▸ Students who do not have equitable access to the educational resources they need are unable to perform at their optimal level, which continues the cycle of poverty (Amadeo, 2021).

▸ Students who fail school are three times more likely to be unemployed, and they are more likely to live in poverty (Breslow, 2012).

▸ In many countries, there is a sizeable gap between male and female literacy rates (United Nations International Children's Emergency Fund, 2019). Yet, for every year of education completed, infant mortality decreases approximately 9 percent because girls and women learn more about health issues, reducing the long-term cycle of poverty (Martínez & Fernández, 2010).

▸ Raising literacy levels improves both employability and wages (Shomos, 2010).

▸ In 2018, in the United States, 25–34 year-olds with a bachelor's degree or higher degree earned 66 percent more than those with a high school degree (Institute of Education Sciences, 2020).

- High school dropouts are sixty-three percent more likely to be incarcerated (Breslow, 2012).

- Among the incarcerated, 70 percent struggle with literacy, and 45 percent lack functional literacy (Davidson, 2020). As a whole, their literacy levels are far below the rest of the population, particularly for people of color (Davidson, 2020).

The Annie E. Casey Foundation's (2010) report *Early Warning!* further traces high drop-out rates in high school to negative middle school outcomes and loss of motivation that relate directly to a lack of reading proficiency beginning as early as fourth grade. Hernandez (2011) confirms this finding:

> Those who do not read proficiently by the end of third grade are four times more likely to leave school without a diploma than proficient readers. . . . children with the lowest reading scores account for a third of students but more than three-fifths (63 percent) of all children who do not graduate from high school. (pp. 3, 6)

To this end, the connection between education, literacy, and societal issues—including poverty, violence, crime, and incarceration—is well documented (Brendtro, Brokenleg, & Van Bockern, 2019; Jensen, 2019). The good news is district and school leaders have an opportunity to positively impact and change this dismal trajectory for students. Consider the following questions as you begin to reflect on your current reality as a leader.

- How can district, school, and collaborative teams identify and eliminate invisible biases that might influence instructional approaches to students and affect trusting relationships?

- What can district, school, and collaborative teams do to avoid excluding any student from access to rigorous learning opportunities in curricula?

- What can district, school, and collaborative teams do to deepen their understanding of and response to students who live in poverty, ensuring high expectations for all students?

- How can district, school, or collaborative teams ensure the resources they select or are asked to use authentically reflect the demographics of students, diverse perspectives, and the experiences of others?

The following sections address each of these questions. We conclude this chapter with an examination of leadership areas related to developing community and relationships and prioritizing students.

Invisible Biases

Consider this scenario: a father approaches you to register his daughter in your school. He is unshaven, sporting facial tattoos, and dresses in ripped sweats with paint splatters on his T-shirt. He provides his electric bill as proof of address. You hide your surprise as you realize the family resides in the most affluent neighborhood of your school. You know your instinctive sentiments are wrong, but part of you wants to ask him for a second piece of identification to prove his address. You check yourself knowing that you are unintentionally allowing bias thinking to cause judgment. As you engage in conversation with him, you are taken completely off guard as he speaks with a sound grasp of the English language.

A week later, you spot an individual in an expensive luxury car in the drop-off lane and notice that it is indeed this parent. On this encounter, he is clean shaven and wears a suit and tie. He asks if he can make an appointment to come in and see you. During the meeting, he explains he would like to volunteer at the school and expresses an interest in being paired with boys who might need mentors. He tells you he experienced much difficulty in his youth and, in early adulthood, was embroiled in serious trouble several times. Because caring adults had given him second (and third) chances, he was able to return to school and complete his high school diploma and college degree; he now works as a coder for a tech company. Grateful for his good fortune, he would like to help others turn around their lives.

How easy would it have been for you to allow perceptions, bias, and judgment to impact your relationship with this parent and, as important, his daughter? How do appearances and what you believe is acceptable or unacceptable in society make you pause when offering—or denying—opportunities to others? Had you not seen this father the second time, would you have reluctantly accepted his request to meet? And lastly, how did completing his education and developing literacy skills positively impact this parent?

One of the most important considerations in ensuring an unbiased culture is the ability to identify and eliminate prejudices that impact classroom practice. Think about the same scenario, except replace the adult with an unkempt student appearing at the door of a classroom. Or consider instances when you have walked into a classroom only to find a student asleep at his or her desk. Your first impressions can create a barrier to learning for a student. How your teachers and you, as the leader, perceive a student's intentions greatly impact his or her access to learning. Before considering equity in instruction, curriculum, and resources, everyone in a leadership capacity and on collaborative teams should begin by examining privately or publicly any intended or unintended biases that might be present in how each individual adult approaches a student or students. Let's look first at how doing so can uncover or lead to areas in instructional practice that will require revision.

REFLECTION

Where do you notice inequity in your building, and how does it manifest itself? What biased thinking or action might lurk among your staff or students that you must address? How do you create an unbiased culture that fosters openness and fairness for all students?

Access to Instruction

Unfortunately, many students confront obstacles to equitable access to instruction by virtue of educators or leaders who create systems and policies that deny them opportunities to learn. This occurs perhaps unknowingly, as part of an invisible bias, such as in a teacher's particular questioning practices. For example, which student does the teacher expect will correctly answer questions? Whom does the teacher call on often, or whom might he or she ignore or overlook? How long does the teacher wait for one student to answer, or how quickly does he or she interrupt another student's thinking to provide the answer because the teacher confidently believes that student is unable to supply a correct response? Which students receive more feedback and opportunities for engagement in a classroom? In many cases, the issue is more wide-reaching, such as when a district or school adopts a biased curriculum from a publisher. Teachers must be altogether cognizant of these and other examples of ways they may harm students, preventing them from excelling emotionally and intellectually.

In thinking about the role of ensuring equal access to instruction in building equity throughout your district or school, it's important for leaders and teachers to reflect on how their *mental maps*—the way their lived experiences influence what they think and believe—often go unexamined (Parrett & Budge, 2012). In *Turning High-Poverty Schools into High-Performing Schools*, Boise State University professors William H. Parrett and Kathleen M. Budge (2012) state, "Although our mental maps (or mind-sets) may be invisible to us, they are important because they are the foundation for our behavior—how we plan, implement, and evaluate our actions" (p. 45). Parrett & Budge (2020) discuss the powerful dynamic between behavior and beliefs, which can help leaders think carefully about situations that can arise when colleagues hold tightly to disparaging and damaging mental maps that would surely impact students adversely. They state, "Educators who are successful in courageously encouraging the examination of mental maps don't do so by challenging peoples' beliefs; rather, they encourage changes in behaviors and norms first. *Changes in behavior most often come before changes in beliefs*" (Parrett & Budge, 2020, p. 81).

Consider the culture of student-centered collaboration you strive to develop in your district or school. How can you inculcate mindsets among your colleagues conducive to fostering a positive culture? What must you understand first, as a leader, as you guide and support others to consider equity part of your expectations and culture? If you suspect or observe that any colleague overtly and reprehensively exhibits biased tendencies, what immediate actions will you take? How can you go about changing negative behaviors and norms that subvert and potentially damage students?

American psychologist and professor Carol S. Dweck's best-selling book, *Mindset* (2016), explains the difference between fixed and growth mindsets. In its simplistic form, a *fixed mindset* believes people possess only a limited supply of intelligence and that they cannot possibly grow their abilities to learn. School and district leaders must be concerned about the mindsets of students, educators, and themselves. When students adopt this mindset—or equally dangerously, when *adults* maintain this mindset about students—everyone faces the difficult challenge of removing barriers to equitable education. Instead, all educators must embrace and encourage in their students a *growth mindset* in which people believe everyone can cultivate their skills through effort and determination. It is a way of thinking of what the word *yet* symbolizes: "I don't know how to do this . . . *yet*."

To help mitigate fixed mindsets in yourself and teacher teams, you can adopt three leadership habits that support moving toward a growth-mindset culture in your district or school.

1. Create instructional expectations that model inclusivity and honor diversity.

2. Observe classrooms and provide supportive feedback to build common understanding of expectations.

3. Engage in critical conversations with educators.

Let's look at other aspects that contribute to or sabotage equal access to instruction and how, as a leader, you can do right by your students. All leaders know their teachers acquire and employ unique instructional styles. Furthermore, core instruction demands teachers be well versed in a variety of strategies and adapt them to differentiate, as necessary, to meet the needs of individual students. Equitable access to instruction must consider that some students require more time to learn, some students will need alternative strategies from their peers, and some students will need both. In a PLC, *time* is the variable and *learning* is the constant (DuFour et al., 2016). Granting access to learning for each student cannot be dependent on his or her demographic profile (such as race, gender, or background) or any other lens that educators might attach to their decisions. Rather, leaders and teachers alike base decisions squarely and explicitly on the academic needs of students.

As discussed in chapter 5 (see Data Are Action Oriented, page 119), there are three tiers of intervention all schools must adopt to equitably meet the needs of students. Figure 9.1 (page 214) illustrates the inverted pyramid that reflects each tier. The inversion of the pyramid is critical because it places Tier 1 core, grade-level instruction at the top (Buffum et al., 2018). Tier 1 is the broadest level, which reflects the importance of *all* students having access to this instruction, with a narrowing focus on those students who require Tier 2 or Tier 3 interventions to reach proficiency with grade-level instruction. Of special note is that the entire pyramid, when inverted, points to the student, which indicates that each and every student must be granted equal access to instruction, support, and intensive remediation, if needed.

Buffum and his colleagues (2018) are careful to define *intervention* as "anything a school does above and beyond what all students receive to help certain students succeed academically" (p. 27). These are opportunities to remediate skill gaps for students as well as extend learning for those who have already acquired skills, encompassing both reteaching *and* extension.

The intervention process stresses *equity* because it begins with the assumption "that every student is capable of learning at high levels, regardless of his or her home environment, ethnicity, or native language" (Buffum et al., 2018, p. 19). Leaders must develop district- and schoolwide understanding and systems of intervention that begin with effective core instruction (Tier 1), then grant support teams deem necessary for each student who can benefit from instruction in Tier 2 (which also might mean extension opportunities), and then utilize Tier 3 to support students who lack foundational skills necessary for success at their grade level.

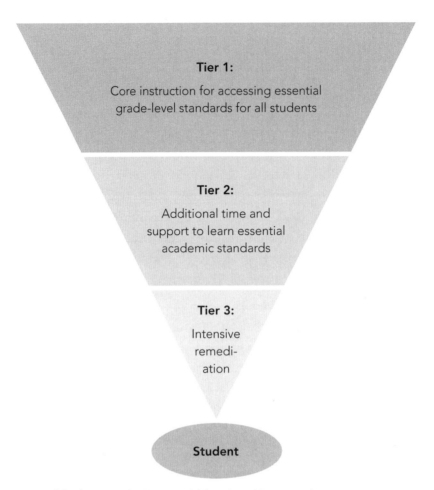

Figure 9.1: A simplified inverted RTI pyramid for tiered intervention.

Pose the questions in figure 9.2 to springboard a discussion with teachers about how they infuse and maintain equitable practices in their classrooms. In doing so, take the time to reflect on your current practices as well. What might be productive actions to take to change and improve your current reality?

While engaging in this conversation, teachers might discover a sense of vulnerability or the need to confront some uncomfortable issues. As you lead this discussion, active listening skills will be necessary to create opportunities for educators to build efficacy and a growth mindset about each student. Spiller and Power (2019) share three habits to foster this kind of attentive listening.

1. Asking clarifying questions

2. Reframing the conversation

3. Closing your mind to other thoughts

Leadership: Guiding Questions for Equity in Access to Instruction	Collaborative Team Notes and Next Steps
What examples of inclusivity within our school or your classroom most likely occur? How can we increase the opportunities for inclusivity?	
How might our instructional approaches foster or inhibit equitable practices in all our classrooms, particularly with regard to literacy?	
What existing or new practices would lead to more equitable outcomes?	
How does instruction reflect invisible biases or suppositions that could send overt and covert unintentional messages to students?	
How is our team ensuring students are included in or excluded from rigorous learning opportunities?	
How can we positively shift our collective mindset and language we use when referring to students who need differentiated instruction and opportunities?	

Figure 9.2: Leadership guiding questions for considering equitable access to instruction.

*Visit **go.SolutionTree.com/literacy** for a free reproducible version of this figure.*

Without active listening that captures these habits, "it is difficult to ask questions, reframe, and stay focused on what the speaker is attempting to communicate" (Spiller & Power, p. 140). Open and honest dialogue is healthy and likely results in identifying one area for teacher (or team) focus to promote the kind of change that benefits all students.

The ability to actively listen and ensure access to instruction is particularly important during challenging times. Teachers rely on leaders to provide consistent and effective leadership, especially when daily occurrences exhaust and overwhelm the system and present emotional strife. Leaders must be vigilant to keep students as the focus and maintain a sense of organization despite distractors, especially with a goal of increasing equitable access to learning. During the 2019–2020 and 2020–2021 school years, the global COVID-19 pandemic provided ample evidence of the need to continue to seek every opportunity to identify gaps in equitable access and to address them expeditiously. Leaders and teachers were called on to deliver instruction, conduct assessments, and provide interventions using a variety of platforms. For some students, there were few disruptions to learning, while other students lacked the technology, intrinsic motivation, and home support to continue learning. As a leader, what lessons learned can aid educators in providing more equitable access to instruction in any situation—natural disasters, pandemics, or other unforeseen and unplanned circumstances—that precludes teachers from delivering instruction and students from fully engaging as they were accustomed to doing? Use the following reflection as an exercise to think about your response to a dire situation as a leader.

REFLECTION

During any dire situation that changes the way school customarily operates, what instructional practices could you and your staff implement to provide unique and thoughtful ways to support meeting the needs of every student? How can leaders and teachers use these practices to diversify instruction and engage students once school resumes in the building? What silver linings pertaining to learning surfaced and might provide a continued opportunity to enhance learning? As a leader, how can you ensure that an equitable culture is an outcome of all instructional practices in your system? What do you need to stop doing? What will you start doing?

Promote High Expectations

Sadly, some educators quickly jump to unfounded conclusions about student capabilities and determine that maybe some students are unprepared or unable to participate in rigorous learning experiences. Or an educator may apply arbitrary reasoning to determine that certain students are incapable of learning all the standards others typically address at their grade level. Both are fallacies and reflect these teachers' limiting beliefs. With the exception of those who have significant cognitive impairment, all students are entitled and obligated to master all standards.

In the first-edition foreword to *Turning High-Poverty Schools into High-Performing Schools* (Parrett & Budge, 2012), educator and professor of educational leadership Michael Copland says the coauthors' work fortifies three foundational ideas that serve all children's learning needs successfully:

> (1) . . . all children *can* learn at high levels, regardless of their race, socio-economic background, language, family situation, or (pick your descriptor); (2) for children from a diverse spectrum to learn at high levels, they need to be taught by people in schools who believe they can learn, who approach teaching with the idea that students will learn if taught well, and who take seriously an ongoing effort to improve their practice in line with best thinking and examples in the field; and finally, (3) for teaching of this kind to be realized across a whole school (or system), leadership at the school and district needs to be squarely focused on supporting the improvement of teaching in an ongoing, routine way. (p. xi)

Parrett and Budge (2012, 2020) present a successful, research-backed framework that has proven to turn high-poverty schools into educational powerhouses, where students perform exceedingly well despite the obstacles they face. Their framework incorporates many of the tenets of the PLC culture, including collective efficacy, shared ownership, and expectations of high standards for all students.

Throughout the PLC process, educators develop collaborative practices around three big ideas (a focus on learning, collaboration, and a results orientation). As DuFour and his colleagues (2016) state:

> The first (and the biggest) of the big ideas is based on the premise that *the fundamental purpose of the school is to ensure that all students learn at high levels (grade level or higher)*. This focus on and commitment to the learning of each student is the very essence of a *learning* community. (p. 11)

In other words, the imperative shifts from teaching to knowing precisely the learning that takes hold. When leaders create a PLC with equitable practices for all students, it means despite gender, demographics, economics, race, culture, or religion, each student is entitled to fair and equal access to instruction that meets his or her individual needs. This might appear a lofty goal for educators; however, many embrace and implement this pursuit successfully in schools throughout the world.

As early as the 1990s, research provided exemplars of high expectations for leaders to follow when working in districts and schools with prevalent high poverty. Reeves (2000) and his colleagues at the Center for Performance Assessment describe a study they conducted with 130,000 students in 228 schools over four years. They aptly named the study *90/90/90* to characterize the schools and findings—90 percent of students from low-income situations who represented 90 percent ethnic minorities met or exceeded state academic standards by 90 percent despite the challenges of poverty and minority status! Research continues to affirm Reeves' (2000) study (Chenoweth, 2017; Reeves, 2020a, 2020b, 2020c; Zavadsky, 2012). Monitoring instructional practices provides evidence that consistently repeating effective teaching strategies proves successful in boosting student achievement despite any obstacles attributed to poverty or ethnicity. According to Reeves (2000), the high-achieving schools shared the following five common characteristics.

1. A focus on academic achievement

2. Clear curriculum choices

3. Frequent assessment of student progress and multiple opportunities for improvement

4. An emphasis on nonfiction writing

5. Collaborative scoring of student work

Throughout this leadership guide and our signature series, we emphasize all five characteristics as effective practices in increasing student success.

In "Seven Practices That Distinguish Successful Schools," Reeves (2020c) asks readers what educators have learned since he published his initial findings (Reeves, 2000). He shares that research continues to support the five core competencies that create equity and excellence in learning systems, including a focus on few priorities, effective feedback, collective efficacy, effective instruction, and leadership effectiveness (Reeves, 2020c). Once again, findings show clarity and consistency in embracing the significance of classroom practice in the pursuit of equitable opportunities for all students (Chenoweth, 2017; Reeves, 2020a, 2020b, 2020c; Zavadsky, 2012).

In the signature series, we feature gender as an example that leaders and collaborative teams must examine when making instructional choices involving students. Undoubtedly, leaders and teams must also consider race, culture, and religion to understand if high expectations for every student are the culture of learning in your district and school. To this end, as a leader, you must be acutely aware and boldly and directly address and take action when you become aware of any bias—intentional or unintentional—that impedes equitable opportunities to access learning for all students in the classroom. Now let's examine some of these opportunities through the lens of curriculum and resources.

Offer Culturally Appropriate Resources

For equity to be a foundation for district and school culture, carefully and seriously consider the selection of curriculum and resources teachers use with students. Although seemingly daunting tasks, representing diversity in all we share with students and families is critical work as we engage students in learning. Suppose you are a district leader, and students in an elementary classroom invite you to attend a presentation. The teacher informs you that each young student will present an opinion paper based on a fictional complex text at the center of instruction. This school, with the most diverse population in your district, represents students from twenty-two countries who speak several languages; the school has also recently been granted an award for its attention to gender-identity issues.

The students begin to present, and immediately, you are surprised and disappointed that the novel their papers are based on reflects characters representing only a white, suburban, middle-class school setting. The students clearly try their best to express their opinions of the text's story elements and what they mean to them. However, you are keenly cognizant that students lack authentic engagement or understanding of what they share in common with the characters and environment portrayed in the book. You are saddened to observe a missed opportunity for students to choose from among a more diverse offering of novels that would have given them options to examine aspects of their own experience, along with a variety of other cultural backgrounds. As you leave the school, you record a note to yourself to build a common understanding and shared learning of how equitable access to instruction must include careful consideration of resources for student use.

When you return to your office, you learn that the text featured in the classroom you visited is currently on the district-adopted literature list. You probe further to review the curriculum for that grade level and, to your chagrin, you discover another resource that is extremely biased and portrays only one culture as part of American school life. With an understanding of the responsibility you have to effect change, you make a commitment: you will ensure teachers not only have resources representative of the majority demographic in their classrooms, but you will also encourage them to be more culturally responsive and broad-minded.

When students of a dominant culture do not experience the rich realities of many cultures, they risk developing a narrow view of an incredibly diverse, multicultural world that limits their own growth (Bishop, 2012). Vow to empower and expect teachers to ask and address the crucial question, "How can I ensure the resources I select or am asked to use authentically reflect the demographics of my students, diverse perspectives, and the experiences of others?" You can help teachers understand and incorporate a mindset that aligns to the metaphor teacher Aline O'Donnell (2019) uses: "Curriculum can serve as a mirror when it reflects your own culture and identity, as well as a window when it offers a view into someone else's experience" (p. 19).

Figure 9.3 provides questions to prompt discussion, foster reflection, and conduct observations. Leaders can adapt or use these questions, for example, to share with teachers so they can self-audit their selections, lead a discussion with collaborative teams, or use them as a template when observing instruction and students at work.

The signature book series discusses several types of culturally responsive texts that teams should consider when choosing core reading material that reflects students culturally and linguistically.

Leadership Area: Develop Community and Relationships

As a leader, when you consider equity in districts and schools, the following statement from consultant Peter Block (2018) speaks to the heart of your collaborative work:

The shift we seek needs to be embodied in each invitation we make, each relationship we encounter, and each meeting we attend. For at the most operational and practical level, after all the thinking about policy, strategy, mission

Leadership: Guiding Questions for Use of Culturally Appropriate Resources	Collaborative Team Notes and Next Steps
What projects, presentations, and individual tasks could you assign to allow students individuality and choice in selecting resources?	
Considering the diversity of the district, school, and classrooms, what do you communicate through social media, visual messages, branding, and so on that models diversity or shows unintentional bias?	
Do the resources you select (or the district or school asks you to use) authentically reflect the demographics and a balanced representation of students in your classrooms?	
How can you learn more about your students' backgrounds to guide the selection of culturally rich resources?	
Do the resources reflect diverse perspectives and experiences of others? Or do the texts predominantly reflect one perspective? If so, how can you positively adjust your instructional plans to be more inclusive?	
How do you know your resources support diverse cultural experiences? Have you engaged with an ally of that demographic background? Have you considered the author of the text and to what degree the author's experience is authentic?	

Figure 9.3: Leadership guiding questions for using culturally appropriate resources.

*Visit **go.SolutionTree.com/literacy** for a free reproducible version of this figure.*

and milestones, it gets down to this: How are we going to be when we gather together? (p. 2)

It is imperative for you to lead with policies, guidelines, and expectations that establish equity as the foundation of your culture. However, how you actually learn about one another, respect differences, and take action to ensure equitable access to learning for all students will determine the value of your stated expectations.

As you consider equity as a foundation of district and school culture, leaders and teachers must know that although people often use the term *diversity* in reference to race, class, or gender identity or expression, it encompasses many aspects—ethnicity, age, sexual or effectual orientation, geographic background, spirituality or religious beliefs, learning style and abilities, marital or partner status, parental or caregiver status, national origin, language, economic status and background, work experiences, personality, and education. Teachers need support to learn about their students' cultural backgrounds and find ways to connect learning to those cultures. As a leader, partner with families and community members, and encourage teachers to connect as well. This creates a more common understanding of family and student needs and helps to articulate high expectations, learn within the context of students' cultures, and show these cultural backgrounds are of value by integrating them into the curriculum (Garland & Bryan, 2017).

Spiller and Power (2019) state:

In our school-improvement work, parents often tell us that teachers assume they do not want to know about curriculum or instructional expectations. Parents often cite examples of times they wished they had known more about what was expected, what the learning should look like, and how to help their child. (p. 160)

Communication, as everyone knows, is a two-way street and a necessary tool in building understanding and relationships. Leaders and educators who take the time to connect with families and communities are more successful in providing appropriate and accessible learning opportunities for students. For example, a representative group from a strong Korean community in your school asks to meet with you. You're unsure why they requested the meeting, but to prepare, you review the classroom placement of all Korean students and their academic progress. You know most are highly successful. When the community leaders arrive, you are pleasantly surprised when they have come to ask for your support. They feel the curriculum lacks challenge for their children and the school day is too short. They explain to you that in South Korean society, the school day ends much later, and the curriculum includes more rigorous expectations. Therefore, they request to extend learning for their children after school using an empty classroom, and they'd pay for an individual to assume the teaching role. Understanding their perspective, you acquiesce to make a classroom available but with the stipulation that any student, regardless of heritage, who wants an enrichment opportunity can attend, and you must also participate in and approve the hiring of the after-school teacher.

When the meeting ends, you think about what you learned from these parents. You recognize the diverse cultural composition of students in your school. However, you have not yet fully considered the opportunities you can make available to capitalize on the colorful mosaic that exists among your student population. In this case, *equitable access to learning* means you need to provide more rigor and extensions for this particular group of students, but that shouldn't prevent other students from benefitting as well. As a school, you will need to address issues like this as part of your focus on creating an equitable culture of learning. Consider what you could do as a principal or district leader to establish more understanding and connections with communities. How could stronger relationships improve access to learning for students? What communication strategies would be beneficial? How do you help teachers understand why this is a valuable practice in their classrooms and with families? To plan for next steps to address these and other questions, use the suggestions in figure 9.4 (page 224).

Leadership Area: Prioritize Students

The last leadership area of focus centers on every educator's reason for becoming teachers and leaders—students. As you read this section, consider how you will maintain a primary focus on students, including making student-centered decisions and establishing an equitable learning environment. *Putting the student first* expressly refers to establishing actions and adopting a mindset that places students as the top priority. It involves equitable school and classroom practices, daily decisions by leaders that reflect an understanding of the student at the center of everyone's work, and collaborative team efforts as part of a PLC culture to meet the needs of every student. As Spiller and Power (2019) remind educators:

> Putting students first also means leveling the playing field and creating a definition of equity that demonstrates equal access to learning for all students in a school. This means quality instruction with rigorous learning opportunities and fair assessment practices that give all students differentiated and various chances to demonstrate what they know and can do. (p. 110)

Leadership Area: Develop Community and Relationships			
District Leader	**School Administrator**	**Instructional Coach**	**Lead Teacher**
☐ Establish tight expectations for equitable access to learning for all students as part of district culture, and involve parents and community representatives in drafting policy and guidelines. Invite opportunities for continuous feedback, as necessary.	☐ Implement district expectations by building a common understanding of the why and what of community connections and relationships to support equitable access to learning for all students.	☐ Support collaborative teams as they develop communication strategies and tools to connect with families and students.	☐ Support district tight expectations for equitable access to learning, ensuring that collaborative teams develop an understanding of their families' and students' diverse cultures and needs.
☐ Provide professional development opportunities for school leaders and teachers to help them understand how to build connections and relationships with students, families, and the community.	☐ Arrange opportunities to meet and connect with families and community leaders to learn about diverse cultures and your students' needs.	☐ Guide teachers and collaborative teams in the acquisition and development of culturally appropriate curricula and resources that will deepen connections with families and students.	☐ Lead conversations to consider ways to connect and understand community, family, and student needs.
☐ Create and lead community focus groups on a regular basis that provide opportunities to connect and learn from diverse communities in the district.	☐ Hold culturally appropriate events and celebrations as part of ongoing school plans.	☐ Support classroom instruction as teachers consider equitable access to instruction through culturally appropriate curricula and resources.	☐ Reflect student diversity needs through the selection of curricula and resources at collaborative team planning meetings.
☐ Consider strategies, including communication in necessary languages, that will demonstrate respect for diversity and increase community connections.	☐ Ensure implementation of a variety of communication strategies with families to respect diversity of language and culture.		☐ Remind teachers that any home-school connection activities, including correspondences, should be available in students' home languages. Discuss ways teachers can obtain translations if they aren't proficient in these languages.
☐ Seek every opportunity to provide a culturally appropriate curriculum and resources that align to community values.	☐ Observe and provide feedback to collaborative teams and teachers as they discuss the needs of students; pay close attention to how teams work with families and the community to support learning.		☐ Spend time in conversation with students to build relationships, understand diverse cultures, and honor each student's unique needs.
	☐ Observe, monitor, and provide feedback and support to teachers on their use of culturally appropriate curricula and resources.		

Figure 9.4: Leadership area guidelines for equity in literacy—Develop community and relationships.

*Visit **go.SolutionTree.com/literacy** for a free reproducible version of this figure.*

Throughout this chapter, we asked you to consider equitable access to instruction, curriculum, and resources for students. A healthy, positive, and equitable school or district culture is only possible when educators make decisions in service to students. Writing student-centered policies and creating student-centered mission statements demonstrate an impressive first step; however, actions determine meaning and impact.

Recall the scenario presented earlier in the chapter when a district leader was invited to watch students' classroom presentations on a book, although few could connect with the experiences it contained. Despite a district and school focus on the student, the teacher chose a complex text from the adopted literature list that failed to aptly represent the learning culture in the district, school, or classroom or diversity in general. This was not an intentional bias; however, it revealed an overlooked opportunity to engage students in personal choice and connectedness, and it did not align to a student-centered mission.

As a leader, seek every opportunity to observe and intentionally consider equity for student learning. Review district and school policies and procedures (including systems of intervention) and observe collaborative teams. Listen for student-centered decisions driven by data evidence rather than teachers' opinions or invisible biases. Visit classrooms and speak with students to specifically notice how each student can (or can't) access learning. Most important, take action to ensure teachers consider students the priority. For example, a teacher organizes students into literature circles (Daniels, 2002) or book clubs (McMahon & Raphael, 2007) based not only on their reading abilities but also their personal preferences. To differentiate by readiness and interest, the teacher first conducts a book talk to introduce each of the text selections. She asks students to rank order their top three book choices. Reviewing her students' input, she assigns each student a book from their ranking to appeal to interest, but she does so knowing their readiness levels. This way, students read a book of interest that presents the appropriate level of challenge.

Further, commit to prioritizing the student as the focus in all decisions. Use a tool such as the student-centered decision-making protocol pictured in figure 9.5 (page 226). Visualizing the student each time you are faced with a decision will ensure that your stated priority is your implementation priority. Operating from this clear-minded laser focus on your most precious commodity—students—you can determine the implications and actions required with regard to safety issues and policies and determine what resources teams might need to address the issue at hand.

What issue requires a decision? _____ Using the following template, complete each square, beginning with the first priority—the student. This is the first criterion in this decision-making protocol; the second priority involves safety, the third policy compliance, and the last focuses on the impact of resources.	
1. Students Describe how this decision will impact students.	**2. Safety** Describe how this decision will impact the safety of students and staff.
3. Policies Will this decision go against any school, district, school board, federal, or state or provincial policies?	**4. Resources** Consider the resources (human and otherwise) necessary to address this issue. Are they available? What will be required?

Source: Spiller & Power, 2019, p. 108.

Figure 9.5: Student-centered decision-making protocol.

*Visit **go.SolutionTree.com/literacy** for a free reproducible version of this figure.*

Use figure 9.6 to consider implementing suggestions based on this chapter as you strive to consider equity in all actions and decisions as a leader.

The Final Word

Reality demands leaders pay attention and respond to the expansive, rich, and varied landscape of students growing and learning in a world replete with defining moments. It is shortsighted for educators to ignore the ever-changing climate of what this implies for students. From racial- and gender-equity movements to

Leadership Area: Prioritize Students			
District Leader	**School Administrator**	**Instructional Coach**	**Lead Teacher**
☐ Create a tight expectation for every student to read at grade level or beyond every year.	☐ Progress monitor student reading data to ensure every student receives access to instruction and intervention that ensures at least reading and writing at grade level.	☐ Provide professional development and support to collaborative teams and teachers as they ensure each student is reading and writing at grade level or beyond.	☐ Ensure collaborative teams establish and monitor a SMART goal for all students reading and writing at or above grade level.
☐ Identify and eliminate bias in district policies, board decisions, communication, and daily actions of district staff.	☐ Provide professional development to teachers to ensure they understand and apply differentiated instructional strategies.	☐ Provide support when teachers are unsure of next instructional steps to support access to learning for all students.	☐ Lead collaborative team progress-monitoring and data-protocol discussions to ensure teachers take timely next steps to meet the needs of students.
☐ Develop a student-centered decision-making protocol or use figure 9.5 as a district leadership tool.	☐ Host appropriate schoolwide student events that reflect the rich diversity of the student population.	☐ Support collaborative teams as they plan for intervention.	☐ Help collaborative teams create Tier 2 interventions immediately as teachers identify student needs.
☐ Through the lens of ensuring diversity, regularly conduct an audit and review of curriculum and resources, classroom practices, grading practices, intervention, and overall district and school policies.	☐ Observe collaborative teams and classrooms with an intentional focus on curriculum and resource choices and instructional practices that include all students or do not include any students.	☐ Observe classrooms, providing support and guidance to teachers on effective differentiated instructional practices to meet all students' needs.	☐ Self-monitor team decisions to ensure teachers use culturally appropriate curriculum and resources that provide "mirrors and windows."
	☐ Observe and provide feedback to teachers as they provide access to learning for all students. Pay particular attention to unintended instances of bias during instruction.	☐ Suggest resources to teachers that mirror the demographics of their students, and provide suggestions for resources that expand students' perspectives of other cultures.	☐ Continue to build a common understanding with collaborative teams of the need to ensure all students' equitable access to learning.
			☐ Bring awareness to any instances of bias, and discuss ways to obliterate it.

Figure 9.6: Leadership area guidelines for equity in literacy—Prioritize students.

*Visit **go.SolutionTree.com/literacy** for a free reproducible version of this figure.*

simply understanding and accepting one's identity, committed people passionately work to generate a society where everyone recognizes and accepts one another's unique qualities. Schools and, more specifically, classrooms provide a venue for students to learn about building toward a more equitable and welcoming society in all its diverse glory. Within the classroom's walls, teachers strive to create a cohesive and inclusive learning environment as a microcosm of a broader, accepting world. In this regard, educators model and teach how to be inclusive of others despite differences—or, rather, because of differences.

Furthermore, leaders must be vigilant in helping to make schools places where educators recognize and eliminate biases that derail sound instruction, demand rigor, promote high expectations, and use resources to reflect students' demographics and the diverse perspectives and experiences of others. Reeves (2020c) implores leaders and staff in every school, particularly those who serve disadvantaged youth, to ask themselves: "What would we do if they were rich?" He asserts:

> Students in elite, expensive private schools . . . have difficulty in reading and math, in organization and behavior. But no one says, "Sink or swim, kid—you should have those skills at home." Rather, they exclaim, "My goodness! We can't let these kids fail, and we will move heaven and earth to ensure their success in this school and in college." (Reeves, 2020c)

The message? Students from wealthier communities are afforded safety nets and benefits that other, less advantaged students rarely, if ever, are given. The inequality of skewed expectations is inexcusable. High-poverty, diverse schools do not have to equate to low-performing schools. This assertion has been proven time and again (Parrett & Budge, 2020). Although it takes a host of factors to bolster the performance of students who live in poverty situations to excellence, it can and has been done.

Equity in all districts and schools is of paramount importance. Students have common needs and are entitled to an education in which teachers reach, extend, and support them with access to learning at the highest levels despite their differences and circumstances. As a leader, take charge to intentionally expect culturally appropriate choices and connections, and relationships with families and students; ensure decisions are evidence based, providing teachers with knowledge of what students know and do not know; mandate timely responses of corrective instruction and extensions; and, most important, require equitable access to instruction for all students.

Literacy—an essential prerequisite for full engagement in our society—equips students with the gateway to widespread learning through reading, writing, speaking, and listening. It is incumbent on leaders to ensure teams infuse literacy instruction across content areas, with careful attention to the gifts a diverse classroom and world afford. As a leader, your challenge remains: to afford students this equitable opportunity to thrive through sound literacy instruction. Please accept the challenge!

EPILOGUE

School and district leaders are undeniably all too familiar with spinning many plates and trying to keep the multifaceted obligations of their jobs in balance. You recognize you want to primarily be an instructional leader, but the reality is your responsibilities pull you in many directions. Too often, district leaders and principals introduce professional development with the intention of learning alongside their colleagues, only to be called out of the room to attend to a pressing issue. Or emails, memos, meetings, and other administrative commitments take leaders away from developing their own understanding of sound, effective classroom learning experiences. By reading this book and using its tools with your collaborative teams, you will have taken valuable steps in expanding your expertise of collaborative team products and classroom implementation of quality literacy instruction, which serves as a gateway for students to participate more fully and meaningfully in the world.

Reeves (2007) writes about how high-performing schools establish literacy as their primary pursuit:

> These schools rightly believe that literacy is as important as the safety and health of their students. Because they know that the health and safety risks of students who drop out of school are markedly higher than the risks of students who succeed in school, these educators and leaders know that the analogy between literacy and health is a sound one. (pp. 237–238)

All of us in education—in whatever capacity we serve—have the privilege of bestowing young people with the means and resources to go forth in this world with an increased propensity for success. As a teacher leader, principal, assistant superintendent—whatever your leadership role—own the fact that you are a pivotal, essential member of a special group fortunate enough to touch lives, make a difference, and foster growth. As leaders, we must each do our part, so together, we can help shape the future lives of those who deserve our commitment to excellence.

APPENDIX A

REFERENCE POINTS, TEMPLATES, AND TOOLS

This appendix contains a variety of reference points for connecting this text to your work as a leader as well as several templates and tools for doing this work successfully.

Reference Points

When we discuss literacy planning, instruction, and collaboration in a PLC in this book, each of our chapters references specific leadership areas that emanate from *Leading With Intention* by Spiller and Power (2019). To better understand these areas, see figure A.1 (page 234), which provides an overview of *Leading With Intention* contents. We also recommend you review table I.1 (page 6), which features the intersection between building literacy in a PLC, as each chapter in this book indicates, with the leadership areas from Spiller and Power (2019). Lastly, we recommend you review all of this book's leadership area guidelines from each chapter, which are also accessible online (visit **go.SolutionTree.com/literacy**). These figures include detailed suggestions that leaders who serve in various capacities—district leader, school administrator, instructional coach, and lead teacher—can implement, as appropriate, to strengthen students' literacy across a district or school.

Chapter 1: Achieving Focus and Staying Intentional		
Key Concepts	**Guiding Question**	**Actions**
• Schools need *effective leadership*, which is a leader's ability to stay intentionally focused on the right work. • Leaders avoid launching and maintaining too many initiatives, use time wisely, and determine a small number of goals that intentionally set the school's direction.	• How can you effectively spend time to guide, monitor, and support what you expect from teams and individuals?	• Implement positive habits for spending time in team meetings and conducting class visitations and observations to provide feedback and support. • Communicate the school vision regularly. • Provide time for teachers to meet in collaborative teams to focus on student results and create instructional plans based on student-achievement data. • Consider what aspects of your school's culture will be tight and loose. • Clarify your intentions and priorities so others understand them, focus on a few goals, minimize distractions, and establish systems.
Chapter 2: Establishing and Maintaining Organization		
Key Concepts	**Guiding Questions**	**Actions**
• Schools need organizational systems and instructional practices that make sense and everyone uses. • Creating collaborative-learning cultures requires leadership to determine and model the necessary systems and practices and demonstrate consistent application and expectations.	• How can you establish and maintain school organizational structures that connect to effective classroom practices? • How does the organizational plan provide support and coaching for collaborative teams to improve student learning?	• Clarify tight and loose expectations. • Revisit system policies and practices; revise policies and practices, as needed, to align with established priorities. • Reflect on current organizational realities to identify the root causes of issues and address these causes with an action plan. • Devise and implement a professional development plan based on priorities. • Provide coaching and classroom support that align to tight expectations. • Identify ways to avoid mixed messages. • Institute instructional coaching for collaborative teams.

Chapter 3: Building Shared Leadership		
Key Concept	**Guiding Question**	**Actions**
• In authentic PLCs, collaboration through the development of guiding coalitions and teacher-led collaborative teams provides increased shared ownership of responsibility that can lead to successful school improvement.	• How can you build collaborative teams and share leadership to strengthen your ability and improve the school?	• Set up interdependency of collaborative teams by achieving a shared goal; gaining the knowledge necessary to impact professional and student learning; meeting regularly to review common formative assessments and analyze data to inform instruction; planning instruction and interventions; and so on. • Create shared leadership among staff members. • Build and focus on a guiding coalition. • Guide teamwork. • Build leadership capacity. • Devise and implement an effective schedule.
Chapter 4: Using Evidence for Decision Making and Action		
Key Concepts	**Guiding Question**	**Actions**
• Leaders gather evidence from multiple data sources, such as state or provincial data, district benchmarks, attendance and tardiness data, needs assessments, and teacher- and team-generated assessments. • Leaders make decisions and develop an action plan based on evidence rather than past experiences and the opinions of others.	• How can you use evidence of student achievement and the current state of the school to make decisions and take necessary actions?	• Acknowledge the current reality and create an action plan based on evidence. • Consider the importance of understanding the characteristics of leading districts and schools. • Identify the root cause of underperformance, and monitor strategies with a continuous review of data. • Use formative and summative assessment data to inform instructional moves. • Create short- and long-term SMART goals to understand and monitor desired results. • Assist teams in aligning their actions with the root causes of student failure to meet learning targets.

Figure A.1: *Leading With Intention* (Spiller & Power, 2019) overview.

Chapter 5: Prioritizing the Student		
Key Concepts	**Guiding Question**	**Actions**
• Leaders take actions and adopt mindsets that place students as the top priority. • Leadership involves having equitable school practices and making daily decisions that reflect an understanding that the student is the center of all educators' work, and collaborative team efforts meet each student's needs.	• How can you maintain a primary focus on students, including making student-centered decisions and establishing an equitable learning environment?	• Develop a district- or schoolwide decision-making protocol that prioritizes students. • Reflect on actions that create a student-centered culture. • Identify and develop an action plan to address inequities in your system.
Chapter 6: Leading Instruction		
Key Concepts	**Guiding Question**	**Actions**
• Leaders understand that quality instruction—a critical area of importance that can change schools—equates to increased performance. When classroom practice improves, educators see remarkable increases in student achievement. • Collaborative teams understand the real purpose of their collaboration is to inform instructional practices to effectively service all students.	• How can you take an active role to lead effective instruction?	• Ensure collaborative teams work interdependently in a cycle of inquiry to address the four critical questions of a PLC. • Guide teachers to implement tight expectations to focus teams' work. • Conduct frequent classroom visits to understand and impact the instructional environment so it's conducive to learning. • Ensure teachers adhere to a research-proven lesson-planning model (for example, gradual release of responsibility). • Monitor the work of collaborative teams by attending meetings or reading meeting minutes to determine how best to support and guide each team. • Provide or make available professional learning, coaching, and growth-producing feedback.

Chapter 7: Fostering Communication		
Key Concept	**Guiding Question**	**Actions**
• Strong leaders communicate well. They reflect on their communication skills, specifically how they listen, what they prioritize, how they communicate their priorities, and how they develop stronger skills so they understand others' needs.	• How can you foster strong communication skills with and among teachers and students?	• Develop focused and intentional means of communication among students, teachers, and staff. • Actively listen to fully focus on a speaker's message by asking clarifying questions, reframing the conversation, and closing your mind to external thoughts. • Develop skills to handle crucial conversations well by taking care of and addressing critical issues, entering a difficult conversation with positive intent, and developing an understanding of others' points of view and needs.
Chapter 8: Developing Community and Relationships		
Key Concepts	**Guiding Question**	**Actions**
• Leaders work beyond the school community to focus on the art of building relationships. • Leaders know there is much to do every day. However, it is critical to leadership success that they value and cultivate strong relationships with parents and the community.	• How can you build and foster relationships beyond the school community?	• Earn the respect and confidence of others by gaining their permission to lead. • Build common understanding of the *why* before the *what*, ensuring communication clarifies expectations through trusting relationships. • Develop a growth mindset focused on strength-based thinking rather than deficit-based thinking. • Create opportunities for parents and community members to understand and be active participants.

Templates and Tools

Collaborative teams can use the reproducible templates and tools in this section as they work to build literacy-focused instruction through their curriculum. Here, you will find a blank PREP template (figure 1.1, page 12) and blank versions of the learning progression and assessments figures from chapter 3 (figure 3.2, page 66, and figure 3.3, page 68), as well as rubrics for measuring the qualitative features of text complexity, which you can find different versions of in the other signature series books. In the appendices for those books, you will also find additional information on the following.

- A process for prioritizing standards

- An overview of Webb's (2002) Depth of Knowledge

- An explanation of essential understandings and guiding questions (as shown in the PREP template)

Based on your leadership capacity, use your expertise to work with teachers to implement these tools and templates.

PREP Template

Unit: _____	Time Frame: _____	Grade: _____
Essential Understandings (optional)	**Guiding Questions (optional)**	

Unit Standards (Indicate priority standards in bold and italic typeface.)

Strand (Reading Literature, Reading Informational Text, Writing, Language, and so on):

-
-
-
-
-

Strand (Reading Literature, Reading Informational Text, Writing, Language, and so on):

-
-
-
-
-

Strand (Reading Literature, Reading Informational Text, Writing, Language, and so on):

-

-

-

-

-

Strand (Reading Literature, Reading Informational Text, Writing, Language, and so on):

-

-

-

-

-

Unwrapped Unit Priority Standards	Knowledge Items	Skills (Learning Targets and DOK Levels)

Unwrapped Unit Priority Standards	Knowledge Items	Skills (Learning Targets and DOK Levels)

Learning Progression and Assessments Template

Priority Standard (or Standards):

Steps	Learning Progression	Assessments
Step ____	**Priority Standard (or Standards):**	
Step ____	Learning Target (Skill) or Knowledge	
Step ____	Learning Target (Skill) or Knowledge	
Step ____	Learning Target (Skill) or Knowledge	

	Step ____	**Learning Target (Skill) or Knowledge**	
	Step ____	**Learning Target (Skill) or Knowledge**	
	Step ____	**Learning Target (Skill) or Knowledge**	
	Step ____	**Learning Target (Skill) or Knowledge**	
	Step ____	**Learning Target (Skill) or Knowledge**	
	Step ____	**Learning Target (Skill) or Knowledge**	

A Leader's Guide to Reading and Writing in a PLC at Work, Elementary © 2021 Solution Tree Press
SolutionTree.com • Visit **go.SolutionTree.com/literacy** to download this free reproducible.

Text Complexity: Qualitative Measures Rubric—Informational Texts

Text Title: _____   Text Author: _____

	Exceedingly Complex	Very Complex	Moderately Complex	Slightly Complex
Purpose	☐ **Purpose:** Subtle, implied, difficult to determine; intricate, theoretical elements	☐ **Purpose:** Implied, but fairly easy to infer; more theoretical than concrete	☐ **Purpose:** Implied, but easy to identify based upon context or source	☐ **Purpose:** Explicitly stated; clear, concrete with a narrow focus
Text Structure	☐ **Organization of Main Ideas:** Connections between an extensive range of ideas or events are deep, intricate and often implicit or subtle; organization of the text is intricate or specialized for a particular discipline ☐ **Text Features:** If used, are essential in understanding content ☐ **Use of Graphics:** If used, extensive, intricate, essential integrated graphics, tables, charts, etc., necessary to make meaning of text; also may provide information not otherwise conveyed in the text	☐ **Organization of Main Ideas:** Connections between an expanded range [of] ideas, processes or events are deeper and often implicit or subtle; organization may contain multiple pathways and may exhibit traits common to a specific discipline ☐ **Text Features:** If used, greatly enhance the reader's understanding of content ☐ **Use of Graphics:** If used, essential integrated graphics, tables, charts, etc.; may occasionally be essential to understanding the text	☐ **Organization of Main Ideas:** Connections between some ideas or events are implicit or subtle; organization is evident and generally sequential ☐ **Text Features:** If used, enhance the reader's understanding of content ☐ **Use of Graphics:** If used, graphics [are] mostly supplementary to understanding of the text, such as indexes, glossaries; graphs, pictures, tables, and charts directly support the text	☐ **Organization of Main Ideas:** Connections between ideas, processes or events are explicit and clear; organization of text is clear or chronological or easy to predict ☐ **Text Features:** If used, help the reader navigate and understand content but are not essential ☐ **Use of Graphics:** If used, simple graphics, unnecessary to understanding the text but directly support and assist in interpreting the written text

A Leader's Guide to Reading and Writing in a PLC at Work, Elementary © 2021 Solution Tree Press
SolutionTree.com • Visit **go.SolutionTree.com/literacy** to download this free reproducible.

	Exceedingly Complex	Very Complex	Moderately Complex	Slightly Complex
Language Features	☐ **Conventionality:** Dense and complex; contains abstract, ironic, and/or figurative language ☐ **Vocabulary:** Generally unfamiliar, archaic, subject-specific, or overly academic language; may be ambiguous or purposefully misleading ☐ **Sentence Structure:** Mainly complex sentences often containing multiple concepts	☐ **Conventionality:** Complex; contains some abstract, ironic, and/or figurative language ☐ **Vocabulary:** Somewhat complex language that is sometimes unfamiliar, archaic, subject-specific, or overly academic ☐ **Sentence Structure:** Many complex sentences with several subordinate phrases or clauses and transition words	☐ **Conventionality:** Largely explicit and easy to understand with some occasions for more complex meaning ☐ **Vocabulary:** Mostly contemporary, familiar, conversational; rarely unfamiliar or overly academic ☐ **Sentence Structure:** Simple and compound sentences, with some more complex constructions	☐ **Conventionality:** Explicit, literal, straightforward, easy to understand ☐ **Vocabulary:** Contemporary, familiar, conversational language ☐ **Sentence Structure:** Mainly simple sentences
Knowledge Demands	☐ **Subject Matter Knowledge:** Extensive, perhaps specialized or even theoretical discipline-specific content knowledge; range of challenging abstract and theoretical concepts ☐ **Intertextuality:** Many references or allusions to other texts or outside ideas, theories, etc.	☐ **Subject Matter Knowledge:** Moderate levels of discipline-specific content knowledge; some theoretical knowledge may enhance understanding; range of recognizable ideas and challenging abstract concepts ☐ **Intertextuality:** Some references or allusions to other texts or outside ideas, theories, etc.	☐ **Subject Matter Knowledge:** Everyday practical knowledge and some discipline-specific content knowledge; both simple and more complicated, abstract ideas ☐ **Intertextuality:** A few references or allusions to other texts or outside ideas, theories, etc.	☐ **Subject Matter Knowledge:** Everyday, practical knowledge; simple, concrete ideas ☐ **Intertextuality:** No references or allusions to other texts, or outside ideas, theories, etc.

Source: Achieve the Core. (n.d.a). Reviewing using the IMET: ELA: Module 101—high-quality texts, evidence-based discussion and writing, and building knowledge. Accessed at https://achievethecore.org/content /upload/Understanding%20the%20IMET_ELA.LIT_Handout_101.pdf on April 29, 2020.

A Leader's Guide to Reading and Writing in a PLC at Work, Elementary © 2021 Solution Tree Press
SolutionTree.com • Visit **go.SolutionTree.com/literacy** to download this free reproducible.

Text Complexity: Qualitative Measures Rubric—Literature

Text Title: _____ Text Author: _____

	Exceedingly Complex	Very Complex	Moderately Complex	Slightly Complex
Text Structure	☐ **Organization:** Is intricate with regard to such elements as point of view, time shifts, multiple characters, storylines and detail ☐ **Use of Graphics:** If used, illustrations or graphics are essential for understanding the meaning of the text	☐ **Organization:** May include subplots, time shifts and more complex characters ☐ **Use of Graphics:** If used, illustrations or graphics support or extend the meaning of the text	☐ **Organization:** May have two or more storylines and occasionally be difficult to predict ☐ **Use of Graphics:** If used, a range of illustrations or graphics support selected parts of the text	☐ **Organization:** Is clear, chronological or easy to predict ☐ **Use of Graphics:** If used, either illustrations directly support and assist in interpreting the text or are not necessary to understanding the meaning of the text
Language Features	☐ **Conventionality:** Dense and complex; contains abstract, ironic, and/or figurative language ☐ **Vocabulary:** Complex, generally unfamiliar, archaic, subject-specific, or overly academic language; may be ambiguous or purposefully misleading ☐ **Sentence Structure**: Mainly complex sentences with several subordinate clauses or phrases; sentences often contain multiple concepts	☐ **Conventionality:** Fairly complex; contains some abstract, ironic, and/or figurative language ☐ **Vocabulary:** Fairly complex language that is sometimes unfamiliar, archaic, subject-specific, or overly academic ☐ **Sentence Structure:** Many complex sentences with several subordinate phrases or clauses and transition words	☐ **Conventionality:** Largely explicit and easy to understand with some occasions for more complex meaning ☐ **Vocabulary:** Mostly contemporary, familiar, conversational; rarely unfamiliar or overly academic ☐ **Sentence Structure:** Primarily simple and compound sentences, with some complex constructions	☐ **Conventionality:** Explicit, literal, straightforward, easy to understand ☐ **Vocabulary:** Contemporary, familiar, conversational language ☐ **Sentence Structure:** Mainly simple sentences

page 1 of 2

	Exceedingly Complex	Very Complex	Moderately Complex	Slightly Complex
Meaning	☐ **Meaning:** Multiple competing levels of meaning that are difficult to identify, separate, and interpret; theme is implicit or subtle, often ambiguous and revealed over the entirety of the text	☐ **Meaning:** Multiple levels of meaning that may be difficult to identify or separate; theme is implicit or subtle and may be revealed over the entirety of the text	☐ **Meaning:** Multiple levels of meaning clearly distinguished from each other; theme is clear but may be conveyed with some subtlety	☐ **Meaning:** One level of meaning; theme is obvious and revealed early in the text
Knowledge Demands	☐ **Life Experiences:** Explores complex, sophisticated or abstract themes; experiences portrayed are distinctly different from the common reader ☐ **Intertextuality and Cultural Knowledge:** Many references or allusions to other texts or cultural elements	☐ **Life Experiences:** Explores themes of varying levels of complexity or abstraction; experiences portrayed are uncommon to most readers ☐ **Intertextuality and Cultural Knowledge:** Some references or allusions to other texts or cultural elements	☐ **Life Experiences:** Explores several themes; experiences portrayed are common to many readers ☐ **Intertextuality and Cultural Knowledge:** Few references or allusions to other texts or cultural elements	☐ **Life Experiences:** Explores a single theme; experiences portrayed are everyday and common to most readers ☐ **Intertextuality and Cultural Knowledge:** No references or allusions to other texts or cultural elements

Source: Achieve the Core. (n.d.a). Reviewing using the IMET: ELA: Module 101—high-quality texts, evidence-based discussion and writing, and building knowledge. *Accessed at https://achievethecore.org/content /upload/Understanding%20the%20IMET_ELA.LIT_Handout_101.pdf on April 29, 2020.*

APPENDIX B

LIST OF FIGURES AND TABLES

*Reproducible figures are in italics. Visit **go.SolutionTree.com/literacy** to download free reproducible versions of these figures.*

REFERENCES AND RESOURCES

Achieve the Core. (n.d.a). *Reviewing using the IMET: ELA: Module 101—high-quality texts, evidence-based discussion and writing, and building knowledge.* Accessed at https://achievethecore.org/content/upload/Understanding%20the%20IMET_ELA .LIT_Handout_101.pdf on April 29, 2020.

Achieve the Core. (n.d.b). *Updated text complexity grade bands and associated ranges from multiple measures.* Accessed at https://achievethecore.org/content/upload/CCSS_Grade _Bands_and_Quantitative_Measures%202015.pdf on March 29, 2021.

Adams, M. J. (1990). *Beginning to read: Thinking and learning about print.* Cambridge, MA: MIT Press.

Ainsworth, L., & Viegut, D. (2015). *Common formative assessments 2.0: How teacher teams intentionally align standards, instruction, and assessment.* Thousand Oaks, CA: Corwin Press.

Amadeo, K. (2021, February 23). *What is educational equity and why does it matter? Why equity is better than equality for the economy.* Accessed at www.thebalance.com /equity-in-education-4164737 on April 1, 2021.

Annie E. Casey Foundation. (2010). *Early warning! Why reading by the end of third grade matters.* Accessed at www.aecf.org/m/resourcedoc/AECF-Early_Warning_Full_Report -2010.pdf on December 22, 2020.

Argyris, C., & Schön, D. A. (1974). *Theory in practice: Increasing professional effectiveness.* San Francisco: Jossey-Bass.

Bailey, K., & Jakicic, C. (2012). *Common formative assessment: A toolkit for Professional Learning Communities at Work.* Bloomington, IN: Solution Tree Press.

Bailey, K., & Jakicic, C. (2017). *Simplifying common assessment: A guide for Professional Learning Communities at Work.* Bloomington, IN: Solution Tree Press.

Bailey, K., Jakicic, C., & Spiller, J. (2014). *Collaborating for success with the Common Core: A toolkit for Professional Learning Communities at Work.* Bloomington, IN: Solution Tree Press.

Bambrick-Santoyo, P. (2016). *Get better faster: A 90-day plan for coaching new teachers.* San Francisco: Jossey-Bass.

Bayewitz, M. D., Cunningham, S. A., Ianora, J. A., Jones, B., Nielsen, M., Remmert, W., et al. (2020). *Help your team: Overcoming common collaborative challenges in a PLC at work.* Bloomington, IN: Solution Tree Press.

Beck, I. L., & McKeown, M. G. (1985). Teaching vocabulary: Making the instruction fit the goal. *Educational Perspectives*, *23*(1), 11–15.

Beck, I. L., McKeown, M. G., & Kucan, L. (2013). *Bringing words to life: Robust vocabulary instruction* (2nd ed.). New York: Guilford Press.

Biancarosa, G., & Snow, C. E. (2004). *Reading next: A vision for action and research in middle and high school literacy—A report to Carnegie Corporation of New York* (2nd ed.). Washington, DC: Alliance for Excellent Education. Accessed at https://production -carnegie.s3.amazonaws.com/filer_public/b7/5f/b75fba81-16cb-422d-ab59-373a6a 07eb74/ccny_report_2004_reading.pdf on January 25, 2021.

Bishop, R. S. (2012). Reflections on the development of African American children's literature. *Journal of Children's Literature*, *38*(2), 5–13.

Blackburn, B. R. (2018). Productive struggle is a learner's sweet spot. *ASCD Express*, *14*(11). Accessed at www.ascd.org/ascd-express/vol14/num11/productive-struggle-is-a-learners -sweet-spot.aspx on December 2, 2020.

Blevins, W. (2017). *Phonics from A to Z: A practical guide* (3rd ed.). New York: Scholastic.

Block, P. (2008). *Community: The structure of belonging.* San Francisco: Berrett-Koehler.

Block, P. (2018). *Community: The structure of belonging* (2nd ed.). San Francisco: Berrett-Koehler.

Bloom, B. S. (1968). Learning for mastery. Instruction and curriculum. Regional education laboratory for the Carolinas and Virginia, topical papers and reprints, number 1. *Evaluation Comment*, *1*(2), 1–12.

BrainyQuote. (n.d.). *Wayne Gretzky quotes.* Accessed at https://brainyquote.com/quotes /wayne_gretzky_131510 on May 10, 2018.

Brendtro, L. K., Brokenleg, M., & Van Bockern, S. (2019). *Reclaiming youth at risk: Futures of promise* (3rd ed.). Bloomington, IN: Solution Tree Press.

Breslow, J. M. (2012). *By the numbers: Dropping out of high school.* Accessed at www.pbs .org/wgbh/frontline/article/by-the-numbers-dropping-out-of-high-school on May 20, 2020.

Brookhart, S. M. (2013). *How to create and use rubrics for formative assessment and grading.* Alexandria, VA: Association for Supervision and Curriculum Development.

Brown, B. (2015). *Rising strong: How the ability to reset transforms the way we live, love, parent, and lead.* New York: Random House.

Bryan, D.-M. (2018). *An earful* [Audiobook]. Columbus, OH: Highlights for Children.

Buffum, A., & Mattos, M. (Eds.). (2015). *It's about time: Planning interventions and extensions in elementary school.* Bloomington, IN: Solution Tree Press.

Buffum, A., Mattos, M., & Malone, J. (2018). *Taking action: A handbook for RTI at Work*. Bloomington, IN: Solution Tree Press.

Butler, B. K. (2015). Collaborating in the core. In A. Buffum & M. Mattos (Eds.), *It's about time: Planning interventions and extensions in elementary school* (pp. 51–80). Bloomington, IN: Solution Tree Press.

Chenoweth, K. (2017, July 18). *For school improvement, demographics aren't destiny* [Blog post]. Accessed at www.edweek.org/leadership/opinion-for-school-improvement -demographics-arent-destiny/2017/07 on January 20, 2021.

Cohen, R. K., Opatosky, D. K., Savage, J., Stevens, S. O., & Darrah, E. P. (2021). *The metacognitive student: How to teach academic, social, and emotional intelligence in every content area*. Bloomington, IN: Solution Tree Press.

Colburn, L., & Beggs, L. (2021). *The wraparound guide: How to gather student voice, build community partnerships, and cultivate hope*. Bloomington, IN: Solution Tree Press.

Collins, J. C. (2001). *Good to great: Why some companies make the leap—and others don't*. New York: HarperBusiness.

Collins, J. C., & Porras, J. I. (2002). *Built to last: Successful habits of visionary companies*. New York: HarperCollins.

Conzemius, A. E., & O'Neill, J. (2014). *The handbook for SMART school teams: Revitalizing best practices for collaboration* (2nd ed.). Bloomington, IN: Solution Tree Press.

Covey, S. R. [StephenRCovey]. (2019, December 3). *"Without involvement, there is no commitment. Mark it down, asterisk it, circle it, underline it. No involvement, no commitment." - Stephen R. Covey #involve #leadership #leadershiptraining #commit #QOTD* [Twitter moment]. Accessed at https://twitter.com/stephenrcovey/status /1201879088111276032?lang=en on March 23, 2021.

Covey, S. R. (2020). *The seven habits of highly effective people: Restoring the character ethic* [30th anniversary ed.]. New York: Simon & Schuster.

Daniels, H. (2002). *Literature circles: Voice and choice in book clubs and reading groups*. Portland, ME: Stenhouse.

Davidson, J. (2020). *The school-to-prison pipeline and prison literacy*. Accessed at https:// bookstr.com/article/the-school-to-prison-pipeline-and-prison-literacy on April 1, 2021.

Donohoo, J. (2017, October 25). *Collective teacher efficacy: The effect size research and six enabling conditions* [Blog post]. Accessed at www.jennidonohoo.com/post/collective -teacher-efficacy-the-effect-size-research-and-six-enabling-conditions on January 6, 2020.

Donohoo, J., & Katz, S. (2017). When teachers believe, students achieve. *Learning Professional, 38*(6), 20–27.

DuFour, R. (2015). *In praise of American educators: And how they can become even better*. Bloomington, IN: Solution Tree Press.

DuFour, R., DuFour, R., Eaker, R., & Many, T. W. (2010). *Learning by doing: A handbook for Professional Learning Communities at Work* (2nd ed.). Bloomington, IN: Solution Tree Press.

DuFour, R., DuFour, R., Eaker, R., Many, T. W., & Mattos, M. (2016). *Learning by doing: A handbook for Professional Learning Communities at Work* (3rd ed.). Bloomington, IN: Solution Tree Press.

Dweck, C. S. (2016). *Mindset: The new psychology of success* (Updated ed.). New York: Random House.

Eaker, R., & Marzano, R. J. (2020). *Professional Learning Communities at Work and High Reliability Schools: Cultures of continuous learning.* Bloomington, IN: Solution Tree Press.

Fisher, D., & Frey, N. (2014). *Better learning through structured teaching: A framework for the gradual release of responsibility* (2nd ed.). Alexandria, VA: Association for Supervision and Curriculum Development.

Fisher, D., Frey, N., & Hattie, J. (2016). *Visible learning for literacy, grades K–12: Implementing the practices that work best to accelerate student learning.* Thousand Oaks, CA: Corwin Press.

Fountas, I. C., & Pinnell, G. S. (2001). *Guiding readers and writers, grades 3–6: Teaching comprehension, genre, and content literacy.* Portsmouth, NH: Heinemann.

Francis, E. M. (2017, May 9). *What is depth of knowledge?* [Blog post]. Accessed at https://inservice.ascd.org/what-exactly-is-depth-of-knowledge-hint-its-not-a-wheel on December 22, 2020.

Fullan, M., & Edwards, M. A. (2017). *The power of unstoppable momentum: Key drivers to revolutionize your district.* Bloomington, IN: Solution Tree Press.

Fullan, M., & Scott, G. (2014). *Education PLUS: New pedagogies for deep learning* [White paper]. Seattle, WA: Collaborative Impact. Accessed at https://michaelfullan .ca/wp-content/uploads/2014/09/Education-Plus-A-Whitepaper-July-2014-1.pdf on January 7, 2020.

Gareis, C. R., & Grant, L. W. (2008). *Teacher-made assessments: How to connect curriculum, instruction, and student learning.* Larchmont, NY: Eye on Education.

Garland, K., & Bryan, K. (2017). Partnering with families and communities: Culturally responsive pedagogy at its best. *Voices From the Middle, 24*(3), 52–55. Accessed at https://library.ncte.org/journals/vm/issues/v24-3/28996 on January 25, 2021.

Gehr, L. (2019). *More than highlighting: Creative annotations—Active strategies for annotation like collaboration work and illustration increase students' comprehension and retention.* Accessed at www.edutopia.org/article/more-highlighting-creative -annotations on April 1, 2021.

Glass, K. T. (2015). *Complex text decoded: How to design lessons and use strategies that target authentic texts.* Alexandria, VA: Association for Supervision and Curriculum Development.

Glass, K. T. (2018). *(Re)designing narrative writing units for grades 5–12.* Bloomington, IN: Solution Tree Press.

Glass, K. T., & Marzano, R. J. (2018). *The new art and science of teaching writing.* Bloomington, IN: Solution Tree Press.

Goddard, R. D., Hoy, W. K., & Hoy, A. W. (2004). Collective efficacy beliefs: Theoretical developments, empirical evidence, and future directions. *Educational Researcher, 33*(3), 3–13.

Graham, S., & Hebert, M. (2010). *Writing to read: Evidence for how writing can improve reading—A report from Carnegie Corporation of New York*. Washington, DC: Alliance for Excellent Education.

Graham, S., & Perin, D. (2007). *Writing next: Effective strategies to improve writing of adolescents in middle and high schools—A report to Carnegie Corporation of New York*. Washington, DC: Alliance for Excellent Education.

Gregory, G., Kaufeldt, M., & Mattos, M. (2016). *Best practices at Tier 1: Daily differentiation for effective instruction, elementary*. Bloomington, IN: Solution Tree Press.

Gregory, K., Cameron, C., & Davies, A. (2011). *Setting and using criteria* (2nd ed.). Bloomington, IN: Solution Tree Press.

Guskey, T. R., & Anderman, E. M. (2013). In search of a useful definition of mastery. *Educational Leadership, 71*(4), 18–23.

Hargreaves, A., & Fullan, M. (2012). *Professional capital: Transforming teaching in every school*. New York: Teachers College Press.

Hart, B., & Risley, T. R. (1995). *Meaningful differences in the everyday experience of young American children*. Baltimore: Brookes.

Hattie, J. (2009). *Visible learning: A synthesis of over 800 meta-analyses relating to achievement*. New York: Routledge.

Hattie, J. (2012). *Visible learning for teachers: Maximizing impact on learning*. New York: Routledge.

Hattie, J. (2016, July 11–12). *The current status of visible learning research*. Presented at the Mindframes and Maximizers Annual Visible Learning[PLUS] Conference 2016, National Harbor, MD.

Henkes, K. (1991). *Chrysanthemum*. New York: Greenwillow Books.

Heritage, M. (2008). *Learning progressions: Supporting instruction and formative assessment*. Washington, DC: Council of Chief State School Officers.

Hernandez, D. J. (2011). *Double jeopardy: How third-grade reading skills and poverty influence high school graduation*. Baltimore: Annie E. Casey Foundation. Accessed at https://eric.ed.gov/?id=ED518818 on December 2, 2020.

Hess, K. (2013). *A guide for using Webb's Depth of Knowledge with Common Core State Standards*. Accessed at https://education.ohio.gov/getattachment/Topics/Teaching /Educator-Evaluation-System/How-to-Design-and-Select-Quality-Assessments /Webbs-DOK-Flip-Chart.pdf.aspx on December 22, 2020.

Institute of Education Sciences. (2020, May). *The condition of education 2020*. Accessed at https://nces.ed.gov/pubs2020/2020144.pdf on April 1, 2021.

International Literacy Association. (n.d.). Science of reading. In *Literacy Glossary*. Accessed at https://literacyworldwide.org/get-resources/literacy-glossary on March 31, 2021.

International Literacy Association. (2020a). *Research advisory: Teaching writing to improve reading skills*. Newark, DE: Author. Accessed at https://literacyworldwide.org/docs /default-source/where-we-stand/ila-teaching-writing-to-improve-reading-skills.pdf on January 7, 2020.

International Literacy Association. (2020b). The science of reading: Supports, critiques, and questions (Special issue). *Reading Research Quarterly, 55*(S1), S1–S360.

Jensen, E. (2013). *Engaging students with poverty in mind: Practical strategies for raising achievement*. Alexandria, VA: Association for Supervision and Curriculum Development.

Jensen, E. (2019). *Poor students, richer teaching: Seven high-impact mindsets for students from poverty* (Rev. ed.). Bloomington, IN: Solution Tree Press.

Johnson, A. (2007). *A sweet smell of roses*. New York: Aladdin.

Johnson, D. W., Johnson, R. T., & Smith, K. A. (2006). *Active learning: Cooperation in the college classroom* (3rd ed.). Edina, MN: Interaction Book.

Kanold, T. D. (2011). *The five disciplines of PLC leaders*. Bloomington, IN: Solution Tree Press.

Kanold, T. D. (2017). *Heart! Fully forming your professional life as a teacher and leader*. Bloomington, IN: Solution Tree Press.

Kelly, L. (2020, November 10). *The Flesch Reading Ease and Flesch-Kincaid Grade Level* [Blog post]. Accessed at https://readable.com/blog/the-flesch-reading-ease-and -flesch-kincaid-grade-level on January 5, 2021.

Kise, A. G. (2019). *Holistic leadership, thriving schools: Twelve lenses to balance priorities and serve the whole student*. Bloomington, IN: Solution Tree Press.

Knight, J. (2011). *Unmistakable impact: A partnership approach for dramatically improving instruction*. Thousand Oaks, CA: Corwin Press.

Kramer, S. V., & Schuhl, S. (2017). *School improvement for all: A how-to guide for doing the right work*. Bloomington, IN: Solution Tree Press.

Kramer, S. V., Sonju, B., Mattos, M., & Buffum, A. (2021). *Best practices at Tier 2: Supplemental interventions for additional student support, elementary*. Bloomington, IN: Solution Tree Press.

Krashen, S. D. (2004). *The power of reading: Insights from the research*. Portsmouth, NH: Heinemann.

Lehman, C., & Roberts, K. (2014). *Falling in love with close reading: Lessons for analyzing texts—and life*. Portsmouth, NH: Heinemann.

Long, J. R. (n.d.). *The fox and the hedgehog*. Accessed at https://aesopfables.com/cgi/aesop1 .cgi?srch&/fabl/TheFoxandtheHedgehog on December 22, 2020.

Louis, K. S., Dretzke, B., & Wahlstrom, K. (2010). How does leadership affect student achievement? Research from a national US survey. *Journal of School Effectiveness and School Improvement, 21*(3), 315–336.

MacLachlan, P. (1985). *Sarah, plain and tall*. New York: Harper & Row.

Many, T. (n.d.). Three rules help manage assessment data. *TEPSA News*. Accessed at www.allthingsplc.info/files/uploads/three_rules_help_manage_assessment_data.pdf on March 31, 2021.

Markel, M. (2013). *Brave girl: Clara and the shirtwaist maker's strike of 1909*. New York: Balzer & Bray.

Marshall, K. (2009). *Rethinking teacher supervision and evaluation: How to work smart, build collaboration, and close the achievement gap*. San Francisco: Jossey-Bass.

Marshall, K. (2013). *Rethinking teacher supervision and evaluation: How to work smart, build collaboration, and close the achievement gap* (2nd ed.). San Francisco: Jossey-Bass.

Martínez, R., & Fernández, A. (2010). *The social and economic impact of illiteracy: Analytical model and pilot study*. Accessed at https://unesdoc.unesco.org/ark:/48223/pf0000190571 on April 1, 2021.

Marzano, R. J. (2003). *What works in schools: Translating research into action*. Alexandria, VA: Association for Supervision and Curriculum Development.

Marzano, R. J. (2004). *Building background knowledge for academic achievement: Research on what works in schools*. Alexandria, VA: Association for Supervision and Curriculum Development.

Marzano, R. J. (2010). *Teaching basic and advanced vocabulary: A framework for direct instruction*. Boston: Cengage ELT.

Marzano, R. J. (2017). *The new art and science of teaching* (Rev. & exp. ed.). Bloomington, IN: Solution Tree Press.

Marzano, R. J. (2020). *Teaching basic, advanced, and academic vocabulary: A comprehensive framework for elementary instruction*. Bloomington, IN: Marzano Resources.

Marzano, R. J., & Pickering, D. J. (2005). *Building academic vocabulary: Teacher's manual*. Alexandria, VA: Association for Supervision and Curriculum Development.

Marzano, R. J., Rogers, K., & Simms, J. A. (2015). *Vocabulary for the new science standards*. Bloomington, IN: Marzano Resources.

Marzano, R. J., & Simms, J. A. (2013). *Vocabulary for the Common Core*. Bloomington, IN: Marzano Resources.

Mattos, M., DuFour, R., DuFour, R., Eaker, R., & Many, T. W. (2016). *Concise answers to frequently asked questions about Professional Learning Communities at Work*. Bloomington, IN: Solution Tree Press.

McMahon, S. I., & Raphael, T. E. (Eds.). (2007). *The book club connection: Literacy learning and classroom talk*. New York: Teachers College Press.

McTighe, J., & Curtis, G. (2019). *Leading modern learning: A blueprint for vision-driven schools* (2nd ed.). Bloomington, IN: Solution Tree Press.

McTighe, J., & Silver, H. F. (2020). *Teaching for deeper learning: Tools to engage students in meaning making.* Alexandria, VA: Association for Supervision and Curriculum Development.

Moss, C. M., & Brookhart, S. M. (2019). *Advancing formative assessment in every classroom: A guide for instructional leaders.* Alexandria, VA: Association for Supervision and Curriculum Development.

Muhammad, A. (2015). *Overcoming the achievement gap trap: Liberating mindsets to effect change.* Bloomington, IN: Solution Tree Press.

Muhammad, A., & Cruz, L. F. (2019). *Time for change: Four essential skills for transformational school and district leaders.* Bloomington, IN: Solution Tree Press.

Nagy, W., Berninger, V., Abbott, R., Vaughan, K., & Vermeulen, K. (2003). Relationship of morphology and other language skills to literacy skills in at-risk second-grade readers and at-risk fourth-grade writers. *Journal of Educational Psychology, 95*(4), 730–742.

National Assessment of Educational Progress. (2002). *The nation's report card: Writing 2002* (NCES 2003-529). Washington, DC: National Center for Education Statistics. Accessed at https://nces.ed.gov/nationsreportcard/pdf/main2002/2003529.pdf on December 2, 2019.

National Assessment of Educational Progress. (2011). *The nation's report card: Writing 2011—Grade 8 national results.* Accessed at www.nationsreportcard .gov/writing_2011 /g8_national.aspx?tab_id=tab2&subtab_id=Tab_1#chart on December 2, 2019.

National Assessment of Educational Progress. (2019). *NAEP report card: Reading.* Accessed at www.nationsreportcard.gov/reading/nation/achievement/?grade=4 on December 2, 2019.

National Association for the Education of Young Children. (n.d.). *Learning to read and write: What research reveals.* Accessed at www.readingrockets.org/article/learning -read-and-write-what-research-reveals on November 19, 2019.

National Governors Association Center for Best Practices & Council of Chief State School Officers. (n.d.). *Common Core State Standards for English language arts and literacy in history/social studies, science, and technical subjects: Appendix A—Research supporting key elements of the standards.* Washington, DC: Authors. Accessed at www .corestandards.org/assets/Appendix_A.pdf on November 19, 2019.

National Governors Association Center for Best Practices & Council of Chief State School Officers. (2010). *Common Core State Standards for English language arts and literacy in history/social studies, science, and technical subjects.* Washington, DC: Authors. Accessed at www.corestandards.org/assets/CCSSI_ELA%20Standards.pdf on December 3, 2019.

New Meridian Resource Center. (n.d.). *Grade 3 scoring rubric for prose constructed response items*. Accessed at https://resources.newmeridiancorp.org/wp-content /uploads/2019/07/ELA-Writing-Rubrics_a11y.6.14.19.pdf on July 26, 2020.

O'Connor, K. (2013). *The school leader's guide to grading*. Bloomington, IN: Solution Tree Press.

O'Donnell, A. (2019). Windows, mirrors, and sliding glass doors: The enduring impact of Rudine Sims Bishop's work. *Literacy Today, 36*(6), 16–19.

Onuscheck, M., Spiller, J. (Eds.), & Glass, K. T. (2020). *Reading and writing instruction for fourth- and fifth-grade classrooms in a PLC at Work*. Bloomington, IN: Solution Tree Press.

Onuscheck, M., Spiller, J. (Eds.), Gord, S., & Sheridan, K. E. (2020). *Reading and writing instruction for second- and third-grade classrooms in a PLC at Work*. Bloomington, IN: Solution Tree Press.

Onuscheck, M., Spiller, J. (Eds.), Martin, E., & May, L. (2020). *Reading and writing instruction for preK through first-grade classrooms in a PLC at Work*. Bloomington, IN: Solution Tree Press.

Organisation for Economic Co-operation and Development. (2009, December). *21st century skills and competences for new millennium learners in OECD countries* (Working Paper No. 41). Paris: Author. Accessed at www .oecd.org/officialdocuments/publicdisplaydocumentpdf/?cote=EDU /WKP(2009)20&doclanguage=en on May 20, 2020.

Organisation for Economic Co-operation and Development. (2014). *Education at a glance: Country note—United States*. Paris: Author. Accessed at www.oecd.org/edu /United%20States-EAG2014-Country-Note.pdf on December 13, 2015.

Paris, S. G. (2005). Reinterpreting the development of reading skills. *Reading Research Quarterly, 40*(2), 184–202.

Paris, S. G., Carpenter, R. D., Paris, A. H., & Hamilton, E. E. (2005). Spurious and genuine correlates of children's reading comprehension. In S. G. Paris & S. A. Stahl (Eds.), *Children's reading comprehension and assessment* (pp. 131–160). Mahwah, NJ: Erlbaum.

Parrett, W. H., & Budge, K. M. (2012). *Turning high-poverty schools into high-performing schools*. Alexandria, VA: Association for Supervision and Curriculum Development.

Parrett, W. H., & Budge, K. M. (2020). *Turning high-poverty schools into high-performing schools* (2nd ed.). Alexandria, VA: Association for Supervision and Curriculum Development.

Pearson, P. D., & Gallagher, M. C. (1983, October). *The instruction of reading comprehension* (Technical Report No. 297). Champaign, IL: Center for the Study of Reading.

Pijanowski, L. (2018). *Architects of deeper learning: Intentional design for high-impact instruction*. Rexford, NY: International Center for Leadership in Education.

Popham, W. J. (2007). All about accountability/The lowdown on learning progressions. *Educational Leadership*, *64*(7), 83–84. Accessed at www.ascd.org/publications /educational-leadership/apr07/vol64/num07/The-Lowdown-on-Learning -Progressions.aspx on November 19, 2019.

Popham, W. J. (2011). *Transformative assessment in action: An inside look at applying the process*. Alexandria, VA: Association for Supervision and Curriculum Development.

Reeves, D. B. (2000). *Accountability in action: A blueprint for learning organizations*. Denver, CO: Advanced Learning Press.

Reeves, D. B. (2002). *The leader's guide to standards: A blueprint for educational equity and excellence*. San Francisco: Jossey-Bass.

Reeves, D. B. (2006). *The learning leader: How to focus school improvement for better results*. Alexandria, VA: Association for Supervision and Curriculum Development.

Reeves, D. (Ed.). (2007). *Ahead of the curve: The power of assessment to transform teaching and learning*. Bloomington, IN: Solution Tree Press.

Reeves, D. (2016). *Elements of grading: A guide to effective practice* (2nd ed.). Bloomington, IN: Solution Tree Press.

Reeves, D. (2020a). *Achieving equity and excellence: Immediate results from the lessons of high-poverty, high-success schools*. Bloomington, IN: Solution Tree Press.

Reeves, D. B. (2020b). *The learning leader: How to focus school improvement for better results* (2nd ed.). Alexandria, VA: Association for Supervision and Curriculum Development.

Reeves, D. (2020c, May). Seven practices that distinguish successful schools. *Principal Leadership*. Accessed at www.nassp.org/publication/principal-leadership/volume-20 /principal-leadership-may-2020/the-e-squared-solution-equity-and-excellence-for -every-school-may-2020 on January 20, 2021.

Reeves, D., & Eaker, R. (2019). *100-day leaders: Turning short-term wins into long-term success in schools*. Bloomington, IN: Solution Tree Press.

Rogers, P., Smith, W. R., Buffum, A., & Mattos, M. (2020). *Best practices at Tier 3: Intensive interventions for remediation, elementary*. Bloomington, IN: Solution Tree Press.

Rylant, C. (2008). *Poppleton in winter*. New York: Scholastic.

Schimmer, T. (2019, February 19). *Should formative assessments be graded?* [Blog post]. Accessed at www.solutiontree.com/blog/grading-formative-assessments on November 19, 2019.

Schmoker, M. (2004). Learning communities at the crossroads: Toward the best schools we've ever had. *Phi Delta Kappan*, *86*(1), 84–88.

Schmoker, M. (2018). *Focus: Elevating the essentials to radically improve student learning* (2nd ed.). Alexandria, VA: Association for Supervision and Curriculum Development.

Shanahan, T. (2018, October 27). *Gradual release of responsibility and complex text* [Blog post]. Accessed at https://shanahanonliteracy.com/blog/gradual-release-of-responsibility-and-complex-text#:~:text=The%20method%20you%20summarize%20as,relinquishes%20more%20and%20more%20of on November 19, 2019.

Shanahan, T. (2019a, September 28). *Five things every teacher should know about vocabulary instruction* [Blog post]. Accessed at https://shanahanonliteracy.com/blog/five-things-every-teacher-should-know-about-vocabulary-instruction on July 11, 2020.

Shanahan, T. (2019b, January 26). *How would you schedule the reading instruction?* [Blog post]. Accessed at https://shanahanonliteracy.com/blog/how-would-you-schedule-the-reading-instruction on July 17, 2020.

Shanahan, T. (2020a, July 11). *Clearing up a couple important misunderstandings about fluency* [Blog post]. Accessed at https://shanahanonliteracy.com/blog/clearing-up-a-couple-important-misunderstandings-about-fluency on January 7, 2020.

Shanahan, T. (2020b, February 1). *If students meet a standard with below grade level texts, are they meeting the standard?* [Blog post]. Accessed at https://shanahanonliteracy.com/blog/if-students-meet-a-standard-with-below-grade-level-texts-are-they-meeting-the-standard on April 21, 2020.

Shomos, A. (2010). *Links between literacy and numeracy skills and labour market outcomes: Productivity commission staff working paper.* Accessed at www.pc.gov.au/research/supporting/literacy-numeracy-labour-outcomes/literacy-numeracy-labour-outcomes.pdf on April 1, 2021.

Simms, J. A., Marzano, R. J. (2019). *The new art and science of teaching reading.* Bloomington, IN: Solution Tree Press.

Smarter Balanced Assessment Consortium. (2014). *Smarter Balanced performance task scoring rubrics.* Accessed at www.ode.state.or.us/wma/teachlearn/subjects/science/assessment/smarter-balanced_scoring_rubrics.pdf on February 5, 2021.

Smith, D., Frey, N., Pumpian, I., & Fisher, D. (2017). *Building equity: Policies and practices to empower all learners.* Alexandria, VA: Association for Supervision and Curriculum Development.

Snow, C. E., & Matthews, T. J. (2016). Reading and language in the early grades. *The Future of Children, 26*(2), 57–74.

Spiller, J., & Power, K. (2019). *Leading with intention: Eight areas for reflection and planning in your PLC at Work.* Bloomington, IN: Solution Tree Press.

Statistics Canada. (2017). *Census in brief: Children living in low-income households.* Accessed at www12.statcan.gc.ca/census-recensement/2016/as-sa/98-200-x/2016012/98-200-x2016012-eng.cfm on April 1, 2021.

Steinbeck, J. (1993). *The grapes of wrath.* New York: Viking. (Original work published 1939)

Thurber, J. (1978). *The 13 clocks.* New York: Penguin. (Original work published 1950)

Townsley, M., & Wear, N. L. (2020). *Making grades matter: Standards-based grading in a secondary PLC at Work.* Bloomington, IN: Solution Tree Press.

United Nations International Children's Emergency Fund. (2019). *Literacy.* Accessed at https://data.unicef.org/topic/education/literacy on April 1, 2021.

Walker, T. (2015). *Shameful milestone: Majority of public school students live in poverty.* Accessed at www.nea.org/advocating-for-change/new-from-nea/shameful-milestone -majority-public-school-students-live-poverty on April 1, 2021.

Weatherford, C. B. (2007). *Freedom on the menu: The Greensboro sit-ins.* London: Puffin Books.

Webb, N. L. (1997, April). *Criteria for alignment of expectations and assessments in mathematics and science education* (Research Monograph No. 8). Washington, DC: Council of Chief State School Officers.

Webb, N. L. (2002). *Depth-of-knowledge levels for four content areas.* Accessed at www .acpsd.net/cms/lib/SC02209457/Centricity/Domain/74/DOK%20Four%20 Content%20Areas%20Webb.pdf on December 22, 2020.

White, E. B. (1980). *Charlotte's web.* New York: HarperCollins. (Original work published 1952)

White, K. (2017). *Softening the edges: Assessment practices that honor K–12 teachers and learners.* Bloomington, IN: Solution Tree Press.

White, K. (2019). *Unlocked: Assessment as the key to everyday creativity in the classroom.* Bloomington, IN: Solution Tree Press.

White, T. G., Sowell, J., & Yanagihara, A. (1989). Teaching elementary students to use word-part clues. *Reading Teacher, 42*(4), 302–308.

Wiggins, G. (2012). Seven keys to effective feedback. *Educational Leadership, 70*(1), 10–16. Accessed at www.ascd.org/publications/educational-leadership/sept12/vol70 /num01/Seven-Keys-to-Effective-Feedback.aspx on March 31, 2021.

Wiliam, D. (2018). *Embedded formative assessment* (2nd ed.). Bloomington, IN: Solution Tree Press.

Wrang, L. (2015). *The sign.* Columbus, OH: Highlights for Children. Accessed at www .commonlit.org/texts/the-sign on November 22, 2019.

Zavadsky, H. (2012). *School turnarounds: The essential role of districts.* Cambridge, MA: Harvard Education Press.

INDEX

"Tremendous, tremendous, tremendous!

The speaker made me do some very deep internal reflection about the **PLC process** and the personal responsibility I have in making the school improvement process work **for ALL kids.**"

—Marc Rodriguez, teacher effectiveness coach, Denver Public Schools, Colorado

PD Services

Our experts draw from decades of research and their own experiences to bring you practical strategies for building and sustaining a high-performing PLC. You can choose from a range of customizable services, from a one-day overview to a multiyear process.

Book your PLC PD today!
888.763.9045

Solution Tree